Psychotherapy of the Borderline Adult

A Developmental Approach

By

James F. Masterson, M.D.

Clinical Professor of Psychiatry
Cornell University Medical College

BRUNNER/MAZEL, *Publishers* • New York

Third Printing

Library of Congress Cataloging in Publication Data

Masterson, James F.
   Psychotherapy of the borderline adult

   Bibliography: p. 359
   Includes index.
     1. Pseudoneurotic schizophrenia.   2. Psychotherapy.
I. Title.
RC514.M36   616.8'914   76-16564
ISBN 0-87630-127-8

*Sorrow may be fated, but to
survive and grow is an
achievement all its own.*

R. COLES, *Children of Crisis*

Contents

vii

Introduction

Psychotherapeutic efforts with the borderline patient were frustrated for many years because the concept of the disorder was vague and its cause was unknown. This made it impossible to design an appropriate treatment.

The conceptual vagueness was due in the main to three factors: 1) a lack of research; 2) the emphasis by the psychiatrists on descriptive and nosologic considerations rather than on the developmental and psychodynamic; and 3) the emphasis by the psychoanalyst on instinctual theory and oedipal conflict between already existing intrapsychic structures—id, ego, superego—rather than on the developmental—how these structures were formed.

This book presents an object relations theory—as amplified by the work of Mahler* on separation-individuation—which lays

* See Appendix.

ix

bare the developmental origins and intrapsychic structure of the borderline syndrome and makes a rational and effective psychotherapy possible. The theory is illustrated through numerous case examples of psychotherapy, thereby providing some answers to many of the most pressing questions about psychotherapy of the borderline. These questions include:

How do you make the diagnosis in view of the complex and shifting clinical picture? What is the difference between the borderline syndrome and borderline state? How do you differentiate the borderline from the psychotic, the narcissistic disorder, or the psychopathic?

What etiologic factors contribute to the disorder? Why does the borderline have such difficulties in close interpersonal relationships? What events pose crucial and severe precipitating stresses?

What kind of psychotherapy is indicated? How often should the patient be seen and for how long? Is intensive psychoanalytically oriented psychotherapy possible? What therapeutic techniques are essential? When, how and why does the therapist intervene? Can the patient's responses to the intervention be predicted? To what extent and how do you deal with the notorious negative transference? What is the effect of intercurrent life events on the borderline patient in therapy? How do you terminate psychotherapy?

The object relations theory suggests that the mother's withdrawal of her libidinal availability at the child's efforts to separate and individuate produces a development arrest at the phase of separation-individuation (rapprochement subphase). This arrest or fixation occurs at exactly that time because the child's individuation constitutes a major threat to the mother's defensive need to cling to her infant and causes her to withdraw her libidinal availability.

The twin themes of this interaction—reward for regression and clinging, withdrawal for separation-individuation—are introjected by the child as self and object representations and thus become the leitmotif of his intrapsychic structure—the split object relations unit. A split ego also develops along with the split object relations unit. These structures are then recapitulated in the therapeutic transference. An understanding of these intra-psychic structures, their relationships to each other, together with their manifestations in the transference, leads to the design of an appropriate and effective psychotherapy.

This theory is described in both its interpersonal and intra-psychic aspects in two chapters. Following a chapter describing the general principles of the psychotherapy, the remainder of the book is devoted to applying the theory to psychotherapy through detailed case reports.

"Supportive" therapy is demonstrated in three chapters. The first two chapters present an interview-by-interview account of two and one-half years of psychotherapy of a 22-year-old woman. The next chapter describes two years of psychotherapy once a week with each of two women, age 40.

Intensive psychoanalytically oriented reconstructive psychother-apy is described in two case reports that occupy 14 chapters: the first of a 45-year-old man seen four times a week for four years; the second of a 40-year-old woman seen from one to three times a week for six years. A final chapter synthesizes the theoretical and clinical and deals with some limitations, qualifications and other questions raised by this work.

It is important to keep in mind that this theory, like all theory, is open-ended and incomplete. It is subject to further validation by others and to revision by myself or others as future evidence should dictate. Perhaps one of the most useful aspects of the theory is that it permits the formulation of hypotheses which can be tested clinically leading to ultimate refinement of the theory. It is a tool for investigation and discovery and not a dog-matic scheme to be followed blindly. When used as the former it can lead patient and therapist alike to even higher levels of crea-tive discovery. When used as the latter it will lead both patient and therapist through an empty, lifeless, repetitive ritual of manipulation.

BACKGROUND

An understanding of how I arrived at the work presented in this volume may shed some additional and necessary light on the work itself.

My interest in clinical research on the personality disorders began in 1955 with a follow-up study of hospitalized adolescents. It continued through a second follow-up study of outpatient adolescents that was published in 1967 (150, 151). The results of this latter study indicated that adolescents with a personality disorder did poorly five years later despite the fact that they may have seemed to improve after one year of psychotherapy. Closer study of the records of this psychotherapy revealed that when patient and parents were seen in psychotherapy once a week for a year the patient did indeed improve. He functioned better, and acting out, anxiety and depression decreased, as did the conflict with the parents. However, what were causing so much trouble five years later—his pathologic character traits—were hardly touched upon in the therapy.

At this point, in 1968, I focused my clinical research on an intensive study of the personality disorder in adolescents in a hospital setting where the patients' 24-hour behavior could be monitored and correlated with the interviews. I was interested in a better idea of how these traits developed and how to treat them.

At the same time the work of Frosch (62-65), Kernberg (100-109), and others with adults in psychoanalytic psychotherapy clarified the clinical picture of the borderline. This led to a shift in emphasis in psychoanalytic theory from the oedipal and instinctual to the developmental and to object relations theory (50, 84, 85, 113-116)—a theoretical model dealing with how intrapsychic structures develop—and therefore ideally suited for understanding the borderline. Developmental theories (94, 209, 229, 245) were elaborated and then put to the experimental test, first and foremost by Mahler (138-147), who studied the contribution of the stages of symbiosis and separation-individuation to normal ego development, and also by Bowlby (16-21), who studied the effects on ego development of separation from the mother during this time of life.

Integration of all that work with our study of the adolescent and his family led to the development of a concept of the border-line adolescent which was quite specific and resembled in most particulars the concept of the borderline adult elaborated by Kernberg and others.

Beyond this, through a unique vantage point—observing patient and family interactions in joint interviews—a theory evolved that the cause of the developmental arrest of the borderline adolescent was the mother's withdrawal of her libidinal availability at the child's efforts to separate and individuate (149, 158). The patient needed the mother's libidinal availability to grow; its withdrawal produced an arrest of growth. A specific psychotherapeutic design—repair of this faulty separation-individuation—emerged and was found to be effective. These findings were published in 1972.

As the theory and therapeutic design crystallized and were found to be effective with adolescents, I began to extend the research to borderline adults in my private practice. They clearly presented many of the same problems in understanding and treatment. Not surprisingly, the theory and technique were found to be just as effective with borderline adults as with adolescents—if the theory is correct that the developmental arrest occurs in the separation-individuation phase between 18-36 months of age, the same level of ego fixation will be present whether the patient is 15 or 35. A general theory of the cause and manifestations of the borderline syndrome emerged that applied to all borderline patients regardless of age.

METHOD

I took process notes—including my own interventions—during sessions. Each session was then briefly summarized. These records were reviewed regularly to keep a close check on the evolution of the data as they emerged in therapy. As I reviewed the sessions I could formulate predictions based on the theory, that could then be checked against succeeding events. A continuous process of hypothesis formulation, testing and feedback could be carried out with each patient. The assets and handicaps of this type of clinical research will be discussed in the *Summary and Discussion*.

The objectives and, therefore, the conditions that guided the collection of the data differed from those that guided its organization for presentation in this book. The data were collected through the vehicle of psychotherapy whose primary objective was to help the patient. The essential condition for this therapeutic objective was the creation of an emotional climate in the interview which would facilitate the patient's experiencing his therapy as an emotional process whose direction and development flowed from his head assisted by the therapist and not the other way around. The patient's autonomy and spontaneous learning had to be carefully respected and protected every step of the way.

The objective of the book was intellectual, not emotional: to outline a theory and illustrate how it is expressed in the case material. The essential condition for this objective was to trace how the psychodynamic themes of the theory weave back and forth in the therapy. For this specific purpose, I reviewed the data collected to focus on, tease out and stitch together the clinical evidence for those psychodynamic threads. This task, complex enough in itself, required minimizing or placing on the periphery some of the patients' auxiliary or secondary problems. This seemed an inevitable and acceptable price to pay since it did not distort the essence of the clinical case, as the reader can determine for himself by the great amount of clinical data presented and by the way the details fit together. At the same time it allowed the clinical manifestations that illustrated the theory to be placed in bold relief.

ACKNOWLEDGMENTS

I am grateful to Miss Helen Goodell, my editor for many years, for her patient efforts to keep my prose clear; to Drs. William Lulow, Thomas Henley and Ralph Klein for reading the manuscript; particularly to Dr. Mary Di Gangi, for her incisive and helpful comments on the clinical sections; to Dr. Donald Rinsley for his help over the years as well as on Chapter 4 of this volume; and finally, to my secretary, Miss Taube Honigstock, for her labors above and beyond the call of duty.

JAMES F. MASTERSON, M.D.

New York
June, 1976

I. THEORETICAL

1

Need for Treatment

To love and to work—Freud's concept of the goals of psychoanalysis—are at the same time the essential building blocks for gratification in adult life. The emphasis on the protean clinical symptomatology of the borderline (5, 26, 27, 32, 38, 62, 92, 117, 175, 176, 252)—i.e., diffuse acting out psychotic-like states, depression, panic, etc.—has obscured the fact that all borderline patients, regardless of overt symptomatology, have serious defects in these two key capacities, to love and to work.

Their capacity to love is crippled by the need to defend themselves against intimacy by clinging and/or distancing; their satisfaction at work is crippled by the need to avoid individuation. Often these two combine—in the better adjusted borderline—to form the very common chief complaint of general discontent or dissatisfaction with life. Small wonder that they are dissatisfied, for they lack the essential capacities to enjoy their lives. These defects which go beyond the florid symptomatology are the preeminent reason they require treatment; without it there is no hope. The brief clinical vignettes which follow demonstrate the extraordinary inroads of the inability to love or to work on these patient's lives.

To Love

First, a few examples of the difficulty in loving or being loved.

Anne

A 27-year-old, blonde, brown-eyed, attractive, married executive secretary complained: "Everything has fallen apart. In the last six months I seem to be trying to ruin my life."

After one year of psychotherapy Anne married an engineer. The couple moved from their home town to New York City where he immediately became busily involved in his work and she took a job as an aide in a therapeutic community.

The first six months passed without apparent difficulty but as the husband became more and more involved in his job and began to work evenings, the patient felt he was withdrawing from her and became angry and depressed. She catalogued her complaints against her husband: that he was unfeeling and selfish; that she had no feeling for him and didn't know if she wanted to spend the rest of her life with him. Nevertheless, she felt that the flaws in her marriage might be in her own mind since he acted as if nothing were wrong.

Her propensity to act out, brought under control by her previous psychotherapy, was now freshly stimulated by the acting out she saw at the therapeutic community. She began to rely on alcohol and marijuana and then started an affair with one of the staff, an ex-addict. The character of the affair gave a clue to the fantasy gratification it provided the patient. The two would meet in a friend's apartment for several hours in the afternoon where they would drink, smoke pot and have sexual intercourse. Despite the fact they spent only occasional afternoons together Anne felt the man loved her. She knew full well, but denied, that he was also having similar relationships with other women.

She confronted her husband with her feelings—that she didn't care about him and the marriage, and that he constantly hurt her feelings by not being affectionate. She was even further annoyed at his seeming lack of response.

In a later interview, she related that when anyone did get close to her she felt angry and withdrew, that she was very sensitive to criticism and assumed that no one would like her if they could see that she was angry. She reported that her confrontation seemed to reverse her husband's attitude, and that he had become affectionate but that she was not able to respond. She wondered if this insatiable need for attention and her fear of being hurt in a close relationship had prompted her affair.

Mary

Mary, a 35-year-old married college professor with one five-year-old child was depressed and complained bitterly about her husband of five years, saying that she was so angry at him that she couldn't stand to live with him any more but that she was so afraid of being alone that she couldn't divorce him.

She described him as being unaffectionate, stingy, depriving, cold, ungiving, insensitive to her needs yet angrily demanding that she comply with his needs. Her complaints focused on his unwillingness to spend money on her—for the apartment, vacations and entertainment—while he compulsively squirreled money into his savings account. The more she angrily demanded that he "come across," the more he withdrew. The more he withdrew, the harder she found it to have sexual relations with him; the lack of sex gave him further cause for withdrawal. A vicious cycle of no money no sex, no sex no money, had resulted.

In the last year she had begun an affair with an older fellow teacher who was divorced and seemed temporarily to fit her needs, as long as she didn't ask too much of him.

The patient had had a few brief sexual relationships with men in college. In her first year of graduate school she had her first emotional involvement with one of her college professors who was 18 years older and married. She recalled that the fact that nothing could come of the affair had been a source of reassurance rather than concern for her. The fact that it was a partial relationship relieved her anxiety about a commitment.

When she finished graduate school and was to go to another state for her teaching assignment her lover suddenly died. While she was still feeling alone and abandoned in her new surroundings she met her present husband. After a few months she married him feeling that "My mother would approve of him." The marriage was fraught with conflict from the beginning.

Parallel with her complaints about her husband was her declaration that she had to hang on to him for without him she would feel destitute, alone, isolated, in a total panic as she had been when she met him. She was so terrified of being alone that protection against it meant more to her than love, sex or romance. She now had to cling to her husband as she had clung to her mother as a child.

Jean

Jean, a tall, slender, attractive married woman of 27, came to therapy at the urging of her husband because she was "frigid." She balked at the last minute at keeping an appointment they had made at a sex clinic because she felt it was degrading and humiliating.

She and her husband had not had satisfactory sexual relations in one and one-half years. She was becoming increasingly anxious, tense, irritable and depressed. She found her life as a housewife and mother boring. She resented her husband's frequent long absences at work, his domineering attitude toward her, and his sexual demands. The more conflict they had, the more she withdrew emotionally. Sex was "something I had to do to please him."

She was harsh and critical of his behavior, felt he didn't respond to her needs and had no compunctions whatsoever about letting him know her views. The husband, for his part, had become increasingly angry, made snide remarks, talked about having affairs, and spent longer periods of time away at work.

She felt she had been an extension of her mother as a child. Her present concept of her self was of being worthless, inadequate. She had married her husband because his accomplishments gave her ego a boost and because he wanted her. Now she felt like an appendage to him.

Phyllis

Phyllis, a 35-year-old tall, blonde, blue-eyed, strikingly beautiful actress complained, "I'm afraid I'm going to make a mess of a romance." She had been going with a 37-year-old doctor almost exclusively for the last year and the relationship had been a roller coaster ride of painful separations and blissful reunions. She found him to be unlike the other men she had been attracted to. He was solid, substantial, but emotionally undemonstrative. He said he loved her but he was neither verbally nor physically demonstrative.

She had long been aware of her inordinate need for affection and the more involved she got the more she felt the need to demand reassurance of his love. She was afraid, and rightly so, that if she did not control this need she would drive him away from her. She was also aware that her need to be loved was so great that it might impel her to suspend her own critical faculties.

When her frustration with his undemonstrativeness built up she broke off the relationship, but then, when he continued to pursue her, she resumed it. Now, however, when she sought a permanent commitment he would procrastinate or back off, thereby exacerbating her fears. They had been through this painful cycle many times. Was it her or him or both of them? Although she was sexually frigid she enjoyed sexual foreplay and being embraced. He had no complaints about her as a sexual partner and seemed to obtain sexual satisfaction himself.

Phyllis continued, "I saw Harry again. He acted very nice with me and we ended up making love. Then I felt terrible and asked him to leave. I felt sick all over, nauseated, tense. I knew I couldn't go back with him. I didn't see him for a couple of days. I felt guilty and lonely so I saw him again, and again felt awful and left him to go back to my apartment. I'm old, there won't be anyone else for me. I can't bear to part with the only person who cares about me. But he's not the right person."

Tom

Tom, a 31-year-old married lawyer, complained of irritability, insomnia and depression which he ascribed to his wife's behavior —she was critical, possessive, extravagant, demanding and insensitive to his needs. She withheld sex on the slightest pretext and was "spending him into the poor house." She refused to entertain for him and devoted herself almost exclusively to the children.

When questioned about how he managed this difficult state of affairs he grudgingly admitted that he was a "hard worker," was not able to get home till very late and had to travel a lot on business, going away several times a month for four or five days at a time. He admitted to having had several affairs which, however, he broke off whenever the girl got "too close, too demanding," because this made him as uncomfortable with his girfriends as with his wife.

Betty

Betty, a short, thin pale brunette who at 31 was a very successful interior decorator, complained of her relationship with Bert, the man she had been living with for the last three years, "I am 31, getting old and want marriage and children. Our relationship neither grows nor terminates. He is younger and divorced. We were instantly attracted to each other and after a few months we decided to live together. He is the first man I've spent this much time with since I divorced my husband in my early twenties. He doesn't want marriage or children and when I suggested it he threatened to leave. We seemed to have no problems until this came up.

"My relationships with men have always been screwed up. I couldn't stand my husband. I can't stand anyone too close to me. I live in a world of fantasy or illusion with men. I ignore what's wrong with them if they tell me they care. I had a two-year affair with an unstable but exciting married man, knowing it could go no further.

"Reality depresses me. I run away from it by being busy. I am very successful at work and have many social friends, but I get very possessive, fearful that Bert will reject me for another girl. I drove several men away with my demands for reassurance.

"Basically I don't trust any man and have little hope that a real relationship is possible. But I'm terrified to be alone. When I confronted Bert with marriage or else and he threatened to leave, I panicked and begged him to stay. I'm at my wits' end. Don't know what to do. Can't stay with him, can't leave him. I'm depressed and resentful most of the time."

Comments

These five patients illustrate one of the most common clinical complaints of the borderline adult: difficulty in loving, in being intimate or close with another human being. This difficulty is often first presented either wrapped in romantic camouflage or projected as being the partner's problem. These maneuvers conceal from the patient the fact that the basic problem is not at the romantic level, nor is it the partner's problem.

The difficulty in loving revolves around the patient's need to use clinging and/or distancing defense mechanisms against his primitive fear of engulfment or abandonment—equivalent to loss of self or loss of object—if a close intimate, loving relationship develops. He must sacrifice the pleasures of a close relationship in order to maintain his inner emotional equilibrium. He must defend himself against the fears aroused by such a relationship by clinging or distancing.

Why must he or she do this? What is wrong with the capacity to love? Ensuing chapters will develop the following theory: The borderline adult's personality development was arrested at the growth state of separation-individuation (18-36 months) (147, 149). The patient's failure to have made a successful separation from his or her mother impels him or her to view all close relationships later in life as repetitions of that unresolved symbiotic relationship which revives the old fears of engulfment and/or abandonment. He must defend himself against closeness in adult life lest it become another "Tie that Binds" (149).

To Work

The second common difficulty is dissatisfaction or inhibitions or both at work. There can be as many reasons for this difficulty as for the difficulty in loving—for example, depression, conflict with authority figures, anxiety about competition with authority figures or peers, a thinking disorder, etc. In these patients, however, it is none of these, but specifically the need to defend against anxiety by avoiding individuation.

Fred, a 20-year-old college student, was so inhibited in his mental process that he literally could not think one consecutive sentence after another. This inhibition was necessary to contain his rage at being abandoned. He could not think; he could not work; he was flunking out of school.

The more usual theme stems from a lack of initiative and assertion at work due to avoidance of individuation. Ralph, a 25-year-old stockbroker, found his income suffering since he was unable to maintain the aggressive activity necessary to keep a full roster of customers. He would have sporadic outbursts of activity, which would bring on great anxiety, which would then lead to avoidance and longer spells of torpor and lassitude. When customers asked his advice he had difficulty in asserting himself or making a decision. His habit of running to the older men in the office for help had alienated them from him.

Peter, a 40-year-old president of his own large company, was an excellent salesman. His success as a salesman was based on his ability to please others, but his administrative effectiveness as the chief executive was severely damaged by his avoidance of asserting himself. He could not say "No"; nor could he set limits to his subordinates or to his board of trustees. He allowed his subordinates too free a rein and too much authority at the cost of company efficiency. He treated his board of trustees as a superior authority rather than a sounding board, constantly sought their approval, and expected them to make decisions that were properly his responsibility. The members of the board, uninformed and unequipped to make these decisions, reacted with resentment toward their president and constantly conspired to defeat him. Peter avoided his anxiety about individuation and self assertion by acting out his dependency wishes. All the while he complained that work offered him little satisfaction!

Jean, a 43-year-old editor of a woman's magazine had been a free-lance writer as a young woman—and a good one. However, the editor's job offered her more money and security (via retirement, pension plans, etc.), as well as a structured authority system with several superiors to whom she reported. She could do the work with her little finger and often had free time on her hands. She fretted and ruminated about changing jobs but did nothing about it. She avoided anxiety about individuation and self assertion by acting out her dependency needs in a job for which she was overqualified. She also complained of dissatisfaction at work.

DISCUSSION

These two themes, difficulty in loving and dissatisfaction with work, when combined, supply one explanation for a most common clinical presenting complaint that has puzzled psychiatrists for a long time.

Most of today's patients do not come to psychotherapy with a specific discrete symptom picture, such as an obsession or a phobia, as was reported to be common in Freud's time. Rather their complaint is more general and vague—of getting too little satisfaction in their lives.

Although the patient has no idea of the source of his dissatisfaction, a careful history usually reveals his difficulties in loving and working. Freud described the goals of psychoanalysis as "to love and to work." Since these are also the essential building blocks for gratification in adult life it is no wonder that the patient with difficulty in loving and in working is getting such paucity of satisfaction in his life.

Overt symptomatology, another common presenting complaint of the borderline adult, is considered in great detail in ensuing chapters.

The presenting clinical picture of the borderline adult may be unfulfilled loving, dissatisfaction with work, overt symptoms, or some combination of the three. In ensuing chapters I shall demonstrate how the separation-individuation theory links these difficulties to their developmental roots, opens the gateway to the clinical mysteries of the borderline syndrome, and leads the way to the design of a specific and effective psychotherapy.

2

Review of the Literature

INTRODUCTION

This review, neither comprehensive nor all inclusive, first sketches the main developments in the emergence of the clinical concept of the borderline syndrome as a stable, fixed diagnostic entity. It then considers in more detail Kernberg's and Mahler's views on normal ego development and on the developmental failure of the borderline in preparation for the presentation of the separation-individuation theory in Chapters 3 and 4. These chapters will link the clinical characteristics of the borderline syndrome to their developmental roots, demonstrating how the developmental perspective enhances understanding of the cause, as well as the varied clinical manifestations, of this disorder and makes possible the design of a specified and effective treatment.

Why is it necessary to delve into such seemingly esoteric concepts as object relations theory or splitting defense mechanisms to understand borderline phenomena? Why are the usual clinical descriptive diagnostic concepts not enough? What is a clinical psychiatrist doing using complex psychoanalytic concepts? The answer is that these conceptual tools best address the heart of the problem.

The review of the literature illustrates that the borderline syndrome has a deceptive clinical appearance. The patient functions very well in some areas, poorly in others, and sometimes has gross psychotic symptoms that, however, remit quickly. At one moment he seems in complete touch with reality and in the next is engaged in some bizarre acting out or is in a trance-like state.

There is no consistency at the level of symptoms or presenting complaints. Indeed, the very inconsistences of the clinical picture are the first signal to alert the clinician to the diagnosis of the borderline syndrome. Consequently, descriptive clinical concepts focus on the most puzzling, paradoxical and superficial aspect of the disorder and serve only to confuse rather than to clarify. It is only those concepts of object relations theory (68, 83, 84, 110-112, 113-116) that stress the underlying psychic structures— ego functions and self and object representations and their attendant affects—that knit the clinical contradictions together into an understandable whole.

CLINICAL CHARACTERISTICS

The borderline syndrome has had a long and undeservedly bad reputation in psychiatry. It has rarely been described in psychiatric textbooks (200, 201) and has been frequently attacked as a misnomer in both the psychiatric and psychoanalytic literature (77, 87, 90, 91, 252).

Originally the term was a wastebasket applied to patients who gave evidence of both a neurosis and a psychosis, and it seemed to convey more about the uncertainty and indecision of the psychiatrist than about the condition of the patient. Knight (117, 118) observed a number of years ago that "most often these patients were called severe obsessive-compulsive cases; sometimes an intractable phobia was the outstanding symptom; occasionally an apparent major hysterical symptom or an anorexia nervosa dominated the clinical picture; and at times there was a question of the degree of depression, or of the extent of paranoid trends, or of the severity of the acting out" (p. 98).

A plethora of labels appeared, varying by the diagnostic style of each psychiatrist, suggesting that the diagnosis might be some form of schizophrenia (26, 67, 90, 91, 252) : for example, incipient schizophrenia, latent schizophrenia, ambulatory schizophrenia, pseudo-neurotic schizophrenia, and chronic undifferentiated schizophrenia. Others favored labels such as chronic severe personality disorder, chronic severe character disorder, narcissistic character disorder. The official APA nomenclature included these patients under the diagnostic category of personality disorder.

This confusion—in retrospect a reflection of the diagnostic emphasis on descriptive symptomatology as opposed to an emphasis on psychodynamics and developmental considerations—persisted, and the ambiguities of the disorder continued to trouble the psychiatrist as he began to see more patients with this clinical picture.

In the last 20 years, as interest in ego psychology grew (41, 48, 124), this disorder became more of a focus of psychoanalytic study (5, 12, 15, 22, 24, 33-35, 38, 40, 43, 49, 53, 62-81, 83, 84, 95-110, 119-130, 160-162, 169, 175, 181, 183-184, 195-200, 216-219, 233, 236, 239, 246). Much of the confusion cleared and a consensus developed that the basic psychopathology was not the presenting symptoms, be they neurotic or psychotic, but a specific and stable form of pathologic ego—a developmental arrest or ego fixation.

Giovacchini (22, 70-76) of the Chicago Psychoanalytic Study Group observed that the clinical manifestations distributed themselves according to their severity and complexity along a spectrum from the less severe psychoneurotic to the most disturbed "borderline" case, which closely resembled the overt psychotic (170, 184). At the healthier end of the spectrum were the patients with narcissistic defenses, giving them an appearance of more or less normality. In the center of the spectrum was the bulk of the cases, who were less stable, less successful, more erratic, and more actively disturbed. They tended to act out more, trying to combat their emptiness with alcohol, excessive sexual indulgence, or some other kind of excitement. However, they did manage to preserve considerable successful adaptation.

Closest on the spectrum to the psychotic were the most disturbed patients, who showed considerable paranoid ideation, marked feelings of void, very tenuous object relations, and the most marginal adjustment (36, 227). In spite of their serious pathology, what seemed to characterize the bulk of the borderline patients was that they resisted psychotic illness.

A corresponding consensus developed as to the general psychodynamics of the syndrome as outlined by Giovacchini from the Chicago Psychoanalytic Study Group. He stated that the dynamic basis of the clinical picture was a developmental arrest, an ego fixation which resulted in defects in crucial ego functions, such as the perceptual and executive. The ego defects deprived the patient of techniques for mastery that were needed to deal with his internal and external world. The fantasies erected to contend with these defects and to protect from the painful memory traces of a traumatic infancy and childhood were of little help in coping with the realities of the adult world.

Ekstein and Wallerstein (42, 44-47) described their concept of the ego defect in children. They postulated an ego mechanism of control that could be roughly compared in its function to that of a thermostat. A reliable thermostat can maintain a somewhat even temperature in a room despite climatic changes. This is analogous to the ego state of the neurotic, which fluctuates minimally and is subject to relative control by the individual. An unreliable thermostat, on the other hand, can lead to unpredictable and inappropriate temperature changes and figuratively represents the unpredictable regulatory and controlling devices in the borderline.

Ekstein and Wallerstein stated that it seemed characteristic of the borderline for ego-state fluctuations to occur many times throughout their day, occasionally with control, but that a large part of their waking life bore strong similarity to the sleep-dream life of their neurotic contemporaries in the lack of control exerted by the dreamer.

The same authors illustrated the intensity of this disorder by saying that the neurotic patient conceived of his problems as leading to dangerous or unhappy consequences, but the possible solutions he envisioned had some real anchorage and were less overwhelmingly catastrophic than for patients in the borderline group who seemed to face absolute dilemmas that admitted of no solution. If we think of the neurotic dilemma in terms of the excursions of a pendulum, we might say that the excursions of the pendulum in the psychological world of the borderline patient cover an infinitely wider amplitude than in the world of the neurotic.

Rinsley (188-191), working with hospitalized borderline adolescents, underlined the fact that the essential psychopathology was a developmental arrest or ego fixation. He made many other contributions. For example, he observed the relationship of Bowlby's studies to the borderline adolescent, and he described the characteristic features of the defective ego, the benefits of separation for ego development, the resistance of parents and patient to separation by hospitalization, the depersonification of the patient by the parents (189), and the "phasic" character of the treatment. He was one of the first to study and advocate the use of intensive analytically oriented psychotherapy for these patients.

Frosch (62-65), working with adults, also emphasized that it was important not to look at the individual symptoms or symptom clusters to make the diagnosis since these could vary so widely. They could be phobias, conversion phenomena, compulsive traits, paranoid features, depression, or anxiety. He suggested, like the other authors, focusing on the defects in ego functions and in object relations.

He distinguished between perceiving and feeling reality and suggested that the basic ego defect involved distortions in perception of reality—both internal and external—that were, however, transient and reversible due to the relative preservation of the capacity to test reality. These perceptual distortions were particularly seen in tendencies to fuse with or be unable to differentiate the self from the non-human environment.

He also suggested that borderlines' object relations had progressed beyond the objectlessness of the psychotic to the point of recognition of need-gratifying objects; however, these relations were still infantile. As with the ego defects, at times archaic psychotic-like manifestations of object relations appeared but, in contrast to psychosis, these were rapidly reversed.

Frosch further elaborated that there was a lack of harmony between the various psychic structures with thinking, feeling and behavior at times and at all levels under the influence of the primary process. Some patients showed a frightening propensity for dipping deep into the unconscious and coming up at times with relatively undistorted and hitherto repressed id-derived material, and primitive libidinal and aggressive impulses which might transiently overwhelm the ego. He suggested that the superego was also primitive, immature and lacunae-riddled. Alongside impulsive breakthroughs were hypercritical, harsh reactions. He emphasized that the weakness of the ego of the borderline was its proneness to regression while its strength lay in its ability to reverse this process. He pointed out the important clinical phenomenon that adaptation was established at different levels and did not follow either the extreme regressive adaptation of the psychotic or the more integrated higher level of the neurotic or normal. Rather regressive and progressive adaptations existed side by side.

Finally, Frosch suggested that the conflict or danger specific to borderlines was the problem of self-non-self differentiation, of maintaining individuation—they needed the object for survival but the object also represented danger—i.e. loss of self vs. loss of the object.

Kernberg's (99-109) prolific and outstanding work on the

adult borderline not only synthesized the prior work in this field but also finally crystallized the clinical concept of a stable disorder due to a developmental arrest with specific observable symptoms, ego defects and psychopathology of object relations. He used the term "borderline personality organization," rather than borderline syndrome or state, to emphasize that these patients presented a specific, quite stable pathologic personality organization rather than transitory states on the road from neurosis to psychosis. This personality organization had typical symptomatic constellations, defensive operations of the ego, pathology of internalized object relations and instinctual vicissitudes.

Kernberg (99) also emphasized that the presenting symptoms did not differentiate the syndrome. He stated that many symptoms could be present in different combinations, that is, "anxiety, polymorphic perverse sexuality, schizoid or hypomanic prepsychotic personalities, impulse neuroses and, in addition, infantile, narcissistic, and antisocial character disorders and many polysymptomatic problems, such as phobias, obsessions, conversions, dissociation, hypochondriasis and paranoia" (p. 648).

Kernberg stressed that the ego defect had two manifestations: nonspecific, such as poor reality perception, frustration tolerance and impulse control, and specific, such as splitting, primitive idealization, projection, projective identification, denial and omnipotence. There was also a failure of normal integration of the intrapsychic structures derived from internalized object relations —i.e. integrated self-image, realistic whole object representations, integration of ideal-self and ideal-object representations into the ego ideal and integration of superego forerunners with more realistic introjections of parental images into the superego.

Kernberg added that, although the borderline, as contrasted with the schizophrenic, had differentiated ego boundaries and good reality testing, he could not synthesize positive and negative introjects and identifications. As a result he resorted to the defense of object splitting to preserve the good self and object images by separation from the bad.

DEVELOPMENTAL CONSIDERATIONS

The above mentioned authors display a consensus on the clinical characteristics which they present with great clarity. However, this clarity fades into vagueness and generalizations when they discuss the developmental origins. For example, Frosch refers to "self-non-self differentiation," and Giovacchini to "developmental arrest." Before presenting the separation-individuation theory of the development of the borderline syndrome it is necessary to consider in more detail Kernberg's views on normal ego development and on the cause of the ego fixation of the borderline.

Kernberg's Contributions to the Object Relations Theory of Normal Development

(Object relations theory may be defined as the psychoanalytic approach to the internalization of interpersonal relations)(105). Kernberg (106) postulated four stages in the development of normal internalized object relations:

Stage 1. This earliest stage of development, roughly coincident with the first postnatal month of life, precedes the establishment of the primary, undifferentiated self-object constellation built up in the infant under the influence of his pleasurable, gratifying experience in his interactions with the mother (94).

Stage 2. The second stage, roughly occupying the first to the third postnatal months, comprises the establishment and consolidation of an undifferentiated self-object image or representation (94) of a libidinally gratifying or rewarding ("good") type under the organizing influence of gratifying experience within the context of the mother-infant unit. Concomitantly, a separate primitive intrapsychic structure comprising an undifferentiated "bad" self-object representation is built up under the influence of frustrating and painful (i.e., traumatogenic) psychophysiological states. Thus, two sets of opposite primitive self-object-affect complexes are built up and fixed by memory traces as polar opposite intrapsychic structures.

Stage 3. The third stage is reached when the self-image and the object-image have become differentiated within the core "good" self-object representation. The differentiation of self-image from object-image within the core "bad" self-object representation occurs later and is complicated by early types of projection, that is, intrapsychic mechanisms which attempt to externalize the "bad" self-object constellation (107, 188, 209). This stage normally occupies the period between the fourth postnatal month and the end of the first year.

(Stage 4. The fourth stage has its inception at some point between the end of the first year of life and the second half of the second year and continues to evolve throughout the remainder of childhood. During Stage 4, "good" and "bad" self-images coalesce into an integrated self-concept; in other words, self-images establish coherence and continuity under the impact of polar opposite emotional-interpersonal experiences; affects become integrated, toned down, and then undergo further differentiation, and the child's self-concept and his actual presentation or behavior in the social field become closer. At the same time, "good" and "bad" object images also coalesce such that the "good" and the "bad" images of mother become integrated into a whole-object conception of mother which closely approaches the actuality or the reality of mother in the child's interpersonal-perceptual field.)

Kernberg (106) emphasized the progressively integrative function of these stages for both ego and superego, and for the development of the capacity for deep and consistent relationships with other persons.)

Kernberg and the Ego Fixation of the Borderline Syndrome

Kernberg (106) theorized that the fixation peculiar to the borderline syndrome occurred in the third stage of this developmental scheme, where there still persisted a dissociation of libidinally determined ($=$ good) from aggressively determined ($=$ bad) self and object representations, i.e., "good" self and object representations and "bad" self and object representations are perceived as separate. He then outlined the structural consequences of this fixation, which determined the clinical manifestations of the borderline (99) : (pathologic persistence of the primitive defense of splitting; failure of development of an integrated self-concept; chronic overdependence upon external objects; development of contradictory character traits in relation to contradictory ego states, resulting in chaotic interpersonal relationships. Superego integration suffered as a result of failure of the guiding function of an integrated ego identity, with persistent contradiction between exaggerated "ideal" object-images and extremely sadistic "all-bad" superego forerunners. Failure of development of an integrated object representation inhibited and ultimately limited development of the capacity for understanding of or empathy for other persons.* Ego strength depends in particular upon the neutralization of "raw" energies, which occurs in intimate connection with the process of integration of libidinally derived (= good) and aggressively derived (= bad) self- and object-images, and it is precisely this integration which failed in future borderline personalities; failure of neutralization in turn compromised specific aspects of ego strength, viz., anxiety tolerance, control of impulses and potential for true sublimations (188).

Kernberg's view of the etiology of this failure placed predominant emphasis upon constitutional factors—an excess of oral aggression, deficiency in the capacity to neutralize aggression or lack of anxiety tolerance (107):

> More characteristic for the borderline personality organization may be a failure related to a constitutionally determined lack of anxiety tolerance interfering with the phase of synthesis of introjections of opposite valences. The most important cause of failure in the borderline pathology is probably a

---

* Associated failure to develop an integrated self representation and an integrated object representation, normally accomplished during Stage 4, may be seen in terms of failure of development of whole-object relations from antecedent part-object relations. It will be recalled that developmental fixation at Stage 3 corresponds with fixation at Fairbairn's late oral stage of infantile dependence (50), during which the (maternal) whole-object is characteristically perceived and treated as a part-object (breast). The borderline's cathexis of whole-objects *as if* they were part-objects leads in turn to a welter of later interpersonal depersonifications or appersonations described elsewhere (189).

quantitative predominance of negative introjections. Excessive negative introjections may stem both from a constitutionally determined intensity of aggressive drive derivatives and from severe early frustrations (p. 250).

A predominantly hereditary constitutional view of the etiology of the developmental failure peculiar to the borderline personality would emphasize the infant's *a priori* propensity to form preponderantly negative introjections, which, in effect, Mahler considers as typical for infantile psychosis. It would be easy, as a result, to underestimate the importance of the mother's libidinal availability to the infant during the developmentally critical period of separation-individuation, which occupies a period from six to 30 months postnatally.

The presence of excessive oral aggression in the borderline leads Kernberg to favor a constitutional etiology for the borderline syndrome.)Although undue degrees of oral aggression undoubtedly characterize the borderline individual, its presence does not per se justify a purely or predominantly constitutional view of the etiology of his psychopathology, and Kernberg adduces no other evidence in support of such a view. There is, to be sure, a parallel deficiency of libidinal cathexis of both self and object representations which could as likely lead to a theory of deficiency of libidinal energy, constitutional or otherwise, a view which was originally put forward by Federn (51). The issue seems academic, however, in view of incontrovertible clinical evidence, drawn from reconstructive psychoanalytic psychotherapy, (that both adolescent and adult borderlines demonstrate a capacity for internalization once their abandonment depression has been worked through)(149, 152-156, 191).

Mahler and the Role of the Libidinal Availability of the Mother in the Development of Normal Object Relations

Mahler's work is replete with references to the fundamental importance of the mother's libidinal availability for the development of normal object relations (138) :

My theory places special emphasis, however, on the interaction of both these factors with the circular processes between infant and mother, in which the mother serves as a beacon of orientation and a living buffer for the infant, in reference to both external reality and his internal milieu. (p. 229).

She continues,

During the course of the normal separation-individuation process, the predominance of pleasure in separate functioning, in an atmosphere where the mother is emotionally available, enables the child to overcome that measure of separation anxiety that makes its appearance at that point of the separation-individuation phase at which a differentiated object representation, separate from the self, gradually enters conscious awareness (pp. 220-221).

In a quasi-closed system or unit the mother executes vitally important ministrations, without which the human young could not survive. The intrauterine, parasite-host relationship within the mother organism must be replaced in the postnatal period by the infant's being enveloped, as it were, in the extrauterine matrix of the mother's nursing care, a kind of *social symbiosis*. The mutual cuing between infant and mother is the most important requisite for normal symbiosis . . . (p. 34).

It is the mother's love of the toddler and her acceptance of his ambivalence that enable the toddler to cathect his self representation with neutralized energy (p. 222).

The question concerning the manner in which the mother's libidinal availability determines the development of the child's intrapsychic structure may be answered in terms of the child's internalization of his interactions with her to form self and object representations, the nature of which will have profound consequences for ego integration (94, 106, 138). Functioning according to the pleasure principle, which comprises his initial orientation in the extrauterine field, the infant will draw away, or will attempt to eliminate or expel the painful feeling state associated with unpleasurable interactions with the mother. Of critical importance, especially in early infancy, is the equation, *"good"* = *pleasurable = minimally stimulating,* as well as the equation, *"bad" = unpleasurable (painful) = overstimulating (i.e., traumatogenic),* as they apply to the quality of the mother-infant interaction.

These interactions are introjected to form scattered "good" and "bad" memory islands which proceed to integrate into the progressively differentiated self- and object-images which Kernberg has described.*

Mahler (138) articulates the mother's role as follows:

It is the specific unconscious need of the mother that activates, out of the infant's infinite potentialities, those in particular that create for each mother "the child" who reflects her own *unique* and individual needs. This process takes place, of course, within the range of the child's innate endowments.

Mutual cuing during the symbiotic phase creates that indelibly imprinted configuration—that complex pattern— that becomes *the leitmotif for "the infant's becoming the child of his particular mother...."*

In other words, the mother conveys—in innumerable ways —a kind of "mirroring frame of reference," to which the primitive self of the infant automatically adjusts (p. 19).

Mahler and the Ego Fixation of the Borderline

Although she urges caution in drawing inferences concerning adult psychopathology based upon observations of childhood development phenomena (147), Mahler notes that there is considerable clinical evidence in support of the inference that the ego fixation of the borderline individual occurs during the rapproche-

---

* It should be noted here that, with reference to mother-infant interactions during the first postnatal year, and in particular during its first half, the term *mother* in fact has reference to the maternal part-object (breast); thus, the term *mother* is employed here in this connection for generic convenience.

ment subphase (16-25 months) of separation-individuation, and in a case illustration she has pointed out the central theme of the patient's search for reunion with the "good symbiotic mother."

Mahler (138) is, however, equivocal about the mother's role in that ego fixation. She suggests the possible developmental consequences of the mother's libidinal unavailability to the infant. She asserts that in instances in which the mother in fantasy or actuality fails in acceptance of the infant, the latter experiences a deficit in self-esteem and a consequent narcissistic vulnerability. She goes on to say,

> If the mother's primary preoccupation with her infant, her mirroring function, is unpredictable, unstable, anxiety ridden or hostile, then the individuating child has to do without a reliable frame of reference for checking back perceptually and emotionally. The result would be a disturbance in the primitive self feeling (p. 19).

On the other hand, while emphasizing the importance of the mother's libidinal availability for optimal infantile ego development, Mahler also points up the normal infant's striking capacity to extract supplies from any available human contact. In support of this view, she cites Spitz's (208, 210-215) investigation of infants who experienced the loss of symbiotic love object during the second half of the first year; although the infants perished if a substitute object was not found, those who found one survived.

In discussing the nature-nurture or constitution-experience issue with respect to infantile psychosis, Mahler suggested the complementary relationship between nature and nurture (138).

> Even those children with the sturdiest constitution can become psychotic if subjected to severe, staggering traumatization during the vulnerable autistic or symbiotic phases of development; while in those with the weakest nature or constitution, nurture does not suffice to overcome their innate defects (p. 48).

Mahler clearly averred that, for her, constitutional defect served as the basis for infantile psychosis, whose victims she described as lacking or failing to acquire the capacity to internalize the representation of the mothering object as a guide for the differentiation of inner from external stimulation.

Mahler also cited studies (54) of children who spent their first year of life in a concentration camp: "While these experiences left their traces on the children's object relationships, the children developed strong ties to each other and none of them suffered from a childhood psychosis." She further cited Goldfarb's studies (79) of children who had been placed in foster homes who ". . . amidst trying circumstances never severed their ties with reality though they may have paid the price for this object loss with neurotic disorders, character distortions or psychopathic difficulties."

Mahler's cited evidence does support her argument for a constitutional etiology for infantile psychosis, since the children studied did not proceed to develop such severe psychopathology despite having been subjected to severe stress, particularly as a result of having been deprived of their mothers. On the other hand, her evidence may indeed be taken to support the concept of environmental etiology of the borderline, particularly in view of her suggestion that these same children might well have developed neurotic-characterological disorders typical for borderline personalities.

It is, in fact, impossible to compare the children reported in these cited studies (54, 59, 208, 210-215) with borderline children. The former had lost their mothers at an early age and were subsequently able to "find" substitutes for them. On the other hand, the borderline child has a mother with whom there is a unique and uninterrupted interaction with a specific relational focus, viz., reward for regression, withdrawal for separation-individuation.

A plausible position on this ancient dilemma could be as follows: The ratio of constitutional to developmental etiologic influence in the borderline patient might exist on a spectrum with the constitutional at one end and the developmental at the other. Some patients would be at either end but most would be somewhere in between.

3

A Separation-Individuation Failure: Interpersonal

Although the theory presented here is my own responsibility, in its construction I have drawn heavily from the work of others, for example, Fairbairn (50), Jacobson (93, 94), Benedek (8-11), Ekstein (42-47) and Kernberg (99-109). I have paid special attention to Spitz's (208-215) studies of the first year of life, Bowlby's (16-21) studies of the reaction of children to separation from the mother by hospitalization at the separation-individuation phase of development (i.e., 18 months), Rinsley's (188-191) important work on the psychodynamics and intensive treatment of the hospitalized adolescent, and Mahler's (138-147) most important studies of the role of separation-individuation in the ego development of normal children.

Spitz's, Mahler's and Bowlby's studies, based on carefully planned direct observation of crucial phases of development

28

rather than on reconstruction from adult analyses (Spitz (209) and Mahler (138) studying the normal, and Bowlby (17-21) the pathological), were central to the development of my own thinking. I will try to indicate the important role these works have played in my thinking by expressing my understanding of them.

The theory is presented in two sections: the interpersonal and the intrapsychic. This division, although arbitrary and not exclusive, enables the borderline problem to be approached on two levels: This chapter will describe a macroscopic or gross view of how the borderline child's interactions with his mother and father distort his early ego development. The next chapter will show in microscopic detail the consequences of this interaction for the borderline's intrapsychic structure.

The theory suggests that separation for the borderline patient does not evolve as a normal developmental experience but, on the contrary, entails such intense feelings of abandonment that it is experienced as truly a rendezvous with death. To defend against these feelings, the borderline patient clings to the maternal figure, and thus fails to progress through the normal developmental stages of separation-individuation to autonomy. He suffers from a developmental arrest.)

As a background for understanding the developmental antecedents of the borderline syndrome let us turn first to the theory of the contribution of the symbiosis and separation-individuation stages to normal ego development.

Role of the Mother in Normal Ego Development During the Separation-Individuation Phase

The concept of separation-individuation as a normal phase of the mother-child relationship is relatively recent and has emerged as an outgrowth of the study of ego psychology and increased interest in mothering patterns. This theory has evolved through the work of many people, but most important are Benedek (8-11), Jacobson (93, 94), Spitz (208-215), and Mahler (138-147), who studied by direct observation the separation-individuation process.

of normal children. It is beyond the scope of this book to give a comprehensive discussion of this vast topic and for further detail the reader is referred to their publications. However, a short outline provides the background essential to understanding the role of separation-individuation in the borderline patient.

Stage of Symbiosis

In normal development the separation-individuation stage is immediately preceded by the symbiotic stage. Symbiosis can be defined as an interdependent relationship in which the combined energies of both partners are necessary for the existence of each. Apart from each other, each member appears to "perish."

The child's image of himself and of his mother in this phase is of one symbiotic unit. The importance of the symbiotic phase, which usually spans ages three months to 18 months, to the normal development of ego structure can hardly be overemphasized. For example, Spitz (209) suggests that it is the mother who mediates every perception, every action, every insight, and every bit of knowledge.

The emotional climate of the mother interacts with that of the infant in a stimulating mutual experience that propels the infant into ever new and more involved experiences and responses. The quality of the mothering, the character, gifts, and talents of the mother, her ability to pick up cues and signals from her child, and her imagination in this complex interrelationship during the first year of the symbiosis seem to be the fertile soil in which ego development takes place (225).

The mother functions as an auxiliary ego for the child, performing functions he is not yet able to perform for himself—i.e., she controls frustration tolerance, sets ego boundaries, perceives reality and helps to control impulses.

Mahler (139) states that the child's dim awareness of the mother as a need-satisfying object marks the beginning of the symbiotic phase in which the infant behaves and functions as though he and his mother were a single omnipotent system, a dual unity within one common boundary. Mahler (139) then emphasizes that the mother, because of the absence of an inner organizer in the human infant, must be able to serve as a buffer against inner and outer stimuli, gradually organizing them for the infant and orienting him to the inner versus the outer world in boundary formation and sensory perception. Thus, in the symbiotic stage, which continues through approximately the eighteenth month, the mother performs many of the ego functions the child will later learn to perform himself.

Separation-Individuation Stage—18 to 36 Months

The symbiotic stage so crucial to ego development should soon attenuate and be succeeded by the separation-individuation stage, which is equally crucial to development. Mahler suggests that this phase begins around 18 months and parallels the development of the child's capacity to walk and therefore physically separate himself from the mother. Mahler further suggests that the two-year-old child soon experiences his separateness in many other ways, enjoying his independence in exercising mastery with great tenacity. Accompanying these events the infant's sense of individual entity and identity—the image of the self as an object—develops, mediated by bodily sensation and perception. The child now undergoes an intrapsychic separation and begins to perceive his own image as being entirely separate from the mother's.

Rinsley (188, 190) has outlined some of the most important dividends of this achievement. There is an end to object splitting and the development of a capacity to relate to objects as wholes. (See object splitting, p. 19.) Aggression becomes separated from positive or affectionate feelings, and energy is made available to the child's ego for further growth and development. The self and object representations have become more progressively differentiated as the child's perceptual apparatus matures and these perceptions of the self and object then become associated with either positive or negative feelings. For example, the child's sense of a worthwhile or positive self-image springs in part from identifications during this phase with the mother's positive attitude toward him.

(Three forces, 1) the infant's unfolding individuality, 2) the mother's encouragement and support, that is, continuation of "supplies," and 3) the mastery of new ego functions (see below), press the child on his developmental pathway through the stages of separation-individuation toward autonomy.)

Mahler (139) states that from the end of the first year on the average toddler seems to become so preoccupied with practicing his newly developed skills that he does not seem to mind his mother's short departures from the familiar playroom. He does not clamor for his mother's attention and bodily closeness during this practicing period. Some infants behave as though they were drunk with their newly discovered ability to walk in space and widen their acquaintance with large segments of reality. The infant does toddle up to his mother once in a while for "libidinal refueling," but his behavior seems to indicate that for the most part he takes his mother's emotional presence for granted.

Mahler further states that as soon as free locomotion is mastered, the toddler only returns to the mother to seek proximal communication with her. This behavior leaves no doubt that the representations of his self and that of the mother are now well on their way to differentiation. As the toddler masters the ability to move from and to the mother the balance dramatically shifts within the mother-toddler interaction from activity on the part of the mother to activity on the part of the child. Mahler concludes that the mother, as the catalyst of the individuation process, must be able to read the toddler's "primary-process" language. She emphasizes the resiliency with which the child's autonomy unfolds from within his own ego if he feels a fair degree of what she calls "communicative matching" on the mother's part. This term describes a process in which the mother perceives and responds with approval and "supplies" to the toddler's nonverbal cues.)

Ego Development

In the course of this separation, the child internalizes into his immature ego through the mechanisms of identification and introjection those ego functions that the mother had performed for him and his ego structure becomes endowed with essential new functions: (secure ego boundaries against both inner and outer stimuli; strengthening of repression that makes more affect available for sublimation; improved reality perception; frustration tolerance; and impulse control. He develops the capacity to be alone (228), to tolerate anxiety and depression (248, 251), to show concern and feel guilt)(230-232).

Object Constancy

Object constancy, equally fateful for later interpersonal relations, also is a fundamental consequence of successful separation-individuation. This concept had origins in both general psychology (177-179) and psychoanalysis. Those interested in a complete discussion are referred to the excellent articles by Fraiberg (52) and McDevitt (159). (The term as it is commonly used refers to the capacity to maintain object relatedness irrespective of frustration or satisfaction.) The relationship has relative autonomy from the fluctuations of need states. The emotional investment of the mother remains stable regardless of fluctuations in the infant's need states or externally imposed frustration.) This quality is associated with, and some believe dependent on, the capacity to evoke a stable consistent memory image or mental representation of the mother whether she is there or not.) The achievement of this capacity has been variously placed, depending on the observer: For example, Spitz (209) places it at eight months. Mahler (139), however, places it around 25 months, specifically linking the attainment with the emergence of a stable mental representation that enables the child to tolerate separation from the mother.*

These new functions can be viewed as benefits of the achievement of separation and autonomy. Clearly, the mastering of this phase lays the foundation of ego structure.

---

* The further importance of object constancy is illustrated by the fact that it is a prerequisite for that process so vital to the repair of an object loss—that is, mourning. If one cannot evoke mental images of the lost object, how can one resolve all the painful feelings caused by this loss to form new object relations? If one cannot mourn, he becomes fatally vulnerable to object loss.

Mahler (141) describes the separation-individuation process as being comprised of four identifiable subphases which blend into each other. It should be kept in mind that while the sequence of the four stages does not vary, the ages given are at best rough approximations and can vary widely in the individual child.

1. Differentiation (3-8 months)—the child differentiates his body image from that of the mother's body image.
2. Practicing (8-15 months)—the child is actively exploring the new opportunities of the real world about him and seems oblivious of the mother.
3. Rapprochement (15-22 months)—his practicing now completed the child again turns to the mother with new demands for her responsiveness to his individuation.
4. On the Way to Object Constancy.

ROLE OF THE FATHER IN NORMAL SEPARATION-INDIVIDUATION

Contemporary psychoanalytic authors have viewed the father's first role as that of drawing and attracting the child out of the symbiotic orbit into the real world of things and people.

Mahler confirmed Greenacre's formulations on this subject and integrated them with her own in the following words:

> The comparative immunity against contamination of the father image . . . can be understood fundamentally in the light thrown upon it by Dr. Greenacre—namely [through] the deep-going difference between the processes by which the two images take shape . . . the mother image evolves by being first differentiated within the symbiotic dual unity complex and then separated out from it; . . . the father image comes toward the child . . . "from outer space" as it were . . . as something gloriously new and exciting, at just the time when the toddler is experiencing a feverish quest for expansion.

The father thus becomes "the knight in shining armor," and sometimes "the rescuer from the 'bad' mother."

Abelin (1) offered the following tentative conclusions from his study of the role of the father in the separation-individuation process.

1. The specific relationship with the father (e.g., the smiling response) begins in the symbiotic phase, somewhat later than it does with the mother and sibling. When the father is reasonably familiar to the infant, the latter shows no stranger anxiety toward him.

2. During the differentiation subphase, attachment to the father increases progressively, but the most conspicuous "turning toward the father" occurs at the beginning of the practicing subphase, when he becomes the "other," the "different" parent. He is a new, more interesting object for the child in the practicing subphase, whereas the mother is by now taken for granted as a "home base," for periodic refueling. The father comes to stand for distant, "non-mother" space—for the elated exploration of reality. A special quality of exuberance is linked with him.

3. Father—and siblings—are only the first landmarks in the expanding practicing space: "Out there" the male adults seem to represent the most different, the most fascinating group of objects. At first, stranger reactions to men are distinct, and often more violent than they are to women. This derives from the sequence and modes in which the specificity of father and mother have been established: The "stranger" is either too unlike or too similar to the parent (s). With the passing of the stranger conflict, a clear preference for men often emerges patterned on the relationship with the father.

4. Girls tend to attach themselves to the father earlier than boys and, conversely, to be more wary of strange men, more discriminating with regard to unfamiliar persons in general. Boys approach male adults earlier and in a more exploratory way. This is associated with their greater interest in distant space and in inanimate objects. Girls have been observed to be amazingly "feminine" and flirtatious as early as at the beginning of the second year, seeking passive physical affection with father substitutes.

5. The father is not consistently experienced as a rival for

mother's loving attention; rather he remains an "uncontaminated" parental love object, while the relationship with the mother tends to become fraught with ambivalence during the rapprochement crisis. The role of the father as a rival may be foreshadowed more clearly and consistently in firstborn boys, or in different cultural settings; in such cases, it may even bear some traits of the later oedipal conflict.

6. The symbolic representation of the father must be distinguished from the actual relationship with him. The rapprochement crisis is at first centered solely on the representation of the self and the mother. A few weeks later, the father begins to appear in the fantasy world of the toddler as the other, more powerful parent. *This father image may be necessary for the satisfactory resolution of the ambivalent rapprochement position.* The simultaneous representation of the three images of the self and both parents would constitute an even more elaborate step—perhaps representing the formal element of the oedipal complex. Thus, the development of these nuclear images after the rapprochement subphase would seem to recapitulate the earlier history of the actual specific relationships—in a distilled and schematized form. In cognitive development, Piaget (177) has called this recapitulation a "vertical lag."

The father becomes the first and most familiar of the "different" adults—the first step into the world of novelty, of external reality. As such, he comes to reflect the exuberant qualities of the practicing subphase, in which the push toward active exploration and autonomous functioning is dissociated in time and space from the "refueling," the periodic returning to the familiar and comforting mother. While this very source of comfort, if exclusive, threatens the infant's need for initiative, attachment to the father is apt to bind the new, wild centrifugal forces. The father responds exquisitely to the "need to function" of the child's newly maturing gross motor apparatuses.

There is implicit opposition between the centrifugal forces involved in practicing and the underlying need for the mother. Increasingly, as this need is brought to light and the two poles confront each other, the centripetal forces of rapprochement threaten to submerge the newly conquered reality in the whirlpool of the primary undifferentiated stage. But when this reality is genuinely anchored in a wide range of nonmaternal objects, when the father is firmly established as the "other," the "different" parent, then we need not be too concerned about the further development of the toddler toward final individuation and intrapsychic separation.

We might summarize the father's contribution to normal ego development in the separation-individuation phase of development as follows: 1) To serve as an object uncontaminated with symbiotic cathexis, to draw and attract a child into the real world of things and people. 2) In his rapprochement subphase to serve as a parental love object which aligns itself with reality and the forces of individuation as opposed to the regressive pull to the need of the mother and therefore to contribute to the successful resolution of the rapprochement phase. 3) To participate in the construction of mental images of the self, the maternal object and the paternal object—the forerunner to the oedipal complex.

Having outlined the essential contributions of the mother and the father to ego development in normal separation-individuation let us now describe what goes wrong in the borderline patient's ego development.

WHAT GOES WRONG IN THE SEPARATION-INDIVIDUATION STAGE IN THE BORDERLINE PATIENT'S DEVELOPMENT

Role of the Mother

The mother of the borderline patient usually suffers from a borderline syndrome herself. The events outlined above do not take place with her child. Having been unable to separate from her own mother, she fosters continuance of the symbiotic union with her child, thus encouraging dependency to maintain her own emotional equilibrium. She is threatened by and unable to deal with the infant's emerging individuality and therefore clings to the child to prevent separation, discouraging moves toward individuation by withdrawing her support (149, 158).

She depersonifies the child (189, 203, 204, 253), cannot see him as he is, but rather projects upon him the image of one of her own parents or of a sibling; or she perceives him as a perpetual infant or an object and uses him to defend herself against her own feelings of abandonment. Consequently, she is unable to respond to his unfolding individuality and he early learns to disregard certain of his own potentials in order to preserve his source of supplies (approval) from the mother.

Feelings of Abandonment

Therefore, between the ages of 18 months and 36 months a conflict develops in the child between his own developmental push for individuation and autonomy, and fear of the withdrawal of the mother's emotional supplies that this growth would entail. He needs her approval to develop ego structure and grow; however, if he grows the supplies are withdrawn. These are the first seeds of his feelings of abandonment (depression, rage, panic, guilt, passivity and helplessness, emptiness and void) which have such far-reaching consequences.

The Six Horsemen of the Apocalypse

The six psychiatric horsemen of the apocalypse—depression, anger, fear, guilt, passivity and helplessness, and emptiness and void—vie in their emotional sway and destructiveness with the social upheaval and destructiveness of the original four horsemen —famine, war, flood, and pestilence. Technical words are too abstract to convey the intensity and immediacy of these feelings and therefore the primacy they hold over the patient's entire life. The patient's functioning in the world, his relationships with people, and even some of his physiologic functions are subordinated to the defense against these feelings.

It is important to distinguish the feelings of abandonment or intrapsychic experience from an actual physical separation and abandonment in the patient's environmental experience. The term "abandonment feelings" refers to the intrapsychic experience of the patient, that is, to what he feels about the environmental experience of separation. Whether the environmental experience results in "feelings of abandonment" depends on the psyche of the patient, not on the experience itself. The abandonment feelings evolve from multifactorial intrapsychic reactions, namely the "six horsemen"; the separation experience is only a precipitating influence.

Components of Abandonment Feelings

The abandonment feelings comprise not one feeling but a complex of six constituent feelings: depression, anger and rage, fear, guilt, passivity and helplessness, emptiness and void. The intensity and degree of each of these component feelings will vary with the unique developmental traumas of each individual. However, each component will be present to some degree in every patient.

Depression

The depression has qualities similar to that emotion described by Spitz (208) as anaclitic depression: feelings that spring from the loss or the threat of loss either of part of the self or of supplies that the patient believes vital for survival. Patients often think of this in physical terms comparable to losing an arm or both legs, or being deprived of vital substances such as oxygen, plasma, or blood. This aspect of the depression illustrates best how it differs in quality from the adult psychotic depression whose dynamics are predicated upon the presence of a sadistically cruel superego that persecutes the ego until it breaks down.

The manner in which the depression emerges in therapy is itself a statement of its motivational power. In the first or testing phase of therapy the patient may complain of boredom or a vague sense of numbness or depression but his affect will appear quite bland and he will not seem to be suffering from a very intense feeling; this is a reflection of the fact that he is now well defended against the abandonment feelings. As the defenses are successively interrupted the depression becomes more intense, repressed memories emerge, and the patient quite obviously is suffering. The patient intensifies his struggle to maintain his defenses but as the doctor interprets them the patient gradually slides into the bottom of his depression where lies, almost always, suicidal despair and belief that it will never be possible to receive the necessary supplies. At this point the patient is a genuine suicidal risk and there is no longer any doubt in the observer's mind about the motivational power of the patient's depression.

Rage

The intensity of the patient's anger and rage and the rate of the emergence of these emotions in psychotherapy parallel that of the depression. The more depressed the patient becomes the angrier he becomes. The content of the rage is first more general and very often projected upon contemporary situations. As memory of his feelings returns, the rage becomes more and more focused on the relationship with the mother. Finally at the bottom of the trough, parallel to the suicidal despair, are homicidal fantasies and impulses directed at the mother. Thus the rage parallels and is companion to the depression throughout the stages of psychotherapy.

Fear

A third component is the fear of being abandoned which may be expressed as fear of being helpless, or of supplies being cut off, of facing death, or of being killed. Two psychosomatic accompaniments of this fear that I have observed in patients in an abandonment panic are asthma and peptic ulcer. It is possible to theorize that these symptoms are an expression of the patient's separation fear. The former is a fear of death if supplies are cut off and the latter a hungering for the lost supplies. The panic itself can dominate the clinical picture to the point that it conceals both the underlying depression and rage.

The degree to which fear participates in the clinical picture seems to be related to the degree to which the mother used the threat of abandonment as a disciplinary technique. The patients live with an almost constant fear of abandonment, waiting for the "Sword of Damocles" to fall. They recall childhood as "it was like living in a permanent funeral as if I might soon be buried."

The threat of abandonment apparently had been used as a disciplinary technique to inhibit the patient's self-assertion or expression of anger and to enforce compliance. Therefore, as the depression and rage emerge in psychotherapy, the fear of being abandoned for expressing these feelings rises in tandem, sometimes reaching panic proportions.

Guilt

Guilt is the "fifth column" behind the front line of the patient's defenses. This guilt, springing from the patient's introjection of the mother's attitude toward him, now becomes the patient's attitude toward himself. Since the mother greeted the expression of his self-assertion and his wish to separate and individuate with disapproval and withdrawal, the patient begins to feel guilty about that whole part of himself which seeks separation and individuation, that is, his thoughts, wishes, feelings, and actions. Consequently, to avoid guilt feelings he suppresses moves in this direction (236) and resorts to a chronic state of clinging and demanding, and thereby sabotages, as by a "fifth column," his own autonomy. This aspect of the guilt is seen most clearly in treatment after the environmental conflict with the mother has been more or less resolved when an intense intrapsychic battle comes to the fore between the patient's wish to individuate and the guilt that this entails.

Passivity and Helplessness

The mother withdraws her approval when the patient attempts to assert himself since she views his self-assertion toward individuation as a threatened "loss" of her child. Therefore the patient associates the fear of abandonment with his own capacity for assertion. When faced with a conflict, he becomes overwhelmed with feelings of passivity and helplessness since the only tool that might give him mastery, self-assertion, brings with it the fear of loss of his mother's love, of abandonment.

Emptiness and Void

The sense of void is best described as one of terrifying inner emptiness or numbness; it springs partially from introjection of the mother's negative attitudes that leaves the patient devoid, or empty, of positive supportive introjects.

Defenses Against Abandonment Feelings

Unable to tolerate the awareness of these feelings, the child handles them by denial (93) of the reality of separation, by projection and acting out of the wish for reunion by clinging, and by avoidance of individuation stimuli (236), all of which are fostered by the widespread employment of the splitting defense mechanism (49, 55, 56) (see Chapter 4). Although separated he continues to cling to the mother to defend himself against the return of feelings of abandonment into awareness (297). The clinging, splitting, denial and avoidance are secondarily reinforced by any number of the various defense mechanisms which later determine the form of the clinical picture: for example, neurotic mechanisms such as those of the hypochondriac, the obsessive-compulsive, the phobic or the hysterical; schizoid mechanisms such as isolation, detachment, and withdrawal of affect.

The abandonment feelings are then split off from awareness; their overwhelming but hidden force is observable through the tenacity and strength of the defense mechanisms used to keep them in check. These defenses, however, effectively block the patient's developmental movement through the stages of separation-individuation to autonomy. He suffers from a developmental arrest. Unlike the autistic or infantile psychotic child, the child with the borderline syndrome has separated from the symbiotic stage and has become fixated in one of the subphases of the separation-individuation stage—possibly the rapprochement stage (15-22 months) where the mother's sharing is such a vital catalyst to the individuation process.

Developmental Arrest or Narcissistic-Oral Ego Fixation

To understand the disastrous consequences of these events for the development of the child's ego structure we must shift to another framework, that is, Freud's psychosexual continuum, which has common meeting points with the one we have been discussing and which, although not specifically emphasized here, is implied as an integral part of the developmental process. Freud spoke of two phases, the autoerotic and the narcissistic (57) phases, that precede the oral phase of development. Symbiosis is a narcissistic phase and separation-individuation is ushered in by orality. It is likely that the developmental arrest of the borderline occurs either in the narcissistic or early oral phase. The earlier the arrest occurs the more likely the patient's clinical picture will resemble the psychotic, and the later this occurs the more likely the clinical picture will resemble the neurotic. In either case the developmental arrest produces severe defects in ego functioning.

Those functions that the mother had performed for the child which the normal child internalizes through identification are not internalized because of the arrest. Consequently the ego defects consist of poor reality perception, poor frustration tolerance and impulse control, and fluid ego boundaries, that is, difficulty in distinguishing between inner and outside stimuli. These are the ego defects referred to by Kernberg (99) as non-specific ego weakness.

The ego structure is further characterized by the persistence of the primitive defense mechanisms of splitting and the specific defenses against separation: projection, acting out the wish for reunion by clinging, denial and avoidance (113-116).

The arrest also causes a failure to achieve object constancy. This has far-reaching clinical significance: 1) The patient does not relate to objects, that is, persons, as wholes but as parts (113-116). 2) The object relationship does not persist through frustration but tends to fluctuate widely with the need states. 3) He is unable to evoke the image of the person when he is not present. When the person is not physically present the borderline patient feels he has literally disappeared and is not going to return. 4) He cannot mourn. Any object loss or separation becomes a disastrous calamity. This can be seen clearly in the transference relationship during the therapist's vacation period; because the patient does not feel that the doctor will return, he sets his defensive operations in motion well in advance to protect himself. Some styles of defense are emotionally withdrawing from the interviews in advance, actually physically leaving the doctor before he can leave the patient, complete emotional detachment, acting out by starting an affair, carrying through a previously tentative marriage possibility, and trying to provoke the therapist by, for example, coming late for appointments.

Role of the Father

Life never seems to be so difficult that it can't get worse. Does the borderline child whose growth is already heavily burdened by the mother's regressive pull get the "average expectable" help from a father who influences him toward growth and reality, who forms a "bridge" out of the symbiotic whirlpool? The answer is no.

The father of the borderline child may have any one of the severe forms of character pathology—i.e. borderline, narcissistic disorder, or even schizophrenia. The key feature is that he is not available to the child as an uncontaminated object to support the forces of individuation and mastery of reality.

Although the specifics vary with each case, the father's influence almost always is towards a reinforcement of the mother-child exclusive or clinging relationship, rather than either opposing or making efforts to lead the child away from it. The marital contact often seems to consist of the mother's permitting the father distance from the home, as long as the father permits the mother exclusive control of the child. It is instructive to note in these cases the amount of absence the father is permitted without any complaint from the mother. Beyond the fact of his frequent absence, the specific dynamics of his relationship with the mother and child when he is present again reinforce the mother-child exclusive relationship. Some of the possible psychodynamic variations are illustrated by the following case examples derived from patients in intensive reconstructive psychotherapy.

Fred, Age 23

This patient's paranoid mother attacked him verbally and physically when the father was not at home. The father spent as much time out of the home as possible. During the patient's childhood, whenever he would attempt to assert himself with the mother or seek the father's assistance in dealing with mother the father would respond as if he were being attacked, being hurt, as if his son were trying to cause trouble. He admonished the boy not to assert himself, to adapt a passive, submissive, accepting role with the mother and when the boy disobeyed this rule the father would leave the house. If the child persisted either in his complaints about the mother or efforts to assert himself, the father would then attack him as being crazy and the source of all the family trouble.

The father would reward his son for his passivity by verbalizing love for him, but in reality the father never played with him or attended any of his functions at school, and actually left him completely in the mother's care. For example, the patient reported his anger at his father's lack of support as follows: "There was nobody there to help. Father valued the house, the neighbors and his relationship with my mother more than he valued me. He sacrificed me for his own thing. He intimidated me if I asserted myself with my brother or my mother. He told me not to take any action. He promised me all kinds of rewards if I would just 'not cause trouble.' Father didn't care. My success didn't matter to him. All he ever gave me was money.

"I was always waiting for father to take action. He let my mother in and let her take advantage of me. Whenever he'd leave the house I'd go crazy because I knew I was alone with her." This is a telling description of the father's failure to serve as the object counteracting the regressive maternal pull. The failure of the normal influence exerted by the normal father could be seen later in Fred's inordinate difficulty in perceiving and mastering reality.

Tom, Age 43

Tom's father spent seven days a week at work with the rationalization that he did it out of love of his children in order to support them. The mother had used the patient to fill in for the father, demanding that he meet her needs in order to receive her love and approval. When the father was around, he reinforced the mother's attacks on the patient's efforts to individuate, put the patient down specifically for those efforts and therefore reinforced the dependence on the mother.

The patient developed an image of himself as being dependent, inadequate and lacking substance, derived from his interactions with the mother. This view was reinforced by the father, whose image he introjected as disapproving and punitive.

Sally, Age 31

Sally had a passive-dependent father who submitted to his aggressive and domineering wife, and, though he verbalized a great deal of affection for the patient, he at the same time dissuaded her from asserting herself with the mother. He consciously urged her by words as well as by behavioral example to adopt his own defense mechanisms of passivity, denial and detachment, thus failing to help Sally to deal with the conflict with the mother and reinforcing her separation-individuation problem. She developed a conscious image of the father as tender, loving, and caring which she later acted out in her relationship with men, where she could only relate as a child with a man who was a care-taking father.

Catherine, Age 22

Catherine (described in Chapter 7) had a father who served as an object to substitute for or replace the mother as a maternal symbol through which the patient acted out the entire separation-individuation problem. This may have happened because the patient received so few supplies of love and approval from the mother but did receive some from the father.

The father, away from home most of the time when the patient was young, demanded that the patient on the one hand be a little girl and comply with his wishes and on the other be protective of him like a mother. When she deviated from this role he would attack her by displaying his fierce temper, sometimes pulling her hair or throwing things at her.

She introjected a father image that was punitive and threatening, best illustrated by the fact that when the patient wrote a letter asserting her independence from the father she developed an intense panic, fearing that her apartment would be broken into and she would be attacked. Only later did she become aware that the fear was related to her fear that her father would attack her if she asserted herself.

Summary

The borderline father by his absence, as well as by the way he relates to the mother when present—surrendering the child to the mother's wishes and reinforcing her clinging, fails to provide that essential opposite pole of valence in reality that would tend to help counteract the regressive symbiotic pull toward the mother. Not only does the mother exert an active pressure for a clinging, symbiotic relationship, but there is also an absence of the usual counteracting pull of the father toward reality.

Thus, in the negative sense the father is as involved in etiology as the mother. Furthermore, the extraordinary degree to which borderline patients avoid and deny reality, i.e., the father, in order to project and act out the wish for reunion fantasy, is more easily understood. The lack of the opposite pole—the father—leaves them with only one pole—the mother—in the rapprochement crisis. Not anchored in father and his reality, they find it easy to deny his existence to pursue the reunion with mother.

CHILDHOOD

Splitting, denial, and the other defense mechanisms enable the child to contain his feelings of abandonment and to function beneath the dependency umbrella of childhood unless he is exposed to an environmental separation from the figure to whom he is clinging. However, the next challenge to his defensive system occurs usually at prepuberty ages 10 to 12, when a second marked developmental maturation of the ego occurs, creating a period of special vulnerability.

PREPUBERTY—A SECOND SEPARATION-INDIVIDUATION PHASE

This growth spurt, manifested by a thrust toward activity combined with a turn toward reality, is similar in scope to the maturation of the ego that occurred in the separation-individuation phase. This maturation, together with the need to separate further from the mother, produces a recapitulation of that early phase of development, that is, a second separation-individuation phase.

Deutsch (37) suggests that prepuberty is a phase in which sexual instincts are weakest and development of the ego is most intense, and that the phase is characterized by a thrust of activity and turning toward growth and independence; thus, it is an intensive process of adaptation to reality and mastery of the environment. The adolescent is caught between the past and the future, between childhood and adulthood, just as the infant is caught between a symbiotic relationship and autonomy. Deutsch emphasizes that the struggle for independence in this period is strongly reminiscent of the processes that take place approximately between the age 18 months and three years, that is, the transition from the symbiotic stage to autonomy. (She gives an example of the girl in prepuberty who, full of hatred and rage, wants to tear herself away from her mother's influence but at the same time frequently reveals an intensified, anxious urge to remain under the maternal protection. She concludes that prepuberty repeats the preoedipal or the separation-individuation phase not only in the struggle for liberation from the mother—the central point of the girl's psychological life at this time—but in other respects as well.)

I found Deutsch's report helpful when attempting to understand why the borderline syndrome in adolescents so often makes its clinical appearance during prepuberty. For example, it often appears during the change from the local elementary school to the larger amalgamated junior high school. In addition, it is not uncommon in adult borderline outpatients to get a history of an untreated symptomatic outbreak at this time of their lives. The theory described by Deutsch (37) seemed to fit the pieces of the puzzle together. It suggested that all adolescents go through a second separation-individuation phase in prepuberty due to the maturational spurt of the ego. In some, this alone precipitates a clinical borderline syndrome while still others manage to traverse this especially vulnerable period without symptoms—perhaps through subtle but unnoticed intensification of the clinging mechanism.

LATER PRECIPITATING STRESSES IN THE ADULT BORDERLINE

The rest of the borderline patient's life history is uniquely dependent upon precipitating events which can impinge upon either aspect of his separation-individuation problem—events which either threaten the clinging relationship or represent a challenge or test of the capacity for individuation or both.

There has been considerable discussion in the literature about the differences between the so-called borderline state and the clinical borderline syndrome. The theory presented here suggests that the borderline state refers to a patient who has a separation failure, an abandonment depression and the ego fixation—but who is currently and probably temporarily able to function with minimal impairment by symptoms because he has adapted to a life-style that conceals his avoidance of individuation. He takes jobs beneath his potential while living at home—and he has not had an environmental separation from the person to whom he is clinging—in other words, he is currently well defended against his borderline problems.

Many borderline patients go through their entire lives this way without ever developing symptoms serious enough to impel them to see a psychiatrist. They remain unaware of the developmental price they have paid for this adjustment. Indeed, they have no interest whatsoever in such awareness because it would create conflicts about this level of adjustment. The clerk who could have been a lawyer, the secretary who could have been an interior decorator, the man or woman in his/her forties without a relationship with the opposite sex—these all are able to deny and rationalize these direct consequences of their borderline disorder.

Beyond this, such borderline patients do not realize the degree to which the ordinary signposts of passage through life represent potentially serious stresses for them. These could be called individuation stresses.

Individuation Stresses

Life events which present a challenge to the borderline's capacity to cope through self motivation (i.e., being motivated by his own thoughts, feelings) stress his denial of individuation and, if severe enough, can precipitate clinical symptoms.

First and foremost, the psychosocial events that signalize normal progress in the life cycle are usually a time of special vulnerability for the borderline: leaving home for school, going away to camp, going from the neighborhood to the larger community high school, going away to college, graduating from college, starting a career, getting married, becoming a parent, being promoted at work. Some borderline adolescents have an abandonment depression at the end of their junior year or the start of the senior year of high school as they anticipate graduation and leaving home. Others break down only later in the first six months of college, when they have left home. Work promotions can so intensify the anxiety about coping autonomously that a clinical syndrome occurs. This particularly applies to the borderline patient who is promoted to a position where he cannot depend on a supervisor and must act on his own initiative.

Separation Stresses

Separation stresses occur when there is any threat to the clinging relationship to the principal person or object. The borderline patient is sensitive to any disturbance in this relationship no matter how minor. It is as if the patient were connected to the object by a set of continuous two-way radar-like emotional impulses. Any disturbance in the harmony or continuity of this two-way communication can arouse some separation anxiety. The spectrum varies from mild disapproval on the part of the object to its complete absence. The mildest separation stresses and their resultant separation anxiety are probably never seen by the therapist except in the transference reactions of his patients, whereas the more serious stresses of death, divorce, etc. usually bring on a clinical syndrome.

FURTHER DEFENSES AGAINST SEPARATION

How the borderline patient, clinging to the maternal object, experiences and deals with separation can be illustrated by Bowlby's study of infants aged 13-32 months who were separated from the succoring maternal figure (16-21). The relationship of Bowlby's observations to the borderline patient, first brought to my attention by Rinsley (188, 191), indicates their excellence and clinical usefulness. I do not agree, however, with the broad theoretical inferences that Bowlby draws from these observations.

Bowlby, studying infantile mourning, described the mourning process as a complex sequence of psychological processes and their overt manifestations, beginning with longing, angry efforts at recovery, appeals for help, then proceeding through apathy and disorganization of behavior, and finally ending with some form of reorganization. He suggested that mourning may take one of several different courses: Those which enable the individual ultimately to relate to new objects and find satisfaction in them are commonly judged to be healthy; those which fail in this outcome are pathological.

If the separation is not successful, Bowlby describes the infant as going through three phases, protest and wish for reunion, despair, and detachment.

Protest and Wish for Reunion

Bowlby states that this phase may last for a few hours to a week or more during which time the child appears acutely distressed at having lost its mother and seeks to recapture her by the full exercise of his limited resources. His behavior suggests strong expectations and wishes that she will return. Meantime, he is apt to reject all alternative figures who offer to do things for him, although some children will cling desperately to a nurse.

Despair

In this second phase the infant's preoccupation with his missing mother is still evident, although his behavior suggests increasing hopelessness, the acts of physical movement diminish or come to an end, and he may cry monotonously or intermittently. He is withdrawn and inactive, makes no demands on the environment, and appears to be in a state of deep mourning.

Detachment

Because the child shows more interest in his surroundings, the phase of detachment which sooner or later succeeds protest and despair is often welcomed as a sign of recovery. He no longer rejects the nurses, but accepts their care, food, the toys they bring; he may even smile and be sociable. When his mother visits, however, it can be seen that all is not well for there is a striking absence of the behavior characteristic of the strong attachment to the mother normal at this age. Instead of greeting his mother he may seem hardly to know her; instead of clinging to her he may remain remote and apathetic; instead of tears there is a listless turning away—he seems to have lost all interest in her.

Should his hospital stay be prolonged and should he, as is usual, have the experience of becoming transiently attached to a series of nurses, each of whom leaves, thus again and again repeating for him the original experience of loss of his mother, in time he will act as though neither mothering nor contact with humans had much significance for him. After the upset of losing several mother figures to whom in turn he has given some trust and affection, he will gradually commit himself less and less to succeeding figures and in time will stop altogether taking the risks of attaching himself to anyone. Instead he will become increasingly self-centered and, instead of having desires and feelings towards people, he will become preoccupied with material things such as sweets, toys, and food. A child living in a hospital or institution who has reached this state will no longer be upset when nurses change or leave. He will cease to show feelings when his parents come and go on visiting days, and it may cause them pain when they realize that, although he has an avid interest in the presents they bring, he has little interest in them as special people.

When borderline adult patients go through the experience of separation which they have been defending themselves against all their lives they seem to react just as Bowlby's infants in the second stage of despair. The patient feels the separation as an abandonment, a loss of a part of himself which brings with it unique and intense fears of death. He initially defends himself against these feelings by clinging to the lost object, that is, expressing the wish for reunion.

The power of this wish for reunion, no small matter by itself, can be extraordinarily influenced or strengthened by environmental experiences such as recurrent illnesses when the mother must care for him, or efforts of the mother to restore reunion whenever any minor separation occurs. When the clinging fails to achieve its aim the patient next passes into a depression which, however, contains such intense feelings of rage, despair, and hopelessness that he further defends himself against this state by splitting, projection, acting out, or by other styles of defense, that is, obsessive-compulsive, schizoid, etc., which in turn protect him against feeling the despair and remembering the abandonment.

Although the rage is precipitated by the separation experience, the content of the rage is also related to the many prior deprivations experienced in the clinging relationship. The clinical picture portrays the repetition in the borderline adult of an infantile drama—the abandonment depression engrafted to the separation-individuation process with a resultant halting of further ego development.

In other words, the patient develops an abandonment depression; his ego structure remains orally fixated; his object relations transpire at an oral level; and his most basic fears are of engulfment or abandonment. His most basic problems have to do with the primitive sense of identity and separateness, as well as of mastery and control of impulses.

4

A Separation-Individuation Failure: Intrapsychic

It is now necessary to take the issue a step further by presenting a microscopic, detailed view of just how this interaction with the mother and father relates to the developing intrapsychic structure of the borderline child—i.e., the split ego and the split object relations unit.

The developmental cause of the fixation of the borderline ego is to be found in the mother's withdrawal of her libidinal availability (that is, of her libidinal supplies) as the child makes efforts to separate-individuate during the rapprochement subphase (16-25 months). Further, the fixation comes into existence at exactly that phase of development because the child's individuation constitutes a major threat to the mother's defensive need to cling to her infant and, as a consequence, drives her toward removal of her libidinal availability.

The twin themes (reward and withdrawal) of this interaction are subsequently introjected by the child, become the *leitmotif* of his psychic structure, and reappear in his pathologic split self and object representations as these are recapitulated within the therapeutic transference.

In view of these considerations, it may be argued that the child's excessive oral aggression is entrenched as a consequence of the mother's withdrawal of supplies in the wake of the child's efforts toward separation-individuation, and further aggravated by the latter's inability to integrate positive and negative self and object representations, since such integration would require further separation-individuation which, in turn, would provoke further withdrawal of libidinal supplies. There thus comes about a situation in which aggression is being repetitively provoked without any constructive means to neutralize it.

The evidence in support of this formulation and of what follows in greater detail is derived from a variety of sources:

1. *Observation:*
   a. Casework-family therapy on a once or twice weekly basis, for as long as four years, of the parents of inpatient and outpatient borderline adolescents (149, 151);
   b. Treatment of borderline mothers of borderline patients in private office practice (149);
   c. Detailed observation and study of borderline mothers in conjoint interviews with their borderline adolescents (149);
   d. Long-term, intensive residential psychiatric treatment of borderline adolescents (149, 191, 191a);
   e. Reconstructive psychoanalytic treatment of borderline adults.

2. *Reconstruction:*

The memories and associated affective responses of borderline adolescents and adults in intensive psychotherapy as they worked through their underlying abandonment depression 149, 158).

INTRAPSYCHIC STRUCTURE OF THE BORDERLINE

The terms *split ego* and *split object relations unit* which have been employed to describe the intrapsychic structure typical for the borderline require further definition:

Splitting: Splitting (55, 56, 99) is a mechanism of defense, the function of which is to keep contradictory primitive affective states separated from each other; both states remain in consciousness but do not influence each other. Splitting also keeps apart the internalized self and object representations mutually linked with these affective states. Used normally by the immature ego, splitting ordinarily becomes replaced or supplanted by repression. The ego of the borderline, however, retains splitting as its principal mechanism of defense, while the capacity for normal repression remains underdeveloped.

Split Ego: Along with its reliance upon the splitting defense, the ego is itself split into two parts, one of which functions according to the pleasure principle, the other according to the reality principle.

Split Object Relations Unit (99): The object relations unit is derived from the internalization of the infant's interactions with the mothering object. The unit comprises a self representation and an object representation which are linked by the affect that characterized the interaction. The object relations unit of the borderline turns out to be split into part-units, each of which in turn comprises a part-self representation and a part-object representation together with their associated affects.

Maternal Libidinal Availability and the Split Object Relations Unit

In the case of the borderline, the object relations unit remains split into two separate part-units, each of which contains, as it were, a part-self representation, a part-object representation, and an affect which links the two representations together. These two part-units are derived from internalization of the two principal themes of interaction with the borderline mother: The mother responds to the child's regressive behavior by maintaining her libidinal availability, and to the child's efforts toward separation-individuation by withdrawing it. Thus are produced, in effect, the two aforementioned part-units, which may be termed the *withdrawing object relations part-unit* (WORU) and the *rewarding object relations part-unit* (RORU), each of which has its own component part-self representation, part-object representation, and predominant linking affect. The withdrawing part-unit is cathected or invested predominantly with aggressive energy, the rewarding part-unit with libidinal energy, and both remain separated from each other, as it were, through the mechanism of the splitting defense. It will be recalled that this situation comes about through fixation at Kernberg's Stage 3 (see pp. 20-21) with ensuing failure of integration of good (positive, libidinal) and bad (negative, aggressive) self and object representations into whole (positive + negative) self representations and object representations which would otherwise be expected to have occurred in Stage 4 (p. 21).

One may summarize the borderline's split object relations units as follows:*

	Withdrawing or Aggressive Object Relations Part-Unit (WORU)	Rewarding or Libidinal Object Relations Part-Unit (RORU)
Part-Object Representation	A maternal part-object which is attacking, critical, hostile, angry, withdrawing supplies and approval in the face of assertiveness or other efforts toward separation-individuation.	A maternal part-object which offers approval, support and supplies for regressive and clinging behavior.
Affect	Chronic anger, frustration, feeling thwarted, which cover profound underlying abandonment depression (rage, depression, fear, guilt, passivity and helplessness, emptiness and void).	Feeling good, being fed, gratification of the wish for reunion.
Part-Self Representation	A part-self representation of being inadequate, bad, helpless, guilty, ugly, empty, etc.	A part-self representation of being the good, passive complaint child.

* The reader will immediately discern the similarity of the split object relations unit to Fairbairn's split internalized bad object and Fairbairn deserves full prior credit for having perceived its basic structure in his analyzands. Thus, the withdrawing part-unit may be seen to correspond with Fairbairn's *rejecting object* (R.O.) while the rewarding part-unit may be seen to correspond with his *exciting object* (E.O.).

These two part-units are ways of conceptualizing the intra-psychic structure which underlies the borderline patient's two prominent feeling states. Their relationship with the split ego and their manifestation in transference and resistance are key concepts and will be used throughout the rest of the book. To avoid the clumsiness of such long terms I will use the initials WORU to refer to the withdrawing object relations part-unit and RORU to refer to the rewarding object relations part-unit. In essence the WORU refers to all three components of that part unit: the image of the withdrawing mother; the image of the inadequate, bad self; and the feeling state that links the images together—i.e., the abandonment depression with any one or all of its six components affects. RORU refers to all three components of the rewarding object relations part-unit: the rewarding or approving image of the mother; the image of the self as a good child who is loved; and the feeling state—i.e., "feeling good."

Maternal Libidinal Availability and the Split Ego

Freud (58) stressed that in the beginning the child's behavior, under the domination of the primary process, is motivated by the pleasure principle, i.e., to seek pleasure and avoid pain. However, Freud states, "As this attempted satisfaction by means of hallucination was abandoned only in consequence of the absence of expected gratification, because of the disappointment experienced, the mental apparatus had to decide to form a conception of real circumstances in the outer world and to assert itself to alter them. A new principle of mental functioning was thus introduced. What was conceived of was no longer that which was pleasant but that which was real even if it should be unpleasant. This institution of a reality principle proved a momentous step."

Freud then traces the development of the use of the sense organs, perception, consciousness, memory and thought as agents of the developing ego's reality testing capacity. He states, "Just as the pleasure ego can do nothing but wish towards gaining pleasure and avoiding pain so the reality ego need do nothing but strive for what is useful and guard itself against damage." Freud emphasized that the ego gradually goes through a transformation from a pleasure ego to a reality ego.

The term ego splitting needs re-evaluation, since it seems to imply that a previously formed structure was split. A more likely occurrence—as indicated by Freud's discussion of the transformation from a pleasure ego to a reality ego—is that a large part of the patient's ego structure fails to undergo this transformation; therefore there is not a splitting of a previously formed structure but a failure to coherently develop the reality principle. This leaves a portion of the patient's ego structure under the domination of the pleasure principle rather than the reality principle. This part of the ego, which Freud called the pleasure ego, in the borderline patient could be called the pathological ego, while the remainder could be called the reality or healthy ego.

Why does part of the patient's ego structure persist as a pathological or pleasure ego rather than developing into a reality ego? The borderline patient is caught between his genetically determined drive for separation-individuation and the withdrawal of maternal supplies that this development entails. As the patient's self representation begins to differentiate from the object representation of the mother—as the patient begins to separate—he begins to experience an abandonment depression under the influence of the mother's withdrawal. At the same time, the mother rewards or encourages those ego functions of the patient—passivity and regressive behavior—that enable her to cling.

The key pathological ego function concerned is denial of the reality of separation which allows a persistence of the wish for reunion, which then becomes a principle defense against the abandonment depression. Thus, part of the ego fails to undergo the necessary transformation from pleasure principle to reality principle, for to do so would mean acceptance of the reality of the separation which would bring on the abandonment depression.

The mother's clinging and withdrawing and the patient's acting out of his wish for reunion promote the failure of one part of the ego to develop, resulting in an ego structure which is split into a pathological pleasure ego and a reality ego, the former pursuing relief from the feelings of abandonment, and the latter the reality principle. The pathological ego denies the reality of the separation, permitting the persistence of fantasies of reunion with the mother, which are then acted out through clinging and regressive behavior, thus defending against the abandonment depression and making the patient "feel good." Extensive fantasies of reunion are elaborated, projected on the environment and acted out, accompanied by an increasing denial of reality. The two, operating in concert, create an ever-widening chasm between the patient's feelings and the reality of his functioning as he gradually emerges from the developmental years into adulthood.

In all likelihood this failure of transformation of the pathological pleasure ego is not just a sudden occurrence at the time of separation-individuation but reflects a persistent developmental failure from the earliest growth phases, beginning perhaps in the stage of differentiation as a response to the mother's withdrawal of supplies on each move toward separation-individuation. The farther the patient was allowed to grow toward eventual separation-individuation, the more reality ego he would possess.

The Relationship Between the Split Object Relations Unit and the Split Ego

As already noted, the splitting defense keeps separate the rewarding and the withdrawing object relations part-units, including their associated affects. Although both the rewarding and the withdrawing maternal part-objects are in fact pathological, the borderline experiences the rewarding part-unit as increasingly ego-syntonic, since it relieves the feelings of abandonment associated with the withdrawing part-unit, with the result that the individual "feels good." The affective state associated with the rewarding part-unit is that of gratification at being fed, hence "loved." The ensuing denial of reality is, in the last analysis, but a small price to pay for this affective state.

An alliance is now seen to develop between the child's rewarding maternal part-image (the rewarding part-unit) and his pathological pleasure ego, the primary purpose of which is to promote the "good" feeling and to defend against the feeling of abandonment associated with the withdrawing part-unit. This ultimately powerful alliance, as it were, further promotes the denial of separateness and potentiates the child's acting out of his reunion fantasies. The alliance has as an important secondary function the discharge of aggression, which is both associated with and directed toward the withdrawing part-unit by means of symptoms, inhibitions and various kinds of destructive acts. The aggression, which gains access to motility through the agency of the pathologic pleasure ego, remains unneutralized, hence unavailable for the further development of intrapsychic structure .*

The withdrawing part-unit (the part-self representation, part-object representation and feelings of abandonment) becomes activated by actual experiences of separation (or loss), or as a result of the individual's efforts toward psychosocial growth, including moves toward separation-individuation within the therapeutic process, all of which *inter se alia* symbolize earlier life experiences which provoked the mother's withdrawal of supplies.

The alliance between the rewarding part-unit and the pathological pleasure ego is, in turn, activated by the resurgence of the withdrawing part-unit. The purpose of this operation, as it

---

* Again, the reader will discern the similarity of these formulations to those of Fairbairn. Fairbairn originally postulated a splitting within the infantile ego in correspondence with the split internalized "bad" object and in effect postulated an alliance between their parts. He postulated, on the one hand, an alliance between the *exciting object* (E.O.) and what he terms the *libidinal ego* (L.E.), and another between the *rejecting object* (R.O.) and what he termed the *anti-libidinal ego* (Anti-L.E.). The E.O.-L.E. alliance fairly directly corresponds with that, here presented, between the rewarding part-unit and the pathologic pleasure ego. For Fairbairn, the Anti-L.E. came to represent the punitive, sadistic aspect of the superego, allied with the R.O. as a split mental structure. The view of mental structure here developed presents no structural components analogous with Fairbairn's Anti-L.E.-R.O. alliance, in part reflective of the fact that Fairbairn had not developed a concept of the tripartite object relations unit or ego state. His profound insights, however, deserve further efforts to explore the possible relationships between his essential structural formulations and those presented here.

were, is defensive, viz., to fulfill the wish for reunion and thereby to relieve the feelings of abandonment. The rewarding part-unit thus becomes the borderline's principal defense against the painful affective state associated with the withdrawing part-unit. *In terms of reality, however, both part-units are pathological; it is as if the patient has but two alternatives, viz., either to feel bad and abandoned (the withdrawing part-unit), or to feel good (the rewarding part-unit) at the cost of denial of reality and the acting out of self-destructive behavior.*

THERAPEUTIC CONSIDERATIONS

It is necessary, now, to consider the impact which this intra-psychic structure exerts upon therapeutic transference and resistance. In brief, the transference which the borderline develops results from the operation of the split object relations unit—the rewarding part-unit and the withdrawing part-unit—each of which the patient proceeds alternatively to project onto the therapist. During those periods in which the patient projects the withdrawing part-unit. (with its part-object representation of the withdrawing mother) onto the therapist, he perceives therapy as necessarily leading to feelings of abandonment, denies the reality of therapeutic benefit and activates the rewarding part-unit as a resistance. When projecting the rewarding part-unit (with its reunion fantasy) onto the therapist, the patient "feels good" but, under the sway of the pathological (pleasure) ego, is usually found to be acting in a self-destructive manner.

The Therapeutic Alliance

The patient begins therapy feeling that the behavior motivated by the alliance between his rewarding part-unit and his pathological (pleasure) ego is ego-syntonic, that is, it makes him feel good. He is furthermore unaware of the cost to him, as it were, which is incurred through his denial of the reality of his self-destructive (and, of course, destructive) behavior.

The initial objective of the therapist is to render the functioning of this alliance ego-alien by means of confrontative clarification of its destructiveness (3, 132, 158, 245-247). Insofar as this therapeutic maneuver promotes control of the behavior, the withdrawing part-unit becomes activated, which in turn reactivates the rewarding part-unit with the appearance of further resistance. There results a circular process, sequentially including resistance, reality clarification, working-through of the feelings of abandonment (withdrawing part-unit), further resistance (rewarding part-unit) and further reality clarification, which leads in turn to further working-through.

In those cases in which the circular working-through process (167) proves successful, an alliance is next seen to develop between the therapist's healthy ego and the patient's embattled reality ego; this therapeutic alliance, formed through the patient's having internalized the therapist as a positive external object, proceeds to function counter to the alliance between the patient's rewarding part-unit and his pathological (pleasure) ego, battling with the latter, as it were, for ultimate control of the patient's motivations and actions.

The structural realignments which ensue in the wake of the working-through process may now be described. The repetitive projection of his rewarding and withdrawing part-units (with their component maternal part-object representations) onto the therapist, together with the latter's interpretative confrontation thereof, gradually draws to the patient's conscious awareness the presence of these part-units within himself. Concomitantly, the developing alliance between the therapist's healthy ego and the patient's reality ego brings into existence, through introjection, a new object relations unit: the therapist as a positive (libidinal) object representation who approves of separation-individuation $+$ a self representation as a capable, developing person $+$ a "good" feeling (affect) which ensues from the exercise of constructive coping and mastery rather than regressive behavior.

The working-through of the encapsulated rage and depression associated with the withdrawing part-unit in turn frees its component part-self and part-object representations from their intensely negative, aggressive affects. As a result, the new object relations unit (constructive self + "good" therapist + "good" affect) linked with the reality ego becomes integrated into an overall "good" self representation, while the split object relations unit linked with the pathologic (pleasure) ego becomes integrated into an overall "bad" self representation; both are now accessible to the patient's conscious awareness as are their counterparts within the person of the therapist. At this point, the patient has begun in earnest the work of differentiating good and bad self representations from good and bad object representations as prefatory to the next step, in which good and bad self representations coalesce, as do good and bad object representations. The stage is now set for the inception of whole-object relations, which marks the patient's entrance into Stage 4 (106).

The de-linking, as it were, of "raw" instinctual energies from the rewarding and withdrawing part-units renders these energies increasingly available to the synthetic function associated with the patient's expanding reality ego, hence available for progressive neutralization. With this, and concomitant with the progressive coalescence of good-bad self and object representations, splitting becomes replaced by normal repression, with progressive effacement, as it were, of the personified or "unmetabolized" images associated with the disappearing split object relations unit (107). The patient is now able to complete the work of mourning for these "lost" images, which characterizes his final work of separation from the mother.

CLINICAL EXAMPLE

A single clinical example is given here to illustrate the foregoing considerations, particularly the operation of the rewarding and the withdrawing object relations part-units and the pathological pleasure ego. Other examples will be described in the next chapter.

Anne, the 27-year-old married executive secretary described in the Introduction, came to treatment with a depression against which she had been defending herself through drinking, abuse of drugs, and an extramarital affair. She complained that her husband did not care for her because he spent too much time at his work.

The patient's history included an alcoholic mother who spent most of her time sitting around the home drinking, and who rewarded Anne, at least verbally, for passivity, inactivity and regressive behavior but who withdrew any form of approval when her daughter demonstrated any kind of constructive behavior. For example, when the patient, as an adolescent, cooked a meal, the mother would withdraw and assume an angry and critical attitude; the same ensued whenever the patient attractively decorated her room or had success at school.

(In what follows the patient clearly describes the withdrawing maternal part-image, i.e., the mother's withdrawal from the girl's assertiveness, activity or need to grow up, with the associated feelings of abandonment and the accompanying part-self representation of being bad, ugly, inadequate, unworthy. She also clearly reports the rewarding part-unit: a rewarding maternal part-image, feeling "good," and the self-image of a child who is taken care of. The mother's commands and the patient's behavior are thus linked together, forming the basis for the alliance between the rewarding part-unit and the pathologic pleasure ego.)

Therapeutic progress had activated the withdrawing part-unit, which in turn activated the rewarding part-unit as a defense, with the patient's behavior coming under the control of the pathologic pleasure ego, e.g., passivity, drinking, the affair. As the patient improved, as if in spite of herself, every step symbolized separation-individuation and proceeded to activate the withdrawing part-unit with its feelings of abandonment. She experienced her improvement as a loss, a frustration of the wish for reunion, and each time she improved she became resistant and hostile, projecting her anger at the mother's withdrawal onto the therapist and the therapeutic situation.

After a year of therapy three times a week, during which Anne had gained control over the behavior motivated by the alliance between the rewarding part-unit and the pathologic pleasure ego, she reported, "This week I pulled myself more into reality . . . I felt you had left me but told myself it wasn't true and the feelings went away . . ." (Note in what follows, however, the activation of the withdrawing part-unit and attendant resistance.) "Yet today I don't want to tell you . . . I'd like to report that I was fucked up all weekend . . . I guess I felt healthy over the weekend. Last night I made a big drink but threw it out rather than drink it." (Note that this improvement brings on further resistance.) "I woke up angry at you this morning. I recognize I'm doing better and I'm afraid you'll leave me. When my work went well one side of me was pleased . . . the other side [Note: rewarding part-unit] said why did I do that and I wanted to drink. I don't think I can maintain a mature way of living. When I have to do something responsible one side of me says no and wants to go out and get drunk. The better I do the more I want to hang onto the fantasies of lovers and drink." (Note: wish for reunion.) "If I'm grown up, independent on my own I'll be all alone and abandoned." (Note: withdrawing part-unit.)

A little later the patient reports that, in effect, the alliance between the rewarding part-unit and the pathological pleasure has become ego-alien: "I had a fight with my bad side—the baby . . ." (Note: the rewarding part-unit and the pathologic pleasure ego.) "I was enjoying myself reading and it was as if I heard a little voice saying have a drink. I could feel myself turn off feeling and then I took a drink. The bad side is my mother's commands . . . I'm ten years old and I can't decide myself . . . I have to follow the command but as I become aware of the command I can now disregard it and decide for myself."

In the next interview the patient reports, "I had two successes —each time it was as if I heard my mother's voice get started but each time I overcame it and went ahead." (Again, however, control of the rewarding part-unit activates the withdrawing part-unit which is then projected onto the therapist as a resistance maneuver.) "I wasn't going to tell you today as you'd think I was better and act like my parents. If I get better you'll leave me. I worry about this especially when you go on vacation. I feel you're leaving me because I'm doing better. My image of myself is that of a person who drinks and has affairs or of a young little girl who has to be taken care of."

As another example of how improvement had activated the withdrawing part-unit and produced resistance, the patient stated: "I didn't want to come today. I saw my old boyfriend. The baby side of me made me feel angry that I didn't want those old satis-factions. I don't want you to think I'm doing too well or I'll have to leave you . . . as if I want to get back at you . . . angry at you, you're doing this, making me better to get rid of me . . . I'm losing you. The baby side of me is angry that you think I can handle myself. Whenever I have five good days the baby side of me gets angry at you but I can't verbalize it or you'll leave me for sure. I like to sit here and say nothing just to piss you off. I see getting better as your withdrawing affection. Last night as I saw I had fixed up my apartment nicely I got furious at you."

This case illustrates the patient's two basic feeling states—the one (RORU) a defense against the other (WORU). She could either feel good (RORU) at the cost of passivity, drinking and the affair, or feel abandoned (WORU). Small wonder she chose to "feel good."

5

The Clinical Picture: A Developmental Perspective

This chapter demonstrates how the separation-individuation theory presented in Chapters 3 and 4 clarifies and gives greater precision to the clinical diagnosis of the borderline syndrome.

STRESSES WHICH PRECIPITATE A CLINICAL SYNDROME

The theory first clarifies understanding of those specific stresses that can precipitate the onset of a clinical syndrome.

Separation-individuation is comprised of two separate but related aspects: Individuation unfolds from within the psyche under the influence of genetic forces, as well as under the influence of the mother, and is manifested by new thoughts, feelings and actions. Separation also occurs in the psyche but it is directly influenced by interaction with the environment—i.e., the maternal object or its substitute. Life events which challenge either or, more often, both of these aspects can precipitate a clinical syndrome. The challenges presented by 1) normal developmental events, 2) accidental separation experiences, and 3) intimacy are discussed below.

Normal Events in the Life Cycle as Stresses

The achievement of ego autonomy via the normal separation-individuation process lays a foundation that enables the child to take on and master later developmental tasks. Failure to achieve autonomy makes the borderline child extremely vulnerable to all those later nodal points in the life cycle that require autonomy for mastery. These life events represent a growth opportunity for the normal child but can precipitate a clinical syndrome in the borderline. Table 1 presents these nodal points in the life cycle with a typical clinical syndrome for each.

The clinical picture tends to shift as the borderline child gets older and encounters the more complex emotional tasks required by increasing chronologic age. Each developmental period poses its own challenges, i.e., childhood, latency, adolescence, young adulthood, middle age, old age.

The normal dependency expected and accepted in the childhood years helps to conceal the borderline child's clinging defenses. When the child has to leave the mother for school the clinging defense is interrupted and the child develops a school phobia.

It is perhaps not surprising that so much borderline symptomatology is seen in adolescence where the dependency is expected to recede and social requirements for independence must be met. At this time the psychopathology tends to shift toward abandonment depression and the acting out defenses.

It is not until young adulthood that difficulties with work, due to avoidance, and difficulties with intimacy, due to clinging and distancing defenses, come to the fore. Prior to this point avoidance of individuation in school work was often camouflaged by a passing but mediocre school record, and the conflict in the rela-

TABLE 1

Time in the Life Cycle	Precipitating Event	Clinical Syndrome
Childhood	leaving home for school leaving home for camp	school phobia phobia
Prepuberty	leaving the local school for the high school	abandonment depression with its defenses
Middle adolescence	sex functioning	abandonment depression with its acting out defenses
Late adolescence	last year of high school; first year of college	abandonment depression with its acting out defenses
20's	a) college graduation or leaving home for work	abandonment depression and acting out defenses
	b) difficulty with work due to avoiding individuation	lack of satisfaction
	c) challenge of intimacy	fear of loss of self or object
30's	a) difficulty with work, intimacy, husband or wife, marital conflict b) difficulty parenting	avoidance, clinging or distancing due to fear of loss of self or object, anxiety depression
40's	a) difficulty as parents with adolescents who rebel against depersonification or who comply at cost of individuation	anxiety, depression
	b) promotions at work where a previously encouraged dependency is lost	anxiety, depression
	c) lack of work satisfaction due to avoidance of individuation or acting out	acting out
50's	failures in work and heterosexual relationships as opportunity runs out and fantasy meets frustration	abandonment depression
Old age	extraordinary difficulty with changes and with loss of loved ones, friends, work	abandonment depression

tionship with the parents held center stage, as the chronologic adolescent who had not resolved his separation problem was confronted with the additional challenge of the need to emancipate from the parents.

As chronologic age catapults the young adult into a world of his own—and many borderlines will defend themselves against this psychosocial maturation by remaining at home—this world confronts his avoidance of individuation and his clinging defenses and impels him more and more to sacrifice life structure to maintain inner equilibrium. He may be able to defend himself quite well with his characteristic defenses (splitting, projection, acting out of the wish for reunion, avoidance, denial, clinging, or distancing) so that he functions, but it is on a far from optimal level even though it is without clinical symptoms. Although not clinically ill he is paying a high price for his comfort and remains vulnerable to all kinds of threats to his fragile equilibrium.

All borderlines, however, do not show poor functioning. Many are very successful at work. Frequently they have an unusual talent in an artistic field—they are actors, writers, painters, sculptors, producers, directors—or in a profession such as the law, medicine, architecture, or accounting. Closer examination will probably reveal that the work contains an illusion of personal closeness, or a closeness that is within very definite limits, such as the relationship of a lawyer and his client, or a doctor and his patient. Furthermore, careful study will probably reveal that they suffer a great deal from anxiety about their achievements and also have quite disturbed personal lives—i.e., poor object relations.

The talented borderline individual is drawn to those areas of activity as a reporter, photographer, psychiatrist, or minister that permit him to experience vicariously, within safe, protective limits, emotions that are inhibited and avoided in his own personal life because of the fear they invoke. The readiness for projective identification, the poor ego boundaries and reality testing facilitate vicarious gratification. The action of playing a role may feel as if it were real; the reporter on the scene may feel as if he were really a participant. These characteristics contribute to the borderline's enjoyment of movies or plays where he can suspend his reality testing and feel as if the play or movie were real.

During young adulthood (20's and 30's) the behavioral, rebellious type of acting out seen in adolescence decreases and the principal presenting problems that take its place are difficulties with work and with close relationships. As the borderline moves into his late 20's or early 30's either his difficulty with intimacy prevents him from a continuous close relationship and thereby confronts him with the problem of loneliness, or he establishes a continuous relationship—married or not—and runs into trouble as the involvement invokes his fear of engulfment and/or abandonment and activates his clinging and/or distancing defenses.

When the borderline marries and has children his difficulty in parenting because of his depersonification of his children comes to the fore—mostly signaled by the children's symptoms and his or her anger and disappointment as a parent. This difficulty yields to yet another type when the children reach adolescence. Prior to this they have tended to comply with the depersonification, but now the pressure for independence brings on a rebellion with acting out that leads to behavior pathology on the part of the adolescent and rage and depression on the part of the parent.

Middle age may decrease the conflict with the grown children as the need for parenting and caretaking decreases, but at the same time depression enters as real life opportunities for satisfaction decrease. Like all people at this time in life the patient must now come to terms with the sad fate of his youthful dreams and fantasies. Reality's confrontation of this fantasy carries a poignant, unique and specific force for the middle-aged borderline, who has lived his life by substituting fantasy gratification for fulfillment in reality. The inexorable exigencies of life break through his denial of reality and force him finally to face what he had been denying— i.e., hoped for achievements unfulfilled, relationships either never attempted or gone sour—all this at a time when the opportunities to recoup are either gone or fast disappearing. This potent force alone can initiate a depression, which, although it occurs in a middle-aged person, is not the customary mid-life depression with its accompanying intrapsychic structure—i.e., an autonomous ego and developed superego—but an abandonment depression in mid-life.

Old age, which brings with it so much environmental change and loss, along with a requirement for emotional responsiveness and flexibility, can be a disaster for the borderline who has never been able to deal effectively with either change or loss.

Accidental Events: Separation Stresses

Beyond the normal consecutive events of the life cycle, border-line patients are exquisitely sensitive to accidental events at any time of life that bring on separation experiences and thereby threaten their clinging defense. If the person to whom they are clinging (mother, father, sibling, lover, close friend, etc.) withdraws approval, becomes distant, leaves the home, becomes ill, or dies, it produces profound emotional reverberations and can precipitate a clinical syndrome through a reinforcement of the abandonment depression.

The Challenges of Intimacy as a Precipitating Stress

Intimacy as a stress deserves special consideration. The mature capacity for love and intimacy is produced by successful resolution of conflicts throughout development. However, there are two key conflicts that must be resolved: separation from the mother in the separation-individuation stage; and giving up of the mother or father as a love object in the oedipal stage.

The separation-individuation phase therefore makes an important contribution to the normal capacity to love, while a failure in separation-individuation leads to difficulties in the capacity to love. During separation-individuation the child intrapsychically separates from the mother and develops an image of himself as being entirely separate from that of the mother. The dividends of successful separation-individuation for the child's ego strength have already been described (see pp. 32-33). Some of these are repeated here as they contribute to the capacity to love: first and foremost, object constancy (as described by Fraiberg) with its companion, the capacity to mourn loss of an object (52, 190); second, the capacity to be alone and to feel concern, as opposed to need for others, as described by Winnicott (228, 231), and the capacity to tolerate anxiety and depression as described by Zetzel (248, 251); finally, the capacity to emotionally commit oneself to another without fear of engulfment or abandonment.

In addition, a successful separation-individuation phase with its intuitive and empathic communication between mother and child forms the anlage of "feeling good" to which the oedipal phase adds the sexual and romantic elements. These two together will later direct the individual to a choice of a mate with whom he or she can repeat this kind of feeling and communication, i.e., the refinding of the object, which Freud stated as follows: "Every state of being in love reproduces infantile prototypes. The finding of an object is in fact a refinding" (59).

The degree to which there has been deprivation or a "bad fit" in the separation-individuation phase will determine the degree to which this early developmental experience will overshadow and influence all later efforts at an intimate or close relationship. Most people suffer at least some minor trauma in separation-individuation which later shows up as minor difficulties in intimate relationships—for what human mother possesses the attributes necessary to be empathic and intuitive to all of her child's unfolding individuality! The endpoint of this spectrum of deprivation is seen in the pathology of love shown by the borderline.

The borderline's conflict over intimacy revolves about a single theme: A close emotional involvement with another person (of either sex) activates and reawakens his fear of being engulfed, i.e., pulled back into the symbiotic whirlpool, or abandoned. If he gets "too close" he feels he will be engulfed; if he gets "too far" he will be abandoned. From the interpersonal perspective the patient is afraid of being engulfed or abandoned by the other person. From the intrapsychic perspective he is afraid of loss of self or loss of the object.

The fear of engulfment relates to the earlier differentiation phase of separation-individuation where the ego boundaries of the self were just beginning to emerge and were weak and tenuous. The fear of abandonment relates to the later rapprochement phase where ego boundaries were more secure and the principal fear was that of loss of the object. All borderline patients have both fears; their relative strength will depend on how far along the developmental pathway of separation-individuation the patient got before the arrest occurred. The earlier the arrest occurred the more the fear of engulfment will predominate, and the later the arrest occurred the more the fear of abandonment will predominate.

The clinical vicissitudes of the conflict in close interpersonal relationships will depend on the patient's exclusive or alternating use of the two principal defense mechanisms against these fears—i.e., clinging and/or distancing. Either mechanism can be used alone, or, more commonly, both are used at different times. In a curious way, the patient's initial complaint or report may sound the same regardless of which defense predominates. The adult patient with the clinging defense is projecting and acting out the wish for reunion on his or her boyfriend or girlfriend. This mechanism contains a wish or fantasy of being the exclusive center of attention and receiving undiluted and constant approval from that person. More than likely, the initial report will list a number of complaints about the partner's inability to fulfill this impossible objective and about his or her shortcomings. In listing these complaints, however, the patient is unknowingly revealing his fantasy of an exclusive relationship. The patient with a distancing defense often picks out a partner whose personality traits make any kind of relationship impossible. Again, the initial report will focus on the partner's shortcomings.

Whatever style of defense the child used to deal with separation from the mother later becomes his pattern to deal with close interpersonal relationships. Later in life, as an adult, any real close personal relationship challenges these defenses, threatens the patient with a real involvement (which would require separation from mother) and therefore activates the withdrawing object relations unit which activates the rewarding object relations unit as a defense. The workings or details of the patient's defenses against closeness come under the direct observation of the therapist in treatment as they are repeated in the transference, where they can be observed, interpreted and worked through.

Some common distancing defenses are:

1. No relationship—isolation.
2. Picks a mate who also has anxiety about closeness and blames the conflict in the relationship on him/her.
3. Keeps relationships superficial either one at a time or many at a time and breaks them off when involvement threatens.
4. Has deep relationships with two people at one time but avoids commitment to either.
5. Relates only with men or women who are involved with others—i.e., partial relationships.

The examples of styles of defense against intimacy described below are taken from the cases presented in Chapter 1.

Anne

This case (see p. 4) demonstrates a marital relationship based on a clinging defense, i.e., acting out the wish for reunion with the husband—which was interrupted by the demands of the husband's career competing with the patient's need for "all" the husband's time and attention. The husband's prolonged absences activated the WORU which the patient then projected on the husband— i.e., he was busy not because he was successful but because he didn't love her and wanted to abandon her.

Mary

The patient (see p. 5) was literally acting out her relationship to her mother with her husband, clinging to him and acting out the WORU by demanding from him what she had not gotten from her mother. The lover also served as a target for the projection of the RORU as long as the affair remained a partial relationship conducive to fantasy gratification. In this case the husband seemed in truth to resemble the mother in his personality characteristics, which were exaggerated and hardened by the patient's angry demands.

Jean

The patient (see p. 6) was clinging to her husband, projecting and acting out the WORU. She saw his sexual needs as a repetition of the mother's demands for compliance and rebelled against these demands by angrily withdrawing, which she had never been able to do with her mother. Thus, her husband's needs precipitated the angry withdrawal from her mother stored up through the years.

Early in therapy constant reality confrontations of her acting out with the husband brought the source of her conflict—i.e., the conflict was with the mother—to her awareness. The marital relationship improved dramatically as the patient understood and returned to the sex clinic to work out a better sexual relationship with her husband.

Phyllis

Over several years of psychotherapy it emerged that Phyllis (see p. 7) had picked a partner who himself had enormous anxiety about closeness and was unable to commit himself to a relationship. This was for Phyllis a distancing device to deal with and conceal her enormous fear of being abandoned if she became committed to a relationship. The separation-reunion cycles came under the therapeutic microscope to the point that the patient realized the man was inappropriate for her and stopped the relationship. Continued psychotherapy enabled her to become fully aware of and control her fear of abandonment to the point that, although she didn't work through the fear, she was able to control it well enough to choose and marry an appropriate partner.

Tom

Tom (see p. 8) was able to defend against and conceal his fear of engulfment in a close relationship by setting up a conflictual and distant relationship with his wife. Several affairs met the same fate. Although he realized there was great conflict in his marital relationship he felt it was all his wife's problem.

The casual observer of couples such as Phyllis and her husband and Tom and his wife always wonders why the two people remain together when they obviously seem to dislike each other and have so much trouble. The fact that this question arises testifies to the extraordinary force of the fear of engulfment precipitated by the challenge of an intimate relationship: The patient feels himself to be better off in a conflictual relationship that defends him *against his fear* rather than in a close relationship which would stimulate that fear—the essential factor is fear, not relationship.

Betty

Betty's problem (see p. 8) was similar to Tom's—i.e., fear of engulfment. However, her distancing defense was more subtle and complicated. She selected men who could only maintain a partial relationship upon whom she projected and acted out a romantic fantasy to deny the reality of the relationship. The repeated failures of these relationships had made her bitter and disillusioned about "men," unfortunately an all too effective defense against any awareness that it was not men but her own desperate fear of engulfment that kept Betty on the partial relationship treadmill.

THE CLINICAL PICTURE

Each level of clinical observation reinforces every other level to build a framework of diagnosis. The history of present illness may often, though not always, reveal a recent separation stress. The patient is usually unaware of the importance of this event so that the therapist must ferret it out.

Following this stress the patient develops acute anxiety and/or depression and his unique defenses against these affects are intensified. The therapist then observes the patient's ego functions and defenses as they have operated in the interview and in his personal life, as well as in his past history. An immature, harsh, critical superego ridden with lacunae can often be observed from the patient's reactions to the interview. Moreover, the past history reveals the typical depersonification of the patient by one or both parents and the tendency of the family to communicate emotions by actions rather than words.

Some of this evidence must be deduced from the small vignettes supplied by the patient, since the patient is more than likely still operating under the influence of the family myth—the series of rationalizations used to conceal the family pathology—and is not aware of the extent of the family conflict. It is as if he presents the tip of the iceberg from which the therapist must deduce the larger but hidden base.

The patient's difficulty with close relationships is quickly evident in his reports of either no close relations with people or great difficulties in his relations with people.

Finally, and most importantly, the manner in which the patient relates to the therapist—the nature of the transference—affords not only its own evidence but is also a testing ground to evaluate hypotheses about the rest of the evidence. As mentioned in Chapter 2, this transference will depend upon whether the patient is projecting the RORU or the WORU on the therapist. If it is the former the patient may form a clinging relationship; if the latter, a distancing relationship; or both may alternate depending on the stimulus provided by the content of the interview. Further evidence to support the specific style of the transference can be found by studying the patient's experience with other close relationships both present and past, where the same features will be found.

To clinch the diagnosis the therapist should be able to map out a specific picture of the patient's unique intrapsychic structure: the rewarding object relations part-unit, the withdrawing object relations part-unit, the split ego with its pathologic defense, and the details of the RORU-pathological ego alliance. Furthermore, he should be able to confirm these observations in treatment as he observes that separation stress or progress in therapy activates the RORU-pathologic ego alliance as a defense.

In the course of this diagnostic process, inconsistencies in the clinical picture should give way to a clear, comprehensive outline, not just of the presenting symptoms or difficulties, but of the entire underlying borderline intrapsychic structure. Three examples are presented below:

Case 1

The patient was a 25-year-old man who was tempted to quit work because of severe depression and a work inhibition. The patient's frankly paranoid mother had openly attacked him throughout childhood for any assertive behavior; the father, rather than come to his son's aid, demanded that the boy submit to the mother as the price for the father's approval.

Analysis of the patient's withdrawing part-unit revealed the following structure: The part-object representation comprised a condensed image which included elements of the attacking mother and the withdrawing father; the predominant affect was, as expected, that of abandonment; the part-self representation was that of a person who had caused the abandonment and was no good, "crazy," inadequate and "bad." The rewarding part-unit included the affect of feeling "good" and the part-self representation of an obedient child, both dependent upon the pathologic pleasure ego's use of inhibition, avoidance and passivity with denial of reality in pursuit of the wish for reunion. The patient's efforts to assert himself to work activated the withdrawing part-unit which, in turn, activated the rewarding part-unit, leading to the defensive use of inhibition, passivity and avoidance.

As the patient improved in treatment and attempted to resume work he would block; however, he was now able to report the maternal part-image, the part-self image and the abandonment feelings (withdrawing part-unit), as well as the results of activation of the rewarding part-unit, i.e., inhibition, passivity, avoidance and blocking. "When I sit there trying to work I feel hurt, stepped-on, crushed and want to give up. I never felt any support or connection with my mother. It's a feeling of complete loss, helplessness, inability to cope with reality. I feel adrift, alone

... mother had no love for me. My image of mother's face is one of an expression of her disliking me. I want her to love me but she hates me and she acts as if I did something against her and she wants to get back and she attacks me. When I appealed to my father for help he was never home and would tell me to cut it out because I was upsetting his relationship with my mother.

"When they left me alone they took part of me with them. They take something with them that leaves me empty. I have no feeling of worth or meaning ... the feeling of being deserted kills me. I feel it's wrong to be myself and I can almost hear my father's voice telling me to cut it out, that if I don't he will leave me.

"Trying to work is tempting fate, risky, treacherous. It brings them down on me. I can almost hear their voices. I can't break their hold ... I feel I'm dying so I give up. I have to block out.

"I feel completely abandoned and I yell, 'Help me out! Where is everybody?' And they say, 'He's crazy!' Father tells me it's my fault ... the way I see things is all wrong. They feel sorry for me. I say, 'Please forgive me for being crazy.' I can't scream or beg anymore because they think I'm crazy. I'm so afraid that if they don't protect me I will die!"

Case 2

This patient was an unmarried 19-year-old girl, a freshman in college who had been an outstanding high school student but who had subsequently dropped out of college because of depression and "panic."

The patient's father, a manic-depressive writer, had had an explosive temper. Throughout the patient's childhood the father had acted as a dependent child in his relationship with the mother, and had openly attacked the patient for her "childhood inadequacies" but envied her achievements. The major role obfuscations within the family arose from the mother's playing the role of the father's mother and demanding that the patient not only submit to the father's attacks but also serve in the role of her own mother.

The patient's withdrawing maternal part-image was that of a mother who exploited her, and who was deliberately cruel and enjoyed her (the patient's) dependency and helplessness; the associated affect included abandonment depression and the fear of engulfment; the part-self image was that of being inadequate, wrong, worthless, guilty, an insect, a bug. The patient harbored cannibalistic fantasies and fears, relieved throughout childhood through masturbation. In the fantasies she was at times the victim and at other times the cannibal. The rewarding maternal part-image was that of a strong, idealized (all-good) mother who would save her from death; the associated affect was that of feeling "good" and the part-self image was that of a helpless, clinging child. This patient's pathologic pleasure ego, shaped by her mother's "rewarding" responses, comprised regressive-defensive behavior, such as acting helplessly, clinging, a variety of somatic symptoms and carrying out the (mother's) assigned role of an inadequate, hysterical child.

After some five months of treatment, the patient had begun to separate, with emergence of the withdrawing part-self image (withdrawing part-unit), which precipitated a near-panic. She reported "I feel everybody's angry at me. I'm about to be attacked. I feel like I'm an insect, a bug. It's all because I don't want to be like my mother, I don't want to hold onto her. The role she put me in fit her needs but also gave me security. She would love me no matter how bad I was. I want her and I want to be taken care of and I can't breathe without her. I don't have a separate existence and I feel guilty if I try. I can't stop wanting my mother like a baby. I can't seem to make a life of my own."

Whenever the withdrawing part-unit was activated as a result of a move toward separation-individuation, the patient projected her anger at the withdrawing maternal part-image and became resistant to treatment, which she then viewed as conducive to abandonment. She thus expressed her wish to kill the therapist, her mother and herself: "Over the weekend I felt completely independent but cut off. I talked about my job very self-confidently, then I got frightened and went into a rage. I wanted to tear myself apart, rip my mother or you apart. I felt terribly depressed. I realize I'm getting better but I don't want to admit it. I don't need my mother. I lost my motivation, my desire to go on. I feel humiliated, defeated, dead and cold. I hate you! I don't think you can help me and I want revenge on my mother and you!"

Case 3

A 22-year-old, unmarried college graduate who lived alone complained of anxiety, depression and hysteriform fears that her legs "might not work" and that she might be unable to eat or swallow; she had, in addition, had several attacks of impaired consciousness. There were also feelings of helplessness and inability to cope, and she almost constantly got in touch with her mother for reassurance.

The mother had idealized the family unit and had rewarded infantile-compliant behavior, which she rationalized as a religious virtue; conversely, she vigorously attacked her child's efforts toward self-assertiveness or originality, an example of which was her refusal to attend the patient's high school graduation exercises when she had learned that the girl had demonstrated against the war in Vietnam. The mother had particularly attacked heterosexual relations as "the work of the Devil." The father, an emotionally distant man, served in the role of the mother's figurehead.

The patient's withdrawing maternal part-image was that of an angry, punitive and vengeful mother who would kill her; the associated affect was a compound of fear and abandonment depression; the part-self image was that of being guilty, worthless, despicably bad. The rewarding maternal part-image was that of an omnipotent, god-like mother; the associated affect was relief from anxiety and feeling "good"; the part-self image was that of a helpless, compliant child. The pathologic pleasure ego, which functioned to maintain the wish for reunion, abetted the fulfillment of the mother's wishes by being "helpless," dependent, unassertive, clinging and asexual. Again, therapeutic progress activated the withdrawing part-unit, which then triggered the rewarding part-unit with ensuing helpless clinging, passivity and symptomatic expressions of a phobic and hysterical nature.

Following resolution of the patient's initial resistance, she reported: "I think I'm destined to die because I'm growing up. I can envision no life apart from my mother or family. I'm made up of two parts—one me, one her. The part that she has worked on, taken care of and given to me . . . if I move away from her the part of her that's in me would turn against me . . . mother will make it turn against me and it will punish me. I don't feel strong enough to battle in spite of myself. Mother insists that I remain helpless and not grow up.

"I'm afraid if I grow up I'll lose her. I will take away her reason for living. I carry out what mother says—I'm an empty shell. Mother puts in the values; otherwise I will be nothing. I'm empty except for her. Mother sees me as a tool for herself. She instructed me that the one thing I can't do is to grow up and leave her—or I'll be punished for it."

The patient felt intense guilt over her hostility toward the mother: "I feel dirty and disgusting. Mother equates growing up with stealing and murder. Defying her is like defying God—you feel guilty and frightened. I've been frightened into believing that growing up is wrong. If I do anything that mother doesn't approve of, like having sex or smoking grass, I'm throwing myself to the winds and anything can happen to me. Mother suggested that sexual intercourse before marriage would make me mentally ill. If I smoke or have intercourse I'm violating the bargain I made with her not to leave her. I'm afraid she will leave me.

"When I assert myself rather than comply I feel that I am nasty and impudent and that everybody will be angry with me. I'm just beginning to realize the extent to which I carry out mother's wishes. If I don't do what she says it's wrong . . . if I reject one thing it's like rejecting all. In other words, having sex is like lying, stealing or rejecting my mother. She would rather I die than go out and do something she did not want. Mother wanted me in order, just like she wanted the nice, clean bathroom in order. When I go and do something that is not in order she goes into a rage and would like to kill me."

The alliance in this case between the rewarding part-unit and the pathologic pleasure ego engendered the patient's feeling of panic over anticipated punishment if she attempted to grow; the punishment she expected would take the form of "going crazy," paralysis of walking, talking and swallowing, and impaired consciousness. In her case, the pathologic pleasure ego discharged aggression by means of symptom-formation.

The information supplied to the therapist by his knowledge of the patient's specific intrapsychic structure—as illustrated by these three patients—enables him to design an equally specific psychotherapeutic approach.

DIFFERENTIAL DIAGNOSIS

The specific delineation of the clinical characteristics of the borderline personality organization described here and by Kernberg has greatly simplified the problem of differential diagnosis. Nevertheless, the fluid ego boundaries, paranoid ideation, transient though reversible psychotic-like episodes, and the tendency to primary process thinking that occur in the borderline syndrome make it necessary to differentiate it from a psychosis. On the other hand, the primitive level of fixation of the ego, as well as the primitive defense mechanisms such as splitting and projection, make it necessary to differentiate the borderline syndrome from the narcissistic disorders.

To differentiate the borderline from the narcissistic disorder it is helpful to think in terms of a clinical picture, intrapsychic structure, and its transference. The clinical picture of the narcissistic personality differs from the borderline: The principal problem is of excessive self-absorption, usually coinciding with a superficially smooth and effective social adaptation but with serious distortions in internal relationships with other people. Characteristics include ambitiousness, grandiose fantasies, feelings of inferiority, overdependence on external admiration, feelings of boredom and emptiness, and an ongoing search for gratification of strivings for brilliance, wealth, power and beauty. Along with these are serious deficiencies in the capacity to love and to be concerned about others. In contrast to the borderline, who clings to others but is afraid of engulfment or abandonment, the patient with a narcissistic disorder shows a lack of the capacity for empathic understanding of others. Others exist principally to satisfy his narcissistic needs. He often exhibits conscious or unconscious exploitation and ruthlessness, as well as intense envy with defenses against it, such as devaluation, omnipotent control and narcissistic withdrawal.

Narcissistic patients lack emotional depth and have an incapacity for experiencing depressive reactions (109). Their ego boundaries are stable and their reality testing preserved. In contrast, social functioning of borderline patients is not as good, at least on the surface. Their impulse control is not as good and they do not have the capacity for active, consistent, successful work, as do those with a narcissistic disorder. However some borderlines do come close.

The differences in clinical picture between the narcissist and the borderline are due to essential differences in intrapsychic structure. The narcissist has a fused grandiose self-object image which is integrated but highly pathological. This integration of the grandiose self probably compensates for the lack of integration of the normal self concept and explains the relatively good ego functioning and reality perception of that patient in the presence of primitive defense mechanisms such as splitting. Kohut (123) defines the origin of this grandiose self as being fixation of a normal growth process, whereas Kernberg (109) describes it as a pathological structure very different from normal narcissism. These differences in origin need not concern us at this point.

The borderline intrapsychic structure, on the other hand, consists not of a grandiose self-object image but of a split self-image, one side of which is good and the other bad, and a split image of the object, one side of which is rewarding and the other side withdrawing. One can see here the profound differences in intrapsychic structure between the two disorders. This underlying psychic difference is often clouded or confused by the fact that the defensive operations of a narcissistic ego are often very much like that of the borderline, i.e., poor reality perception, poor frustration tolerance, defective impulse control, and primitive defensive functions such as splitting and projection.

These observations about differences in the intrapsychic structure between the two disorders can be confirmed in the transference. The narcissist forms a transference based either, according to Kohut, on projecting the idealized infantile object on the therapist from whom he expects to receive gratification and supplies, or on a mirroring process in which the purpose of the therapist is to mirror the patient's exhibitionism. The borderline, on the other hand, projects either the rewarding object relations unit or the withdrawing object unit on the therapist and either clings or distances himself accordingly.

The fact that the borderline at times can resemble a psychotic was instrumental in Frosch's (63, 64) designating the borderline as a psychotic character. He emphasized the following important difference between the psychotic and the borderline: The borderline has evidence of having had previous object relations, of having progressed beyond objectlessness to the point of recognition of gratifying objects, but primarily at a need-for-gratification level. Although thinking, feeling, and behavior at all levels are at times under the influence of the primary process, these disturbances are reversible as there is still a large portion of the ego intact enough to function as an observer and evaluater even if it not always in control—a preservation of the capacity to test the reality. The weakness of the ego of the borderline lies in the proneness to regression; however, his strength lies in his ability to reverse regression. Evidence of regressive and progressive adaptation may be seen side by side in the borderline when, in spite of severe disturbances, he makes in the main a syntonic, i.e., stable, integrated, adaptation to objective reality.

The intrapsychic structure of the psychotic reveals a fused self-object image, poor ego boundaries and poor reality testing which is persistent and not reversible. These contrast with the separate split self and object images of the borderline which are consistent, as well as the borderline's stronger ego boundaries and better contact with reality.

The pervasive presence of the acting out defense pattern in the borderline makes it necessary to distinguish the adult borderline from the antisocial personality or psychopathic personality. The acting out of the adult borderline is rarely antisocial and usually occurs as a result of interpersonal conflict or as reaction to separation experiences. The superego of the borderline is punitive, harsh and often filled with lacunae but nevertheless present and operative. The borderline patient does learn from experience. The most important difference comes in the potential in object relations: The borderline's object relations, though primitive, are definitely present, the patient relating in either a clinging or distancing fashion. The psychopath's capacity for object relations is practically absent. The psychopath relates to objects in a manner similar to that of the infants described by Bowlby (19) in the phase of detachment where there was no emotional relationship— the other person being seen as something to be manipulated for gratification.

To summarize, the separation theory throws a unique light on the clinical picture of the borderline syndrome: the stresses that can produce a clinical syndrome, as well as the signs and symptoms of that syndrome. Beyond that, it greatly simplifies the problem of differential diagnosis by clarifying and specifying the underlying and enduring intrapsychic structure of the disorder.

6

The Psychotherapy

The psychotherapy compensates for the two developmental defects of the borderline character, i.e., object relations and ego structure, by two therapeutic techniques: The therapist must be a real person who supports the patient's individuation, and he must confront the denial of the destructiveness of the pathologic ego.

THE THERAPIST

First and foremost, the therapist must be a *real person,* who maintains a consistent, positive supportive attitude. He supports moves towards individuation in order to provide the patient with an appropriate external object that he can internalize.

What do I mean by support? Is it any effort to share the therapist's own life with the patient or to meet the patient's regressive needs? The answer is no. By support I mean two most important things: First, the therapist must maintain a positive attitude towards the patient's individuation. This entails a constant and consistent expectation that the patient will act in a realistic, healthy, mature fashion, combined with an attitude of curiosity, concern and investigation when he does not. This extends as far as congratulating the patient for realistic achievements, empathizing with his realistic defeats and disappointments.

Second, the therapist must continuously lend the patient his reality perception via limit setting and confrontation of avoidance and denial to help the patient overcome defects in perception of reality due to splitting, poor reality perception, as well as denial of reality. In other words, the therapist confronts the patient with the destructiveness of the pathologic ego's defense mechanisms: splitting, avoidance, denial, projection, and acting out the wish for reunion.

At the same time that he is being a real person who supports individuation and lends his reality perception to the patient, the therapist must keep in mind that the patient may be tempted to react to these therapeutic activities as he did to his mother—to use them as a set of directions or rules to which he can comply for approval, thus using therapy as a resistance to, rather than a stimulus for, individuation. To minimize this tendency the therapist has to bend over backwards to ensure that therapy for the patient is a feeling experience. The development and direction of therapy must come from the patient's head rather than from the therapist's directions. The therapist has to try to be "tuned in," as empathetic to the patient's immediate feeling state as possible, so that his activities will correspond to that state. He must cultivate patience and restraint in order to allow the patient to learn his own insights which carry the most therapeutic force. For the borderline patient it is the *act* of learning these insights himself that is as important as the insights.

Despite all these cautions on the part of the therapist it is inevitable that various degrees of compliance will play a role in the patient's motivations. These must be brought to the patient's attention and their influence investigated. This last step—analysis of the transference—is the final protection against the patient's using the therapy as a resistance to, rather than a stimulus for, growth.

THE TWO FORMS OF PSYCHOTHERAPY

"Supportive" Psychotherapy

Most borderline patients, except for those in crisis, begin treatment on a supportive basis—i.e., one or two times a week. During this period the therapist has an opportunity to evaluate the patient's potential for reconstructive psychotherapy more carefully through a study of his transference reactions as well as review of his history.

"Supportive" psychotherapy aims to enable the patient to learn conscious control of the defense mechanisms of his pathologic ego, and thereby to strip from the reality of his life structure these defenses along with their destructive effects. The term "supportive" is used because it is widely known and because it helps to differentiate this form of psychotherapy from reconstructive psychotherapy. The quotation marks are used to emphasize that it is actually more than supportive and more than short-term, sometimes stretching into years and bringing about dramatic changes in the life of the patient.

In supportive therapy the testing phase lasts longer, regressions are more frequent, and the transference and the therapeutic alliance are less intense than in reconstructive therapy. However, it is still possible to go beyond confrontation and do some minimal working-through of the depression. Further, there can be dramatic change in the patient's clinical picture in supportive therapy as he moves from resistance to a therapeutic alliance. Although the patient's efforts to control the pathologic ego are less intense and the connection with the underlying affect less obvious, the patient still is able to strip from the reality of his life structure the projected and acted out wish for reunion with its destructive effects.

Often when the patient has learned to identify and consciously control his pathologic mechanisms, has improved his life adaptation, is achieving greater gratification through self-assertion and expression in the reality of his life, he decides to stop treatment. Occasionally, this type of patient will have to be seen once or twice a week for up to 10 to 20 years or even longer. More commonly, these patients will stop after the presenting episode has been adequately controlled and will return again when life events create further difficulties.

It is vital for the therapist to maintain his availability as long as necessary. Many patients after a course of supportive therapy later receive a great deal of assistance through a letter, a phone call, or a short series of interviews. Frequently a later life crisis produces a regression with loss of previously learned insight which may, however, be rapidly relearned in contact with the therapist.

Effective treatment of the borderline requires a time perspective which differs from ordinary reality perspective. One is working with tenacious resistances and early fixations which require much time and input to resolve. I have often been asked when discussing the subject why "briefer" forms of treatment could not be found to be effective. My answer has been that when we find briefer means of development then we will have briefer forms of therapy. The therapist must be prepared to engage and take on the responsibility of the treatment for long periods of time, which will inevitably invoke endless repetitions of the same issues. He must be willing to accept small gains which will, however, begin to look larger when viewed over a longer time perspective.

Reconstructive Psychotherapy

Intensive reconstructive psychoanalytically oriented psychotherapy is usually an expansion and outgrowth of supportive psychotherapy and aims to work through the abandonment depression associated with the original separation-individuation phase, leading to the achievement of ego autonomy together with the transformation of the split object relations part-units into a whole object relations unit and the split ego into a whole ego.

With a separate and defined self-image, an autonomous and reality oriented ego, and a whole object relations unit, the patient's individuation flowers and new capacities emerge for love and work that are the true building blocks for gratification in adult life.

CHOICE OF PSYCHOTHERAPY

Introduction

The choice of treatment in the past has often seemed to depend more on the therapist's theoretical bias than on the patient's clinical condition. For example, Zetzel (244) argued that the borderline patient should only have supportive psychotherapy as she felt that he could not work through the abandonment depression. I have not always found this to be true and therefore feel that all borderline patients who have the potential should have the opportunity for reconstructive psychotherapy, since it offers the greatest and most enduring change.

The amount of treatment a patient desires or will accept depends on his awareness of his suffering. The more he is aware of his suffering, the more he recognizes the destructiveness of his defenses, and the more likely he will be to accept what might otherwise seem to be heroic efforts at treatment.

The unique defenses of borderline patients make it difficult for them to accept reconstructive psychotherapy, because the purpose of the destructive behavior is to relieve the suffering, and the destructiveness of that behavior is denied. Consequently, there is minimal awareness of the suffering whose cause is externalized or of the destructiveness which is denied—the two important ingredients of motivation for treatment and change. Beyond that, the borderlines' use of the defense mechanism of avoidance to deal with individuation—which is the prime focus of reconstructive psychotherapy—further erodes their motivation. These patients are not willing to take on the separation anxiety that reconstructive psychotherapy generates until and unless they become aware of the mainspring of suffering and/or the destructiveness of their defense mechanisms.

Thus, the defense mechanisms of acting out, denial and avoidance pose formidable synergistic barriers to motivation for reconstructive psychotherapy. The therapist who recommends reconstructive psychotherapy before these defenses have been dealt with will only heighten the patient's resistance—and perhaps impel him to flee from treatment to avoid anxiety.

Clinical Factors

The clinical evaluation must take into account many variables which themselves vary so widely from patient to patient that it is not possible to give a simple outline or scheme of criteria. Instead I shall discuss the major clinical variables, together with some indications of how they vary, as food for thought to guide the therapist in his study of his patient. Only when he has put the entire picture together for his individual patient can he make the final decision.

Chief Complaint and History of Present Illness

The presenting clinical pictures can be roughly divided into the acute and the chronic. The former consists most often of a panic or an abandonment depression following a recent traumatic separation experience. These patients should probably be seen three times a week from the outset to deal with the acute symptomatic crisis. It can require this much contact with the therapist to activate the patient's clinging mechanisms in the transference and thereby relieve the acute symptoms. If seen less often the patient will have to look elsewhere—to other people, to more acting out—for relief. During this period, which can last from weeks to months, the therapist can evaluate the patient's potential for reconstructive psychotherapy.

A unique problem occurs with those patients who have suffered a recent, realistic and severe separation trauma such as loss by death of a parent, spouse or surrogate to whom the patient has been clinging. If possible, these patients should be seen three or four times a week to try to work through the depression at the recent loss without further consolidating the pathologic defenses against earlier losses. This is a difficult task since the patient tends to react to this later loss as a repetition of the earlier ones and success will depend to a great extent upon how much separation trauma the patient was exposed to in his earlier, developmental years. If this effort fails the patient should enter reconstructive psychotherapy.

There are a variety of chronic presenting clinical pictures. The patients ages range from the late 20's to the early 40's. Their problems are longstanding and unrelated to any recent separation experience. Some complain only of work difficulty and are quite unaware of their conflict in interpersonal relations. It is difficult to get these patients to come more than once a week at the beginning. Others complain more of their difficulties in interpersonal relations which are due to fears of engulfment or abandonment. When these difficulties predominate clinging will be a prominent mechanism and, combined with conscious awareness of the loneliness and isolation associated with having no close relationships, this can motivate the patient to start psychotherapy twice a week. If the fear of engulfment predominates, distancing defense mechanisms will be prominent and psychotherapy should be started once a week in order not to reinforce the patient's fear of being engulfed.

Patients whose presenting complaint is a chronic longstanding marital conflict pose special problems. The marriage bond is usually a regressive one based either on mutual clinging or on some combination of clinging and distancing. Unless the patient is in a crisis from a recent separation experience therapy should begin twice a week. Once a week rarely permits the therapist to get beyond the day-to-day marital battles.

The decision of one partner to start therapy upsets the balance of the relationship and exposes the other partner to separation anxiety, which he or she often handles by attacking the psychotherapy. The popular trend toward marital therapy—i.e., both partners, one therapist—is, I think, contraindicated in borderline patients. The dyadic transference of the borderline suggests that one cannot treat both partners. Neither will allow enough of a transference to develop for intrapsychic change to take place. Joint interviews can be used to confront both partners and deal with the other partner's resistance so that he or she can enter psychotherapy with someone else.

Past History

The past history provides clinical evidence on the two most important factors affecting the patient's capacity for reconstructive psychotherapy: his ego strength and the amount of separation trauma he experienced in his developmental years.

Ego Strength

How far the patient's ego developed along the separation-individuation axis before the arrest occurred is crucial since it indicates both how much of a reality ego developed and how primitive the defense mechanisms are. This can be seen partly in the history of present illness—i.e., the more neurotic-like the stronger the ego, and the more psychotic-like the weaker the ego. A careful early history which reveals either an absence of early symptoms, or symptoms of developmental lag combined with evidence of early sublimations that persist into latency suggests an ego that has demonstrated some capacity to cope with or master early developmental tasks.

A parallel consideration is whether or not the patient had a positive, close relationship with one or more persons in the family other than the mother in his early years—with grandparents, uncle, aunt, older sibling, etc. These relationships create nuclei of basic trust which can be enlarged in the therapeutic relationship.

Separation Trauma

The number and severity of separation traumata the patient experienced in the early years determine the degree and amount of abandonment depression he will have to work through. Minimal experiences in the vulnerable 18- to 36-month period, such as birth of a sibling who falls ill and requires the mother's attention or a mother's getting depressed, suggest that the patient, if not too severely exposed to later traumata, is a good candidate for reconstructive psychotherapy. The most common story of an early separation trauma is the birth of a sibling reinforced in latency or puberty by another separation trauma such as a divorce. Patients with such histories are good candidates for reconstructive psychotherapy.

There are some patients, however, whose separation trauma has been so massive and so repetitive throughout all the crucial developmental stages, that their repetitively reinforced defenses represent a contraindication to reconstructive psychotherapy. Such patients can often be considerably helped by supportive psychotherapy.

Age

The upper age limit for the capacity to "work through" is unknown. My oldest patient in successful reconstructive psychotherapy was in his mid-forties.

Behavior of the Parents

The more the mother's behavior was characterized by clinging rather than distancing or verbal and physical attacks, the more likely the patient will be a candidate for reconstructive psychotherapy. The exception is the patient whose mother's clinging appeared so early in the separation-individuation phase and was so intense that the patient has overwhelming fears of engulfment —of being sucked back into the symbiotic whirlpool. The more the father was neutral or even supported growth rather than reinforcing the mother's clinging, the better the candidate for reconstructive psychotherapy.

Transference and Defense Mechanisms

The greater the clinging mechanism in the transference and the lesser the distancing mechanism, the more likely the patient is a candidate for reconstructive psychotherapy.

IQ

The patient does not require a high IQ to be able to work through—this is an emotional, not intellectual, experience. The lowest IQ I have worked successfully with was around 90 (WAIS).

STAGES OF THE PSYCHOTHERAPY

The treatment is a process, a continuous series of changes, one laying the groundwork for and flowing into the other. Although natural and logical to the therapist observer, it will not appear so to the patient who may go through many ups and downs as each new therapeutic issue brings with it its own resistance.

Although for purposes of exposition I divide the treatment process into three phases*—1) testing (resistance), 2) working-through (introject work or definition), and 3) separation (resolution)—the reader should keep several points in mind. These are only major trends and there may be much regression, overlapping and back and forth movement. Patients in supportive psychotherapy get into the working-through phase very little, if at all. Each phase has some identifying clinical characteristics which will be briefly outlined. They will be developed in later chapters on treatment.

Testing Phase

This phase which initiates the therapy of all patients—supportive or reconstructive—extends from the onset of treatment to the

---

* The terms in parentheses are those used by Rinsley (191, 191a) to describe these phases.

overcoming of the initial resistance and the establishment of a therapeutic alliance. It can last from a number of months to a number of years.

The borderline patient by definition enters therapy with a great deal of resistance. He has been relying exclusively on the alliance between the rewarding object relations unit and the pathological ego for defense against the WORU with its abandonment depression and for the regulation of his internal equilibrium, denying the reality of the destructiveness involved. What the clinical observer calls symptoms of life difficulties are for the patient the ignored byproducts of his brittle and desperate efforts at regulation of his inner emotional life. He is not about to give up this effective but destructive system of defense without a struggle and without an assurance of something to substitute for it. Since the transference relationship and psychotherapy are to comprise that substitute, the patient must test out the effectiveness and reliability of psychotherapy before investing his emotional equilibrium in it. Thus, the borderline adult patient goes through a lengthy testing phase much like an adolescent.

This testing is further motivated by his poor object relations; in other words, his conflictual relationship with both parents has left him with little trust in other human beings and he must learn through testing to be able to trust, as well as rely upon, the therapist. If the therapist proves himself to be trustworthy and competent a therapeutic alliance develops, the patient controls his pathologic ego's mechanisms of defense, becomes depressed and then uses therapy to deal with the depression. Therapy and the therapist substitute for the rewarding object relations unit-pathologic alliance for dealing with uncomfortable feelings.

Confrontation

Confrontation, the principal therapeutic technique of this phase, throws a monkeywrench in the patient's defense system by introducing conflict where there previously had been none. The patient had been regulating his internal equilibrium or making himself feel good by acting out in ways that were harmful, but because he denied the harmfulness he felt no conflict. When the therapist points out the harm the patient can no longer act out without recognizing the harm. Therefore conflict and tension are created. The patient can no longer act out freely without conflict. He has to recognize the cost of "feeling good." As the therapist brings to the attention of the patient's observing ego that which had been split off and denied, the patient often responds with anger at the loss of a mechanism which he had regarded as ego-syntonic.

It is important to keep in mind that confrontation is needed throughout the therapy. The observing ego will lose its awareness when the patient undergoes a regression, i.e., previously learned insights will temporarily disappear and confrontations will have to be resumed.

Confrontation is not without its own dangers (2, 3). The therapist must be able to be "really there," empathic and "tuned in" to the patient's feeling state in order for the confrontation to work. The confrontation must be faithfully wedded to the content of the patient's associations and the patient's feeling state. It must be clearly in the patient's best interest. If it is not, the authority inherent in the dynamic theme itself is replaced by the therapist's authority. And what might have been a useful confrontation becomes a manipulation on the part of the therapist. The therapist's chief protection against this danger is his awareness of his own feeling states and of the degree of his own narcissism. Only then can he be sure that the confrontation does not spring from his own emotions to gratify his own narcissism.

The therapist must be able to confront quietly, firmly and consistently without being angry or contentious (60, 61). He must be able to disagree without being disagreeable. If the patient senses that the therapist is angry he will use the anger to avoid the validity of the confrontation—i.e., the therapist is saying it because he's angry, not because it is true.

There is one carefully chosen exception to this rule. When resistance persists despite major confrontations and seems to be defeating therapeutic progress a certain amount of therapeutic astonishment is necessary in order to alert the patient to the dangers of the tenaciousness of his resistance.

Working-Through Phase

Confrontation overcomes the resistance and engages the patient in a therapeutic alliance. He enters a transference relationship based on projection of the wish for reunion on the therapist. In intensive reconstructive therapy at this point the patient enters the abandonment depression associated with separation from the symbiotic mother.

As the patient develops greater control of the RORU-pathologic ego alliance he moves deeper into therapy. His day-to-day problems diminish and move to the periphery as the momentum of therapy is taken over by dreams, free associations, fantasies, and memories.

Transference Acting Out

To avoid the pain of depression (WORU) the patient frequently defends against the emergence of each segment of it by acting it out in the transference. This is such a constant temptation for borderline patients that it is probably the most prominent single resistance to treatment. The patient is impelled to "replay" his conflicts using the therapist as mother and/or father, thereby relieving his inner tension without having to face the suffering of the original conflicts that remembering and working-through imply. Whether the patient is projecting the RORU with its attendant positive affect or the WORU with its attendant negative affect on the therapist, he is able to obtain regressive satisfaction or gratification that he is unable to achieve anywhere else in the reality of life. The acting out must be confronted and interpreted, after which the patient will return to working-through.

It is also necessary to interpret the secondary defenses against the abandonment depression, such as blocking, denial, avoidance and emotional withdrawal in the interview. The therapist encourages verbalization as an alternative to acting out for release of the hostility underlying the depression and investigates the origins of the depression in the conflict with the parents.

Communicative Matching

Mahler's (141) reports of normal separation-individuation describe the toddler in the rapprochement phase insistently returning to the mother for "supplies." The mother provides these supplies by responding to the child's nonverbal cues in such a way as to provide approval for his further individuation—a process she calls "communicative matching."

This key developmental experience has been minimal in the borderline patient. The clinical indications of the poverty of communicative matching become apparent in the latter part of the working-through phase for the first time when the patient has worked through the abandonment depression and his own individuation process begins to flower, i.e., new interests, thoughts and feelings emerge. Rage and depression seem to occur in parallel with these newly emerging thoughts and feelings despite the fact that the abandonment depression has been worked through. Reinterpretation of the rage at the mother's withdrawal seems to promote regression.

This has led me to efforts to provide communicative matching by discussing with the patient from my own knowledge general and universal aspects of the particular new interest or feeling presented. In other words, the therapist supports his or her individuation. This is most easily illustrated by discussion with patients of their new interests—i.e., sports, the stock market, literature, history, music, art, current events, etc. A great deal of information can be imparted in these discussions about various styles of coping with and mastering reality problems (4). Discussion might focus on such varied topics as the amount of planning and effort required to succeed at a sport or in business or the arts, or the need to see and deal with people as they are in reality rather than as the patient might wish them to be. For example, a 20-year-old borderline college student planned to become a constitutional lawyer. It was without doubt the strongest and most consistent sublimation he possessed amidst a welter of paranoid psychopathology. In the calm between therapeutic storms we spent a great deal of time discussing the implications for constitutional law of the various legal moves in the Watergate scandal. As his paranoid suspiciousness decreased he made some tentative and hesitant moves towards women and it was necessary to not only deal with his fear of rejection but also to discuss many of the universal reality problems that exist between the sexes. Similarly, in both male and female patients who are driven to "instant intimacy" one eventually discusses the realistic manner in which healthy people get involved in a relationship.

Another woman patient had worked through her abandonment depression, during which she had expressed a great deal of rage and depression at the mother's attacking her whenever she attempted to do anything on her own, including attempting to buy her own clothes, decorating her own room, cooking, or taking up any outside interests at school, and particularly initiating what had been a budding interest in gardening. As her individuation emerged, her interest in plants intensified and she began to develop her own indoor greenhouse, buying plants and spending a great deal of time taking care of them. Despite the fact that she seemed to have worked through the abandonment depression, these activities were accompanied with less intense but still substantial rage and depression. Interpretation of their origins seemed to have no effect. I then began each time she brought up her interest in gardening to discuss gardening experiences in general. This seemed to attenuate the anger and depression and to promote further individuation.

This type of "therapeutic communicative matching" is indicated whenever the material the patient presents seems to reflect an expression of a newly emerging self. The same cautions that applied to confrontation also apply to communicative matching. The therapist must be empathetic and "tuned in" to the patient's newly emerging self. It must be in response to the need of the patient, not the narcissism of the therapist.

Separation Phase

The patient's clinical picture shows a decided change as he enters this phase. He has controlled the mechanisms of this pathologic ego and is using more constructive defenses so that his life structure is substantially free. He has worked through the homicidal-suicidal affect of the frustration of the wish for unconditional love and he has done all these within the framework of the transference with the therapist. Depression is now markedly reduced but the patient experiences anxiety over separation from the therapist and over his capacity to function on his own— anxiety about autonomy. This revives the old conflict over separation as being an abandonment and a new conflict arises which the therapist must interpret. Ideally the decision to stop treatment should come from the patient with the therapist's support and termination of therapy should be graduated, the therapist being available at later times should the patient require it.

THE THERAPIST'S REACTIONS*

Partner for Growth or Regression?

The borderline patient projects so much and is so provocative and manipulative, particularly in the beginning of therapy, that he can place a great emotional stress on the therapist. Unless the therapist can understand both what the patient is doing and how it is affecting his own emotions he will be unable to deal with it therapeutically. It is important to keep in mind that the patient is a professional at provocation and manipulation while the therapist is an amateur at the use of these mechanisms.

Borderline patients, after they have overcome their denial and entered the working-through phase, often will refer to their childhood as having been a concentration camp in which they learned to survive through manipulation of the omnipotent guards, i.e., their parents. They are exquisitely sensitive to the daily emotional state of the therapist, to his tone of voice and to nonverbal messages conveyed by gestures and body posture. They use this sensitivity to seek out the therapist's personal "Achilles' heel," to provoke and manipulate him in order to test his competence, to fulfill their pathologic needs and also to resist treatment. They seek personal information not only out of the hunger for emo-

---

* See pp. 342-346 for more on the therapist's reactions.

tional contact and to act out the wish for reunion as a resistance to therapy, but also to provide ammunition for their rage reactions. The therapist must be prepared to have his own personal idiosyncrasies exaggerated and trotted out for critical scrutiny. The therapist must not react to that behavior but rather use his own reactions to these maneuvers as a signal, a kind of litmus paper to diagnose the meaning of the patient's behavior.

The borderline patient often cannot distinguish between feelings and reality; to him these are the same thing. His denial of reality, his poor reality perception, the urge to project and act out the wish for reunion—all combine to make him unaware that what he feels is not true in reality. He must learn this perception from his therapist. However, the mechanism of projective identification tends to suggest to the therapist that the patient's feelings have a spurious sense of reality so that it is easy for the therapist to be caught up in the patient's distortions. For instance, if the patient is attacking the therapist by projecting on him the WORU image of the attacking mother, pretty soon the therapist begins to feel as if he is in truth the attacking mother. I have often seen resident psychiatrists, like actors using the Stanislovsky method, summon up dynamics from their own personal past to support the feelings associated with the role the patient was projecting on them. For example, a female resident I supervised who had done well with other patients became extremely sarcastic with a new female patient. When, over a period of time, it became clear that the patient was projecting the WORU part-unit onto the therapist in an extremely intense way the therapist had to search through her own development and past to find a psychodynamic cause to support the hatred the patient was projecting onto her and impelling her to feel towards the patient. Investigation revealed that the therapist had had a sister, the parents' favorite, who died before she was born. The resident felt that since her sister was dead she could never compete with her for the parents' favor. The therapist then projected this image of her dead sister back onto the patient to support her own feeling of hate.

The therapist must be careful to maintain a consistent positive approach which is grounded in reality and not to give ground and therefore reinforcement to the patient's projected emotions. The therapist's firm grounding in reality is what guards the patient against his projections. It is of paramount importance that the therapist cut in, confront and clarify in order to prevent the therapy from becoming stalemated.

The pitfalls related to the therapist's personality are many. The compulsive therapist whose compulsiveness springs from a reaction formation to his own tendency to act out may become angry and anxious at his patient's acting out and his confrontations then will be defeated by his own anger. The submissive therapist never confronts the patient adequately and therefore activates the withdrawn WORU projection and transference acting out takes over, i.e., the patient feels the therapist does not care. The dependent therapist who needs his patient's approval activates the rewarding object relations unit and so repeats the patient's developmental problem and treatment stops.

If the therapist has been temporarily caught up in the patient's acting out or projections, he must be secure, honest and direct enough to admit his own mistakes either in perception or response. For example, has he confronted where he should have interpreted or vice versa? The patient's shaky hold on reality requires this kind of understanding on the part of the therapist. The patient will forgive the therapist's mistakes if his treatment in general is proceeding satisfactorily but he will not forgive the therapist for dishonesty or covering up. The patient has had more than his share of both during his childhood.

The therapist must be flexible enough to switch from one therapeutic technique to another almost at the drop of a hat or at a moment's notice as the patient's clinical state changes. One moment interpretation is necessary which may induce a regression, which will require confrontation, from which individuation may ensue, which will require communicative matching. A therapist who is able to confront and set limits will be able to initiate the therapy but if he is unable to shift in the working-through phase when an empathic response is required the therapy will stop and the patient will begin to project the WORU on the therapist. Some therapists are able to both confront and be intuitive and empathic during the working-through phase but have great difficulty with communicative matching or letting go, in which case the treatment founders in the last phase.

The poor object constancy of the borderline suggests that the therapist should be as careful as he can be to maintain the consistency of all the environmental arrangements of the therapy to provide a framework against which a patient's projections can be understood. The hours of therapy should be changed as infrequently as possible; the therapist should be on time and should give clear apologies and explanations for any changes or cancellations.

The Non-Directive Passive Therapist

The therapist who adopts a consistently passive stance appropriate for the neurotic patient will meet with failure with the borderline patient since the two developmental necessities—a real object and a reality ego—will be lacking. The therapist's passivity will so correspond to the patient's projection of his withdrawing maternal part-image that the patient will not be able to distinguish between his WORU projection and the reality of the therapist's behavior. Consequently he will enter a transference psychosis. This will activate the RORU unit which will produce resistance and the therapy will stop. Moreover, the therapist's failure to confront the destructiveness of the mechanisms of the patient's pathological ego—avoidance, denial, projection, acting out of the wish for reunion—will leave the patient at the mercy of these mechanisms. The therapy may stop in a dramatic, catastrophic fashion with the patient abruptly not returning or refusing to return; however, more often there is a prolonged stalemate, since the borderline patient is a master at compliance with the therapist's unconscious wishes. The patient's lack of involvement remains hidden beneath his defenses while he presents the therapist with an illusion of therapy.

The Directive Therapist

The other side of this therapeutic dilemma is the directive

and seductive therapist who attempts to "take over" and manage the patient's life for him in a vain effort to make the patient feel that he really "loves" or "cares about" him. This creates a deadly trap for the borderline patient who feels so deeply deprived of maternal affect and approval and is therefore so needful of such approval that he will soak it up like a dry sponge in order to "feel good."

When this occurs growth in psychotherapy or separation-individuation will cease since both patient and therapist are bent upon activating the patient's RORU. Neither will be able to recognize the reality of this relationship. As time progresses the patient will only indirectly note that the price he has paid for "feeling good" is the ancient and historical one of giving up his growth and development. He will begin to notice that although he enjoys seeing his therapist he is not getting any better. I have seen a number of patients who had several years of this type of "therapy" before stopping because of insufficient improvement. Even years later, after they have realized what happened, they still have high regard for the therapist who so fulfilled their very basic and infantile need to be taken care of and their wish for reunion.

The message is clear: The patient's feelings of infantile deprivation are so fundamental, so deep, and the feelings of abandonment so painful that he is willing in therapy, as he was as a child, to sacrifice *anything* to fulfill the fantasy of reunion while at the same time avoiding the pain of abandonment. The therapist whose manner reflects the overly directive and approving approach springs the trap by reinforcing the RORU and bringing growth and development—progress in therapy—to a halt. It is the cruelest of deceptions which repeats for the patient the scapegoating he received as a child from the parents: The authority figure who is supposed to and pretends to act in the patient's best interest actually is doing the patient the greatest damage.

Transference

What then is the appropriate attitude of the therapist? Although he doesn't "love" the patient or wish to take care of him as a child, he has a professional—not a personal—interest in the patient and his problems and wants to help the patient to help himself. This crucial reality differentiation has to be taught to the borderline patient by various limit setting statements of the therapist and by subjecting to investigation the patient's projections of the wish for reunion fantasy (the RORU), as well as of the WORU, on the therapist. The latter are investigated first while the former are allowed to lie dormant, unless they also begin to impede therapy. Usually, as the patient works through his WORU and establishes a true therapeutic alliance, he gradually becomes aware of the RORU on his own. The tenaciousness of this RORU projection is seen in the fact that for a long time, long after he has become aware of the RORU projection, it continues to exert its influence.

The transference relationship of the borderline is paradoxical. It is dyadic, not triadic. It is notoriously unstable—due to the object splitting and the excess of aggression—the patient being excruciatingly sensitive to rejection and to minor separation stresses. On the other hand, the patient does project on the therapist his fantasy of reunion with the mother—his rewarding maternal part-image—which forms a powerful tie. As a child the patient would do anything in order to receive supplies from the mother, including the suppression of his own growth and development. This situation becomes reversed in therapy. The patient's projection of his reunion fantasy on the therapist enables the patient to endure the pain of the inevitable abandonment depression that ensues as soon as he begins to make therapeutic progress. The RORU projection is the carrot that impels the patient to endure the stick of working-through the WORU projection.

Countertransference

Countertransference refers to the therapist's transfer of unconscious attitudes which he had towards important people in his childhood onto the patient. For a full discussion of all the implications of this complex subject the reader is referred elsewhere

(13, 30, 31, 135, 185, 186), as we shall concentrate on it only as it applies to the borderline therapist.

The vicarious emotional involvement that occurs in therapy, seemingly within safe limits and without the risks that occur in the usual close emotional relationships in real life, attracts therapists who are borderline themselves to the treatment of these patients. Unless these therapists have had treatment and are aware of their own borderline propensities they cannot perceive their own unconscious mechanisms defeating the therapy. If the therapist's principal mechanism is that of distancing he either does not see the patients more often than once a week and thereby probably does disservice to those patients who can benefit from a more intense therapy or he starts therapy more intensely under intellectual motivations and will not permit a therapeutic relationship to be established. Generally, this type of therapist will not perceive the patient's emotional state and will respond with irrelevant topics or questions whenever the patient happens to move deeper into his feelings. Finally, the patient will feel this as a rejection and project the WORU on the therapist. At this point therapy will stop.

If the therapist's prominent mechanism is clinging, a mutual clinging relationship results which triggers or activates the RORU unit. The patient then "feels good" but his therapeutic process stops. (One often wonders if this may not explain some of those therapists who end up marrying patients—perhaps because they cannot separate.)

Probably the most difficult of all for the patient is the therapist whose mechanisms alternate between clinging and distancing. At one moment the therapist invites the patient into a relationship and at the next he cuts off the relationship, thereby repeating the maternal pattern. The borderline therapist with either mechanism becomes a true partner for regression because, not having solved his own separation-individuation problem, he is unable to perceive and support his patient's individuation through communicative matching.

SEPARATION STRESS IN THERAPY

The failure to develop object constancy with persistence of the fear of abandonment makes the therapeutic relationship exquisitely sensitive to the least separation stress, which immediately activates the WORU followed by the RORU as a defense. The more involved the patient gets with the therapist the more his fears of being abandoned or engulfed are enhanced and then projected on the therapist.

The patient's fears of abandonment and engulfment are often so great that he cannot tolerate any more involvement than interviews once or twice a week. On the other hand, at times of crisis the stability of the patient's inner equilibrium, as well as of his relationship with the therapist, is so dependent on contact that it is sometimes necessary to see the patient every day, even several times a day, as well as to be available by phone, or to permit the patient to come and sit in the waiting room for periods of time with the therapist having only very brief contacts in person.

The external separation stress produces an overwhelming, catastrophic response, the patient undergoing a regression, losing the ego's observing capacity, as well as previously gained insight, which brings inquiry and investigation to a temporary halt. The withdrawn WORU is activated, the patient's inner regulation of his emotional equilibrium goes off the rails and the alliance between the RORU and the pathologic ego takes over. This change in the patient's clinical state dictates a corresponding change in the therapeutic technique. At this point interview technique has to return to reality confrontation. It is necessary to again help the patient gain an observing distance from his feelings. The judicious and appropriate use of humor can be helpful to defuse some of the feeling of pain as well as to teach the patient to maintain some distance from his feeling state.

II. CLINICAL

A. Supportive Psychotherapy

Introduction

The art of supportive psychotherapy of the borderline adult consists of keeping up the therapeutic pressure by raising the patient's anxiety through confrontations of the destructiveness of the defenses of the pathologic ego—splitting, avoidance, denial, projection, and acting out—while at the same time remaining alert to and empathetic with the enormous fear of engulfment or abandonment which these confrontations stimulate. The therapist must walk a tightrope adjusting the therapeutic pressure to that which the patient is able to tolerate within the limits of the transference relationship.

Should he relax his confrontations too much, therapeutic progress will stop; should he increase them too much the patient's fear of engulfment or abandonment will become too great and more than likely the patient will stop therapy. This art uniquely depends upon the capacity to judge from moment to moment

117

throughout the course of therapy how much confrontation the patient can tolerate in order to progress without feeling so much anxiety that he has to disrupt treatment, to titrate the separation anxiety against the strength of the transference relationship.

The next three chapters present the "supportive" psychotherapy of three patients. Chapters 7 and 8 describe the first two and a half years of supportive psychotherapy of a young woman whose fears of engulfment and abandonment produce great resistance to entering psychotherapy. Chapter 7 illustrates the long struggle with the defense mechanisms of the pathologic ego. Chapter 8 illustrates that as these defenses are reached the patient enters a true therapeutic alliance. Her self begins to emerge as she at the same time begins to face the underlying conflict with the parents. The 124 consecutive interviews over this period are included in order to demonstrate in great detail the extraordinary intrincacy and tenacity of her resistance, as well as the therapeutic intensity and activity necessary to confront the resistance and allow the patient to enter psychotherapy. I think this patient clearly demonstrates that a very frightened and defensive borderline patient will enter psychotherapy if given the proper therapeutic support.

Chapter 9, presenting the supportive psychotherapy of two older women, has a different focus. The patients began therapy with vague and superficial complaints about "life not being satisfying." The initial therapeutic task consisted of making the patients aware of their emotional problems through confrontation of the defenses of the pathologic ego. All three women's difficulties with intimacy prevented them from having satisfactory relationships with men. However, the latter two, in their 40's, had reached an age where men were less available even if they did get over their problems. The former patient, at age 25, had much more to look forward to in her relationship with men if she could learn to master her emotional problems. This is a persuasive argument for doing as much psychotherapy as is possible with young adults, both men and women, before age has limited their heterosexual horizons.

7

The Perpetual Student:

"Frightened, Unloved, Without a Self"

CASE REPORT OF CATHERINE

Catherine, a 22-year-old, short, slender, blue-eyed attractive blonde, was casually dressed in a miniskirt. She was referred to me by a colleague after an evaluation which was unduly prolonged by her fearfulness about treatment as expressed verbally and by being late or missing appointments. She complained that since receiving her college degree a year ago she had been "running around," unable to make a decision about herself or her life. She suspected that she was running around because on the one hand she could not deal with living at home, but on the other hand, she was not able to be completely away from home—a clear articulation of the borderline dilemma!

She had spent the year in travel and temporary jobs while awaiting admission to a graduate program at a local college.

119

When the college accepted her she suddenly realized she didn't want to attend and, disturbed by this dilemma, she sought psychiatric consultation.

She added that her return to the United States, which had required her to settle down in one place, had led her to feel "more lonely and nervous." She felt she "needed people," was afraid of being alone, never felt independent. She had had only one good relationship with a man in the last four years; however, she felt she had probably suffocated him and destroyed the relationship with her need for security. She tended to date men who were both egotistic and sadistic and for whom she felt sexual attraction but no affection.

Family History

Father was a successful broker who had a self-centered, domineering personality around which the family revolved. He was moody and hot-tempered, would frequently blow up, and on occasion would explode into physical attacks, mostly at the brothers, but occasionally at the patient. The mother and brothers placated the father completely, and Catherine was the only family member who on rare occasions fought with him. He perceived Catherine as still a child, expected her to comply with his wishes and was annoyed and sulked if she did not. If she did not visit on weekends he was annoyed, but when she did visit he paid no attention to her. He was particularly annoyed at her plan to live and work in the city. Although her childhood memories of him were vague she recalled him as being very interested in her as an infant and young child, this interest decreasing as she got older. She said, "I think the trouble began with him when I started to walk and talk." She recalled him as being oversolicitous about her physical and material welfare while being completely oblivious to her real interests and feelings. He would indulge her with various gifts more appropriate to his interests than hers and if she pointed this out he sulked. He expected her to conform to the role of perpetual child and to cater to him like the mother and brothers did. She felt she was not able to talk to him about her own thoughts and feelings.

Mother presented a much more subtle but equally conflictual problem. The patient described her as rather dependent, helpless and fearful, placating and catering to the father's outbursts. She clearly favored the older brother whom she flagrantly overindulged. While on the surface she acted as a go-between with Catherine and her father—ostensibly to show her interest in Catherine by protecting her—actually it was to act as a reinforcing agent for the father's demand that Catherine placate him like the mother and brothers. Whenever the mother's relationship with Catherine conflicted with the relationship with her husband or older son it was Catherine's interest that was sacrificed. For example, Catherine's assertions upset the father which upset the mother. When Catherine expressed her own interests and feelings the mother accused her of being self-centered. This attitude was subtly concealed beneath more overt attitudes of overindulging Catherine and treating her as if she were a helpless, fearful child —probably a projection of the mother's image of herself.

The older brother, age 26, was a dependent, self-centered, stingy man who was flagrantly overprotected and indulged by the mother. He continued to live at home despite a good job. He was the frequent butt of the father's hostility and related to the father with the same pacifying compliant manner as the mother. He had yet to date and seemed afraid of girls. He was patronizing and hostile to Catherine who felt, nevertheless, superior to him.

The younger brother, age 18, was a shy, withdrawn, young man who was a senior in high school and who sided with his brother against Catherine.

Past History

Catherine was the second of three children in a middle-class home. She recalls very little of her earliest years except that in the first five years she had frequent upper respiratory infections, a mild case of asthma, and received a great deal of attention from both parents. She recalls that even then the home was dominated by the father, and that as long as his mood was good there was little difficulty. In fact, one would have to suspect that even during these times the mother's and father's infantilizing attitudes were having their effect. There was a lot of rivalry and battles between her and her brother. She started the local school without difficulty and did well. When she was eight, in the third grade, she fell ill with vague gastrointestinal complaints which lasted for one year —a time which she again recalls as one in which she received a lot of attention. However, during this period, in the third grade, the family moved to another city. She had great difficulty adjusting to the change and making new friends and consequently was depressed and lonely for a year. She recalls the years between ages seven and 12 as being particularly bad because of the father's temper outbursts; she would run away from the house when he came home. At the same time he spent most of his time away traveling and was only home on weekends. When she was 13 and in the eighth grade the family moved again, and again she had trouble adjusting and was depressed and lonely for a year. She reports no difficulty in high school where she was a good student, nor in going away to college where she finished her studies and graduated without trouble. She chose to travel to avoid a final decision about a career since she didn't know what she wanted to do.

From her high school years on she had always had an active interest in boys and had dated a lot. However, she described a pattern, which evolved over several years, of always having relationships with two or more men—one of whom she fantasied as the "caretaker" whom she loved but did not have sexual relations with, and another whom she was attracted to but had no affectionate feelings for and with whom she did have sexual relations. If she did have sex with the former it never led to orgasm, while sex with the latter usually ended in orgasm. For the last three years she had had an intermittent relationship with Charles (the "caretaker"), whom she felt she loved and might eventually marry, and with Fred (the sexual outlet).

Comment

Catherine defended herself against her anxiety about being on her own—against separation-individuation and autonomy—by avoidance of committing herself either to a career or to a relationship with a man. The career avoidance had been concealed beneath the smokescreen of being a perpetual student. She could go away to college and travel as long as home was her base. This smokescreen, however, dissolved when she had to commit herself to a life as an independent, responsible adult by entering a graduate program. She was also vaguely aware of the splitting in her relationship with men; she tended to cling to one man while she acted out her hostility with another—having a realistic relationship with neither.

I suggested to Catherine that she had concealed her emotional problems about leaving her parents and becoming independent through the device of being a perpetual student and through various dependent relationships and that she should get a job and settle down in one place while she worked this problem out. I suggested interviews once a week since I felt that Catherine's fear of psychotherapy—i.e., fear of engulfment—was so intense that she could not tolerate greater involvement at this time. In the interviews that follow it is important to note Catherine's preoccupation first with men and then with her father. The focus on these two areas is initiated and continued by her as a reflection of her problem. I am principally responding to what she considers important.

THE THERAPY

Interview #3

Catherine immediately demonstrated the extraordinary transference fluctuations that occur in borderline patients by reporting that my writing as she spoke in the previous interview made me seem mechanical and nonpersonal and made her feel like crying.

My writing, which took my exclusive attention away from her and exposed her to separation anxiety—anxiety about loss of the object—interrupted the projection of the wish for reunion fantasy—RORU—on me and triggered the WORU. To set reality limits to this projection I stated I was just doing my job and when I queried as to where she had felt this way before she recalled that when her father shouted at her she would cry instead of standing up to him because if she stood up to him "we'll kill each other." She then reported hating his attacks, wishing him dead but nevertheless loving him. She also reported memories of his attacking her, pulling her hair and throwing shoes at her. Catherine had thus defined the arena of the initial therapeutic encounter.

Interview #4

She reported provoking the sexual interest of two men without intending to follow through. I did not mention the transference implication but instead emphasized the reality that if she provoked sexual interest without intending to follow through she was liable to get into trouble.

Interview #5

There was a long silence after which Catherine described that she felt "faint," "like shaking" and that she was very depressed after the last interview.

Interview #6

She reported that one night when she was alone for the first time in a girlfriend's apartment, she had panicked and felt there was someone in the house coming to get her. She recalled that she often had felt that way. She had also been upset by hearing that a friend of the family was placed in a psychiatric hospital.

She described her relationship with men as being either physical or protective. Charles was protective; she held on to him. "This image of him is very important to me."

Interviews #7, #8, #9

During the next three weeks interviews #7, #8, and #9 dealt with the patient's procrastination and avoidance about finding an apartment of her own; she had been living like a nomad or gypsy moving from one friend's apartment to another. I confronted her by saying that this behavior was symptomatic of her whole problem—i.e., avoidance of dealing with anxiety about committing herself. She accepted the confrontation without comment.

I repeated the statement. She responded, "It must come from overprotective parents but there's nothing wrong with that!" I challenged this statement! The patient remained silent and cried. I then pointed out her resistance to facing the conflict with her mother and father as evidenced by this response to my challenging her stereotyped view. Suddenly she replied, "Today you said something that's both familiar and unpleasant and you are getting closer to home."

At this point it may be helpful to digress a moment from the psychotherapy to summarize Catherine's borderline problem.

ANALYSIS OF CATHERINE'S BORDERLINE PROBLEM

This patient was precipitated into treatment by the fact that her defenses of avoidance of commitment to a career or to a relationship and her acting out of the wish for reunion were challenged by her chronologic age of 22. Heretofore she had been able to conceal her conflict over being independent beneath the façade created by living the life of a perpetual student. This life permitted the acting out of dependency needs, and physical distance from her parents allowed her to avoid confronting the conflicts with them. Her anxiety mounted when she could no longer be a student and had to make a choice of a career.

The defenses of the patient's pathologic ego were avoidance of independent action or assertiveness in work or in interpersonal relationships combined with denial of the destructiveness of this behavior. Emotional involvement in relationships was handled by distancing mechanisms (both physical and emotional) and isolation.

She played the role of the good child with her parents in order to receive their supplies.

She maintained a similar distance from real involvement with a man and instead used her present relationships with men to deal with the residue of anger and depression left over from her past conflict with her parents—i.e., she projected the wish for reunion on the man and then acted out her need to be taken care of with him. Transient relationships that did not entail emotional involvement were used to obtain sexual release. Beneath this defensive façade lay her fear of being engulfed or abandoned if she allowed real emotional involvement.

Catherine's original symbiotic attachment to her mother was probably characterized principally by her fear of engulfment and to a lesser degree by her fear of abandonment; to defend against these feelings, she displaced this symbiotic attachment from the mother to the father. This displacement was encouraged and facilitated by the mother who complied with and subordinated herself to the father. The displacement was probably further facilitated by: 1) the mother's defects in nurturing which may have produced severe feelings of deprivation which only added to the already existent threat of regression back into the symbiotic whirlpool; and 2) the fact that in all likelihood the father may have actually provided more supplies than the mother. However, clinging to the father to defend against the mother became a two-edged sword since the father not only reinforced the tie that binds ("remain the good child to receive supplies"), but also reinforced the patient's fear of abandonment with his severe, explosive temper outbursts.

It is important to keep in mind that the relationship with the father starts out as a direct displacement of the symbiotic relationship with the mother—i.e., the father emotionally became a mother to the patient—rather than a male figure in his own right for whom the patient could compete with the mother. In other words, the relationship continues to be dyadic, not triadic. This is further complicated later in development when the symbiotic level condenses with the oedipal and a relationship that had been a source of support becomes burdened with oedipal guilt feelings.

A common mistake is to diagnose such a patient as hysterical and to conceive of the psychodynamics as being solely related to the father in the oedipal phase of development. This point of view overlooks the severe ego defects this patient possesses which must have originated in a developmental arrest at a stage earlier than the oedipal; this, in turn, leads to a failure to provide the proper support for the patient's weak ego. In addition, the emphasis on sexual and oedipal content leads both patient and therapist away from the more fundamental symbiotic nature of the problem and probably encourages, rather than sets limits to, sexual acting out. Since borderline patients are extremely sensitive to and compliant with the therapist's unconscious wishes they often strive both directly and indirectly to provide him with what they think he wants in order to get his approval as they did with their mother. This can result in long periods of fascinating oedipal content in interviews, including dreams and fantasies which are obligingly provided and which give the illusion of therapeutic progress, beneath which there is a therapeutic stalemate. The therapist who keeps this distinction in mind will avoid being led down the garden path of investigating oedipal features in the patient until the earlier preoedipal developmental problems have been thoroughly worked through, at which time the oedipal conflicts will emerge in their true triadic form and the patient will be emotionally ready to deal with them. Even then the form of the oedipal conflict will be severely influenced by its condensation with the preoedipal features described above.

As a result if the displacements described above, the entire separation-individuation conflict was played out around the father, who served as a substitute or replacement for the mother. Thus, the wish for reunion with the mother was displaced on and acted out with the father. This later showed up in therapy through the patient's use of heterosexual relationships to act out the wish for reunion to defend against the abandonment depression—i.e., activating the RORU to defend against the WORU.

Catherine's WORU consisted of an image of an angry, explosive, attacking father who would withdraw at any efforts to assert herself, express her individuality, or be on her own, with resultant profound depression, emptiness, rage and a self image of being inadequate, helpless and hopeless. The WORU contains another earlier, deeper maternal representation of a "smothering or engulfing mother." The RORU consisted of an image of the father and mother as loving, caring, providing supplies and a self-image as a good child with an affect of feeling good. This caring was dependent, however, on the patient's not expressing herself.

It is important to recognize the severe threat that therapy posed for Catherine. Her splitting, distancing, avoidance, denial, projection and acting out defenses protected her from the overwhelming fears of engulfment and abandonment that involvement in a relationship threatened. They also protected her from the abandonment depression involved in confronting the enormous conflicts with both her mother and father.

If she allowed a relationship to develop with the therapist she not only would encounter the fear of abandonment but also would have to confront the conflicts with the parents. In more technical words, involvement in therapy activated the WORU. Therapy would require her to stop activating the RORU as a defense, and instead work through the painful affect associated with the WORU in interviews. Consequently she tested the therapist almost as an adolescent tests the therapist, before she was willing to become fully involved.

As anxiety about involvement with the therapist rose (as involvement activated the WORU), she acted out the wish for reunion as a defense (i.e., the RORU). What lay beneath the acting out and the distancing from the therapist was the original involvement with the father with its enormous fear of abandonment and, beneath that, the fear of being engulfed by the mother. The former had to be dealt with in therapy before the latter could come to the fore.

The first task of therapy was to confront the pathologic ego defenses of splitting, avoidance and denial. The therapist made reality confrontations of the destructiveness of this behavior. As the confrontations impelled the patient to change her behavior, depression and anger came to the fore and were handled either by blocking and avoidance or by acting out the wish for reunion in relationships with men. These behaviors were pointed out as defenses against the underlying depression and anger. At the same time, the splitting of the conflict with the father from the conflict with men was also pointed out.

As the patient began to give up the acting out of dependency needs (avoidance of commitment) at work and in relationships with men, an inevitable consequence was the mobilization of the underlying anger and depression related to conflict with the mother and father. Whenever the patient controlled the activation of the RORU to defend against the WORU the depression came to the fore. Concomitantly, the patient was becoming progressively more involved with the therapist and now began to more clearly reveal fears of abandonment if she got involved with him just as she had with her father, which brought the problem in her relationships with men to the surface.

Now to return to the psychotherapy, interview #15.

Interview #15

The confrontation in interview #14 brought on the abandonment depression and in this next interview Catherine reported an attempt to act out the wish for reunion to deal with the abandonment depression.

"I went to see Charles but got very upset because he has changed, was into drugs, kept pointing out how childish I am and was cold and critical." Charles' behavior shattered her wish for reunion fantasy. I pointed out that she was upset because Charles was no longer playing the old game with her and that therefore she could no longer hold on to the old fantasy.

She then reported that her father had made a special point of calling her on a visit to the city to offer her a ride home despite the fact that he knew she had not intended to visit home. This led me to point out that the father holds on to her just like she clings to Charles. She recalled that as a child she used to lock herself in the bathroom when her father got angry. "Since I was so afraid I don't like to think about my father but maybe you're right. I should try to understand my parents."

I interpreted that she clung to her childhood view of her parents to preserve her security. She responded "Father wants me around but maybe I don't like it. Why would father hold on to me as he has mother?"

This confrontation of her defenses and the beginning investigation of her conflict with the father brought on a dramatic defensive response—transference acting out.

Interview #16

She reported having had sexual relations with Fred, again acting out the other side of her split object relations unit—sex without emotion.

Interview #17

Catherine was silent. Finally she said, "I had a cold feeling about you all week; you didn't care about me." This was a transference projection of her feelings about her father which she had just begun investigating in interview #15. I said, "You're mad at me." She replied, "Yes." I asked, "Was it because I said your behavior with Charles was a defense against your feelings about your father, which in turn appalled you?" Catherine replied evasively, "I don't know, I can't remember."

Interview #18

I used a dream Catherine reported that Charles had married to point out the large amount of fantasy in her relationship with both Charles and Fred. She replied, "After the last interview I called Charles because I cannot forget his 'taking care of me.'"

Interviews #19 and #20

The next two interviews, #19 and #20, she reported feeling better, being able to be alone in the apartment, sleeping well and not wanting to call Charles.

Interview #21

Catherine reported a transference dream in which she tended to see me as strong, powerful and confident to deal with her own feelings of dependency and weakness.

She also reported beginning to look for an apartment for herself, although she was tempted to move in with Fred despite her lack of feeling for him. I pointed out the destructive impact of living with a man for whom she had no affection.

Interview #22

I confronted that her relationships with both Charles and Fred were heavily influenced by fantasy, the one to be taken care of, the other for sex, that both were efforts to deal with her difficulty in feeling both sex and affection for one man. This increased her resistance, leading to a series of interviews during which she blocked out all feeling.

Interview #23

She remained silent throughout the interview.

Interview #24

She continued to block but reported that she stopped calling Charles and planned to live alone for the summer.

Interview #28

She reported that after spending a weekend in a commune she was very anxious, had dreams of Charles and Fred leaving her and became depressed and very upset. I connected this anxiety about losing her fantasy of Charles' and Fred's taking care of her with my previous interpretation.

Interview #29

Catherine had visited home and reported a new perception of her father as "saying nothing to her, taking little interest in her and just going about his business." Her denial was decreasing. She felt he knew nothing about her; this thought was followed by suicidal thoughts. I noticed and brought to her attention that she described her father's lack of interest with a very indulgent smile which led to her awareness that her anger at the father was suppressed out of both fear and guilt.

Interviews #30 and #31

A job offer led to enormous anxiety about being on her own. I related this to the relationship with the father, saying that he placed her in an impossible bind, demanding success but at the same time wanting her to remain an obedient child.

Interview #32

She reported a dream of two aunts "sending an ape to murder me," which was probably a response to my interpretation about the father. However, I did not interpret the dream. She decided not to take the job.

Interviews #33-36

Charles had called and the patient had now perceived for the first time that he had a need to take care of someone else and that she had responded to this need, not wanting to let him know of her improvement for fear of losing him. I pointed out again that she was treating him as if he were a father, not a boyfriend.

As the therapeutic pressure mounted on the use of avoidance and the acting out of reunion fantasies to deal with the abandonment depression, Catherine's resistance rose and she had to defend herself by establishing distance from the therapy.

Interviews #37-51

In the next 14 interviews she blocked, denied feelings and talked about details of her job.

Interview #52

Catherine now returned to report the abandonment depression that had been stirred up by the therapy and had led to the distancing defenses: "I am feeling unloved and without a self."

Interview #53

Catherine began silent and blocked but then moved a little bit further into the abandonment depression. She remembered that when she was a child her father had traveled a lot and was not interested in her when he was home. Consequently, she had withdrawn from him. Their first house was associated with violence and with her having asthma and respiratory infections as a child. She then reported a weekend trip during which she had an encounter with a man, felt herself "getting attached in the old way" and stopped the relationship. She was beginning to curb the acting out of the wish for reunion fantasy.

Interview #56

Following a visit home Catherine made some new perceptions. Her denial about her parents was diminishing and she began to question whether or not they cared. "Mother was oversolicitous; father just wanted me around. I'd like to take something from them. I feel bitter without their support. I have to work for it rather than get it freely."

Confrontation of the patient with her defenses against her abandonment depression—her avoidance, denial of conflict with father, and projection and acting out of the wish for reunion on Charles, together with her distancing from me—interrupted these defenses, initiated the abandonment depression and allowed the patient to investigate and understand the conflict. Catherine was now beginning to talk about feelings about her parents, not actions with men.

Interview #57

Overcoming the denial of her perceptions of the parents' real attitudes to her exposed her to the feelings the denial had been a defense against—the abandonment depression (or the WORU). She projected this feeling state on to the psychotherapy rather than face that it had to do with her parents, and defended herself against it by distancing herself from the therapy. "I really didn't want to see you today." "I fell asleep and almost missed coming here, feeling I'm nowhere."

I confronted the patient by saying the opposite was true. "The treatment has made you more aware of the anxiety and depression you felt about your parents."

Catherine replied, "I don't want to talk about it anymore because it would just mean further depression. I think I should stop." She then added, "I had a dream this week of my mother and brothers being against me. . . . I just can't handle close relationships; I just have to find someone to take care of me."

I followed the confrontation through: "You seem caught between being upset at recognizing how much you need your parents on the one hand and on the other seeing how many problems they have relating to you. These perceptions are a product of trying to become independent but seem only to bring on more depression. Seemingly you can't win: You're depressed if you stay as you are and more depressed if you change." I suggested the possibility of a third alternative—working through the depression in therapy so that she could be independent of the parents. Catherine had no response.

Whenever Catherine felt depressed she projected the withdrawn object relations unit on the therapist, feeling that the depression came not from the relationship with her parents but from therapy; she wanted to manage the depression now as she had before by denying and blocking out feelings, stopping therapy and finding a man to take care of her. These defenses are again illustrated by the next interview.

Interview #58

"I'm so upset about coming that I'm crying. I feel caught and all week felt as though you were following me around. I imagined your face and wished it would go away and had serious thoughts about stopping treatment. I felt under so much pressure from you."

I interpreted that she seemed caught between her life-style and her therapy. She used her job, her relationship with men and her parents to foster her dependency and when treatment pointed this out she became anxious and depressed and wanted to get rid of the anxiety and depression by getting rid of the treatment. I raised doubts as to whether this technique would work. Catherine then revealed that she had been so upset after the last interview that she had cried bitterly because her parents wouldn't come to visit her and had then called her mother and feigned illness in order to get attention.

Interview #59

This resistance continued in interview #59, Catherine again distancing herself from me, saying she felt nothing and didn't want to come anymore. Avoidance, denial and projection held sway. I asked if she were angry at me. She replied that she had to grow up and be independent sometime. I suggested that she was mad at me for confronting her with her dependency on, and conflict with, her parents.

Interview #60

The resistance continued; Catherine was angry and almost didn't come to the interview. I again confronted her with her anger at my pointing out her depression and dependency and her wish to avoid both by avoiding me.

This finally overcame the denial as she described a visit from her father with again seemingly new perceptions about his behavior. "I'm angry at him but pacify him, like mother." I interpreted that she was caught between being afraid of increased friction with her father if she confronted him with her anger and her feeling of loss of her sense of self if she did not. In addition, I said that up to now she had chosen the latter course.

She replied, "I am myself with other people." I used this comment to interpret the splitting defense: She split the conflict with her father from the related conflict with men; maybe she sought men to take care of her as a way of dealing with her conflict with her father. For the first time a connection was made between past and present, father and men.

She responded, "I just want to be protected and left alone, that's pretty bad, eh?" I interpreted that she seemed to be saying that she felt that there was no hope either with the father or with any other man.

Interviews #61 and #62

Catherine now reviewed her entire history of relationships with men who always had turned out to be either narcissistic or sadistic or impotent, inadequate and dependent. She recalled the occasional use of one-night stands to relieve her anxiety and depression. To concretize and symbolize the ego-alien quality of the kind of men she had picked I used the nickname "Catherine's Zombies."

Such a technique provides an effective shorthand which promotes self-awareness of the ego-alien and destructive quality of the RORU-pathologic ego alliance and also tends to set some limits to the emotional pain associated with this awareness through the injection of some humor. It must be used cautiously and with proper timing; otherwise it will boomerang and be reacted to as a criticism.

Interview #63

The confrontation with the denial of the destructiveness of her acting out the wish for reunion with men stripped her of this defense and again the feeling state against which it had been a defense—the abandonment depression (WORU)— emerged. This in turn led her to reactivate the defense by again acting out, which produced more resistance.

She saw her old fantasy boyfriend Charles but again her new perception of his difficulties made it impossible for her to project her wish for reunion fantasy on him. As the patient's observing ego was strengthened and reinforced in therapy, as her denial was overcome and her reality perception improved, she was no longer able to deny the destructiveness of her acting out and therefore she came into conflict about acting out the wish for reunion.

Interview #64

She had visited home again and continued to revise her perceptions of her father and his relationship with her, which was further evidence of the strengthening of her observing ego. She reported being annoyed that he expected her to be dependent on him and thus forced her into playing a role for him. Mother reinforced this role by expecting her to obey him and be quiet.

I again asked, "Why don't you express your feelings to him?" She replied, "I'm afraid. I want to be dependent on them but the price is too high. It affects every other aspect of my life." For the first time the patient's splitting of the parental conflict from her present life adjustment was overcome.

This inevitably led to depression, with the patient reporting feelings of being smothered and thoughts of suicide. A beginning urge to stop acting out the fantasy of reunion with men was suggested when she revealed that she told an older man she didn't want to see him. "I'm tired of being a little girl." I replied, "Yet you're depressed at the idea of giving it up."

Interview #65

Resistance, although present, was somewhat less as the patient said, "I don't feel like talking because it's painful." She reported that her mother told her not to come home if she were upset. She denied any reaction to this startling pronouncement.

She reported having decided to enroll in the graduate program in journalism at a local college and that she wanted to pay for it out of her savings rather than ask her parents for money. At the same time she reported great anxiety about her capacity to do anything.

Definite evidence of therapeutic progress is now seen by: 1) Catherine's beginning to curb the acting out of the wish for reunion, followed by depression; 2) more realistic perception of her parents as well as the relationship between the conflict with the parents and her present life difficulties—i.e., reduction of avoidance, denial and splitting defenses; 3) beginning of a desire to commit herself to a career and quality as a journalist—i.e., to individuate—which brings with it anxiety about autonomy.

Interview #66

She began this classic resistance interview with silence. I said, "What's going on?" Catherine replied, "I'm upset, I don't want to talk. I'm in a destructive mood." More silence. I said, "Why do you go along with the destructive mood?" Catherine replied, "I'm a child." Silence. I confronted the pathologic ego's denial of the destructiveness of this defense mechanism of avoidance by again questioning, "Must you go along with it?" She announced that she was under great pressure from the WORU and therefore was impelled to activate the RORU-pathologic ego alliance at any cost. This confrontation was the necessary support that her ego state required. The confontation in this interview met with little success; however, at the end of the interview the patient reported turning down several other men who had presented opportunities for sexual acting out.

Interview #67

This interview indicated again the clear and unequivocal change in the patient's condition. Avoidance, denial and acting out were now being replaced by constructive efforts to individuate—to become a journalist and confront and deal with the environmental conflict with the father and mother at home—and by the intrapsychic consequences of individuation—depression—in the interview. She elaborated further on her desire to attend the graduate program. For the first time she told her father she was in treatment and that she had conflicts with him and that she wanted to become a journalist. In addition, she accused her father of blaming her problems on the mother's overindulgence to avoid any responsibility himself. She reiterated to me that she would never be able to deal with her feelings about her father. I said, "Perhaps you avoided becoming independent because it meant dealing with these feelings about her father." Catherine replied, "I'll be in treatment forever," and then she blocked. I interpreted the block as her way to avoid dealing with her feelings of hopelessness about both her father and her relationship with men.

Interview #68

The interpretation of the blocking decreased her resistance as she immediately reported depression and fantasies of killing her father—those feelings she had been defending against by blocking in interview #67. I pointed out that her only two alternatives seemed to be either to be submissive and withdrawn or to kill him.

She responded with silence. Then, "I have nothing to say." I again offered confrontation support: "This is crazy when your interviews take so much effort and money." She responded, "I feel hopeless and want to cry. It's better not to bring ugly things into the open." I stated, "You sound very much like your mother." She replied, "I'd rather have peace than friction." I countered, "That's fine if that's all there is to it." She then reported that she was afraid that her father might attack her, that he used to hit her, throw shoes at her and pull her hair.

Interview #69

Resistance mounted. She began with silence and then said, "There's no continuity unless I see my parents." I pointed out that she suppressed her feelings about her father and then denied that she had any feelings about him between interviews. She reported that she had thought about giving up journalism, saying she didn't want to move ahead. "Why?" I questioned.

She gave no answer. I interpreted that her giving up was a reflection of her feelings of hopelessness about her parents. After a long silence Catherine replied, "It hurts me that my father doesn't come to the city to see me more often but I don't tell him."

Then she quickly attempted to deny the emotional pain by saying that she shouldn't feel so badly. I confronted the denial by questioning if she shouldn't feel upset at the fact that her wish to see her parents more often was frustrated and disappointed. She replied, "These things never were discussed in my family." She told her parents that she was going to visit a friend for the weekend rather than come home. Her father had responded, "That is no place for you; you come home." Catherine had not responded to this remark, saying, "It wasn't convenient." I confronted the denial implicit in this statement by pointing out that her failure to deal directly with her father affected her current relationship with men.

She replied, "Father wants me home but there's no communication when I get there. I feel like crying. I don't want to get into it." I questioned, "Do you have a choice?" Catherine replied, "I get along fine with people." I confronted this denial: "No, you don't." She then reported feeling very horny because there were no men in her life at the moment. I pointed out that she was not about to take a chance with a real relationship with a man until she worked out her feelings about her father. This led to further silence and resistance.

Interview #70

She exploded, "I'm angry at you and the treatment. It's like true confessions. You reinforce it." I confronted the projection by saying. "You have two options: to face the problem and be upset, or to deny the problem and be angry at me." The denial is the core of the resistance to facing the conflict with the father. Catherine responded, "I can't do it. I don't have it in me. I'm not able to." "Why not?" I questioned.

Her resistance dealt with by confrontation, Catherine resumed the work by reporting that she had told her mother on the phone that she didn't want to come home and then she and her mother talked about treatment and the conflicts with her father, which revived old memories.

Now Catherine cried bitterly, saying that she was just bitching to her mother about her father. Mother had again urged her to accept the father as he was, emphasizing that he would not change. Finally the mother accused Catherine of being unforgiving. Catherine then recalled that she had run away from home between ages seven and 12 when the father had tantrums, that the father was away a great deal during those years traveling from Monday through Thursday, that when he returned home the patient would immediately leave the room, which the father resented.

Then she reported a date with a new man with whom she got stoned on pot and had sexual relations. She was astonished to note that although she didn't like him she kept seeking his affection and approval.

I asked her why he didn't turn her off, as would have happened with most women if they didn't like a man. "I didn't have a strong enough ego to say 'No.'" I interpreted this incident as a response to interview #70 about her father's lack of affection; she was looking for affection from men to replace what she did not get from her father. She responded, "I could never get it from my father; it's a dead end." This interview reflected all three fundamental themes: greater perception of the conflict with the father leads to depression and anger (WORU), which are projected on the therapist as a resistance and combined with acting out of the wish for reunion with other men as a defense. By the end of the interview she was facing her feelings of hopelessness about father's love. This again, however, brought on resistance.

Interview #72

Catherine again exploded, "The treatment is a waste of money. I want to stop in the fall. You made me realize that it's all up to me so I don't need you. I'm very angry. You're not helping me. I haven't accomplished anything. Nothing changes." I said, "It seems to me you're saying that if I won't be a father and take care of you, you will leave me."

Catherine responded, "I don't think I can put it all together. I don't think it's in me." "Why?" I questioned. She then reported having dated a seemingly appropriate man who was very interested in her, but she was surprised to find that she could not allow him to get close. "I don't feel good enough about myself. I have no self worth and nothing to offer." I said, "Perhaps this is the reason for the zombies." She then linked her low self-esteem to the way her father related to her and said she felt hopeless, and must work it out without dealing with him.

Interview #73

Catherine now began to act on her new awareness. She went home for the weekend and told her father his manner was insulting. He gave no reply. She also began to assert herself with her roommates and friends. She wistfully mentioned wishing her father would say that she looked nice, but then excused him, saying it wasn't natural for him. I confronted her by saying, "That doesn't stop the wish." She replied, "I'm disappointed but what can I do about it? I don't like being so sensitive about his lack of concern."

Interview #74

Catherine continued to assert herself, calling Charles to tell him that she wouldn't see him anymore. Having confronted the father, she could now give up acting out the fantasy of reunion with Charles. However, she then reported the inevitable symptoms of depression: "Now there's only me to take care of me; it's so hard to be just me."

She further reported that with new men who seemed to be realistic possibilities for her she felt mostly depressed and wanted to demand from them without giving anything of herself. "I have to know they like me before I respond. I want a total commitment from them. I don't want the man to know what I'm like." I interpreted this behavior as a protection against her fear of rejection. Catherine replied, "If there's no guarantee in a relationship I'd rather have none at all." I replied, "Other people manage relationships without guarantees—why do you need them?" I further questioned, "Where does the fear of rejection come from?" Catherine replied, "I can feel independent until I have to deal with a man. I have such a desperate need to be accepted that when I become involved with a man I get depressed." At this point she became acutely depressed, cried and said, "I can't go any further."

Interview #75

This breakthrough of feeling led to depression and resistance. In this interview Catherine was again silent, talking about being lonely and vulnerable, a little girl who didn't know who she was. She constantly reiterated her desire not to talk. I made no comment.

Interview #76

Catherine was resistant again and silently suppressed her feelings but talked about having fantasies of verbal battles with her father. She said that she was trying to keep her emotions level and avoid relationships with men.

Interview #77

Resistance continued. She did not want to come to the interview, did not want to discuss anything. I pointed out that she was suppressing and denying feelings, which were harmful to her treatment. She said she could not remember what we were talking about. I recalled for her that it was conflict with her father. Catherine responded that after her last encounter with a man from whom she'd gotten an infection she turned off and decided not to be involved with men. "I'm too hurt and too angry. It's better to avoid. I'm better off when I don't confront people with my feelings." She then reported having visited home again and feeling all alone, with no support, battling all four of them by herself. "They avoid discussing anything emotional. Mother covers up and placates. I tell them what I think but they try to stop me."

Interview #78

Catherine's mood had now improved and she was quite verbal and active. She reported having confronted the boy from whom she'd gotten the infection, again noting her lack of sense of self and how she gets her image of herself from others. She then reported having masturbated several times, feeling good about it as an act of independence; she then said, "Part of me is depressed and thinks communication with men is hopeless while another part is slowly growing towards a sense of self."

This was the first small evidence that Catherine was beginning to cathect or emotionally invest her self-image as she faced the conflict with her parents in the interviews. She was beginning to support her individuation rather than act out her dependency.

Interview #79

Catherine's resistance was lowered, her new self was in control and she reflected rather realistically on her behavior: "Can't understand why I don't want to go home, is it guilt or is it anger? Mother doesn't want me home if I'm upset. The balance is shifting to not going home in order to feel better. I think about my mother, father and brother and I know home won't be pleasant."

Her roommate was moving out and she was depressed and resentful at having to assume the responsibility for the apartment by herself. "Why?" I asked. She said, "Me and those things and I'm all alone."

She then reported that mother blames the father's resentment on her, that father had given her special treatment as a child and the mother saw her as the one who stirred the father up and gave her a lot of trouble.

After this interview I went on a three-week vacation. The extent of the patient's denial is indicated by the fact that at no time did she allude to the fact that this was the last interview. During my vacation Catherine acted out again with Charles but her perception of Charles as emotionally disturbed kept the acting out from fulfilling the wish for reunion.

Interview #80

The first interview after vacation she wondered why she had a soft spot for misfits who were brilliant but couldn't function. I pointed out that she tended to romanticize and idealize these misfits and then let them take advantage of her. I suggested that she didn't expect enough from them. Catherine responded, "It frightens me to give up the need to be liked to get down to what I'm really like." I said, "You're afraid of yourself beneath the façade plastered over it." She replied, "Maybe there's nothing there."

Interviews #81-84

Catherine was now living alone in an apartment by herself, working in the morning and attending college in the afternoons. She reported a general improvement. "I am more together. I am alone more. I can do things myself more. On the other hand, I'm depressed. I've come to like living alone and I enjoy the work at school but I get depressed at the thought of involvement with men."

Interview #85

A final exam impelled a panic that she would fail. I interpreted this as a reflection of her anxiety about her capacity to cope on her own.

Interview #86

Catherine reported a totally irrational sensitivity and outburst of anger at her instructor for a minor criticism. I pointed out that since she can't tell her father off she seems compelled to tell off all other people who put her down. She replied, "Anytime I need anything from mother and father I get a lot of shit and I don't want to handle that." I said, "You deny the anger there and then act it out on the teacher. The degree to which you avoid your father is the degree to which you are compelled to sound off at other people." Catherine replied, "It's not a pretty choice." I said, "The consequences of not making the choice are not pretty either." She responded, "The subject is too distasteful," and lapsed into silence. I pointed out that she was handling the issue with me the same way she handled it with her father by avoidance. Catherine replied, "I'm not going to face him. I can't stand to talk about it; it's too emotional. I don't have to be reminded of it." I questioned, "You don't?"

Interview #87

Catherine continued to avoid, saying she couldn't change her emotions. "I'm damaged; I can't change at 23."

Interview #88

She reported flashes of memories of childhood anger at the mother and father, of having a fantasy on the subway of wanting to kill the father, of feeling lonely and isolated.

Interview #89

Exhibiting more resistance, Catherine had nothing to say and wanted to stop therapy. "I feel depressed every morning I have to see you." I interpreted this as a wish to avoid her feelings about her parents which she externalized on to the interview. She then reported that she'd been home over the weekend but that there was no conflict. I suggested there was no conflict because she suppressed herself to avoid the conflict.

Interview #90

More resistance. Catherine started, "I have nothing to say. I don't want to come anymore. It costs too much money. I'm getting nothing out of it." I replied, "Yes, you are getting something out of it but you're angry at having to look at your parents and so you start to put the lid back on by suppressing feelings.

Interviews #91 and #92

Catherine was now doing well at school and she reported a visit home where she fought with her mother over an inappropriate Christmas gift and then became overwhelmed with guilt.

Interview #93

Catherine reported, "I have to set up a system so my parents don't hurt me. Why didn't I become independent?" I suggested that Catherine was trying to make up with men the dissatisfactions she had felt with her parents. Catherine then queried, "How do I control the dependency with men?"

Interview #94

Catherine reported a phone call from her mother and father that left her depressed. She continued, "I didn't want to come to the interview today and talk about them because there is no communication and I feel left out." She then reported a dream that her father saw her boyfriend in her closet and ran away upset and hurt." I interpreted that the dream reflected her unconscious contract with her father: She had to remain a little girl to get his approval; if she tried to become a woman he would be upset and withdraw; therefore she couldn't be a woman with a man for this would mean loss of father's love.

Interview #95

She reported having done well in the first part of her exam and then having blown the second section—the essay—on purpose. I interpreted this behavior as her way of avoiding her anxiety about functioning as a successful adult.

Interview #96

Catherine reported having resisted the temptation to act out the wish for reunion with another man who asked her to go away with him for two weeks. She told him she wanted more of a relationship than a two-week trip and commented that she felt good about telling him. She had been more responsible than ever before. She had kept her own life and direction and had asserted herself. Then she remarked, "I didn't realize I had changed that much."

Interview #97

She began with a comment made by her boyfriend that he felt she would stay with any man who would take care of her, that the man himself didn't matter. I reinforced this observation that her relationships with men have been based on her wish to be taken care of and not on love. Catherine replied that she had noticed in herself an angry demand for affection that was truly childish but was only quelled by receiving unqualified affection.

Interview #98

Catherine finished the term successfully and received a call from her father. "All I heard was perform, perform, perform. I had fantasies of taking up that offer for a two-week trip I had just turned down. I slept with Fred again to deal with the depression I felt." I asked, "Can't you manage the depression by yourself?" Catherine answered, "I'm depressed but I have to continue taking care of myself." I commented, "You want men to take over although you resent the fact that your father does it so much." "Father smothered me; I have to keep my distance from him." Catherine then reported having had a fantasy of being helpless and wanting her boyfriend to pick her up and hold her in his arms. I said the fantasy expressed her feeling of childish helplessness.

Interviews #99 and #100

The interpretation increased the resistance and Catherine acted out the role of being helpless in the next interview. "No one is helping me. I have to do everything myself." Catherine then called to cancel the next interview saying she was sick. In the following interview she reported that she hadn't been sick, but that she was angry and depressed and wanted to stop therapy because she was running out of money and, in addition, because, although she'd finished the term, she wasn't looking for a job.

I pointed out that stopping therapy and not looking for a job were related, that she wanted to do both in order to feel better; meanwhile she was sacrificing both her growth and her functioning. In order to avoid the anger and depression brought on by my interpretation Catherine denied that she was sacrificing growth but I countered the denial and asked, "Why is the anger so threatening?" She said, "I can't deal with it; it frightens me. I'm picking on everybody. I'm also having fantasies of wanting to go home more often."

Interview #101

This confrontation again decreased resistance and Catherine talked about having done well in her courses and having started to look for a job as a journalist. She also reported a visit to her home, where her father seemed happy to see her. She, however, had felt sad, had cried and had had fantasies of his becoming ill and dying, of losing him; she then told of having to block these thoughts out of her mind in order to get along at home.

I pointed out that she used distance to deal with the conflict in her feelings about leaving her father; therefore she also had to maintain distance to deal with the conflict in her feelings about men. She can't relate to men without first dealing with the conflict with the father.

I had been seeing Catherine once a week for two and a half years and had never raised the possibility of seeing her more often, feeling that the suggestion would only increase her fear of being engulfed and therefore also increase her resistance. However, the improvement in her functioning, the lessening of her acting out, the strengthening of her observing ego as well as the establishment of a therapeutic alliance, and her perceptual breakthrough into the central issue of the conflict with her father all suggested that she should come more than once a week. I raised but did not press the point.

She responded that she didn't have the money. However, even now the suggestion greatly increased her resistance for the next six weeks (interviews #102 through #107). She reported much depression, no sense of self or desire to do anything; she stopped looking for a job again because her depression increased every time she went out.

Catherine's response suggested that my caution was well advised. Despite obvious clinical indications she was not ready. However, she had already come a long way in the last two and a half years and she was committed to therapy as a way of dealing with her problems.

8

The Perpetual Student:

"I'm Beginning to Find a Self"

The interviews that follow have been given a separate chapter in order to emphasize the emergence of Catherine's self image.

Interview #107

My suggestion was dropped, her resistance lowered and the therapy continued once a week, but only for a short while.

Her depression had lifted some and she was back to looking for a job, saying that she could only be satisfied with herself when she made an effort. I reinforced the fact that effort alone satisfied self-esteem. Catherine responded, "I'm now managing all right without games or fantasy. I feel content. What will happen when I get close to my goal?"

Interview #108

Her improvement continued. She reported, "I'm feeling more independent, having positive fantasies for the first time about writing jobs, and even thoughts about getting my own apartment and car. I've been masturbating with a fantasy containing only a body with no face. I had never masturbated before the last few months. I can spend the whole weekend alone in the apartment. Two and a half years ago I would have gone bananas." This newfound capacity to be alone in her apartment was by itself a solid, substantial achievement.

Interview #109

Catherine discussed a visit home for the first time in two months during which she had felt quite independent. At first she had felt depressed and sad and couldn't understand why, particularly because she was well aware that her mother and father expected her to play a dependent role to get their approval.

I pointed out that she had used distancing to defend herself against this perception so that when the distance was overcome by visiting home the depression surfaced. She responded, "I wish I could have warmth from them. Father doesn't go out of his way for me once I'm home. He wants to control my life; talking to him is like talking to a wall. He can't accept the idea of my having boyfriends." She then said, "I didn't think this interview would go this way. I was thinking how angry I was at you and that I didn't need treatment." I interpreted these thoughts as an externalization of the depression and anger at her father brought out by the visit.

Interview #110

She reported having had a fight with her father; she had to avoid him to be independent, to keep him out of her business. I asked how avoiding the father affected her relationship with men. She replied, "They're all like my father." I pointed out that distance from the father meant distance from men, which in turn meant no involvement.

Interview #111

Her mother had called to get her to make peace with her father, which only upset Catherine more. She continued to be anxious, depressed and angry.

Interview #112

After this interview Catherine's use of distance and compliance as a defense was dramatically overcome. She wrote her father a letter saying that he expected too great a price for his favor, that she had no communication with him, that he considered her a part of himself, and that she was not coming home again until she was completely independent of him. Following the letter she had acute anxiety attacks, being afraid her father might attack her. She asserted that she was not going to "take any shit" from any man, that she was going to be healthy and realistic; nevertheless, she was still tempted to have an affair. She hadn't had a date in five months. She continued, "Fathers can really fuck up daughters. I can't stand the thought of a man who can't at least give what I can."

Catherine was now raising realistic questions about her relationship with a man for the first time; however, her depression deepened and she reported suicidal thoughts.

Interview #113

Catherine said she felt much better after interview #112. "This could become a habit," she said suspiciously. I picked up on this statement to point out that she was afraid of being dependent on me as she had been on her father, that she was afraid I would reject her or put her down as he had, that she either wanted a man to take care of her like Charles had done or she set up distance from men by picking inappropriate men like Fred. She replied that she had felt the need to call Charles after the interview—a need to be taken care of. I reinforced the interpretation, saying she wanted myself or Charles to fulfill the needs her father hadn't. Having finally asserted her independence from her father, Catherine now returned to my suggestion of having treatment more than once a week and asked to come two times a week. This decision, which deepened her involvement in therapy, also raised her anxiety, which had to be defended against by transference acting out.

This patient's readiness to move from supportive to a more reconstructive analytic psychotherapy was dramatically signaled by her willingness to forego the ancient submissive role with her father, assert herself with him and take on her fear of being abandoned, attacked or engulfed. This dramatic act signaled that she had formed a strong enough transference relationship—albeit on the basis of the wish for reunion—to be able to forego the use of a life structure to deal with her problems and to deal with them more constructively in her therapy.

Confrontation of the denial of the destructiveness of the RORU-pathologic ego alliance—i.e., the patient's acting out the wish for reunion was at the cost of her growth and individuation —created conflict about the use of this mechanism. As the patient controlled it, the abandonment depression (WORU), against which it had been a defense, emerged. As the patient began to deal with the abandonment depression in interviews rather than by acting out, her self began slowly to emerge on its own.

Interview #114

Catherine had obtained a job as a journalist with a magazine, cried all night and started to panic, thinking that she couldn't do it. I pointed out that her fear of being unable to cope on her own drove her back to the wish to be taken care of. She began to investigate the origin of this fear: the feelings of helplessness, as well as her feelings about her father who made her feel incapable. She had told her mother whenever she ran away from home that she wished he were dead, but her mother, rather than make her face her father, interceded for her. She continued that she still didn't want to face her feelings about her father: "I'm getting weak. I'm getting close to you, my therapist, in spite of myself and I hate it." I again interpreted her fear of dependency on me with distancing as a principle defense, and again related this defense to her difficulties with men.

Interview #115

Catherine reported feeling very good after interview #114. But, although she had relaxed and unburdened herself, she now felt she was blocking: She had had thoughts of my dropping dead and she was cutting off her feelings today. I interpreted her being cut off as a defense against her losing me now that she had become involved in the treatment—that she had two fears, being smothered and being left.

Interview #116

Catherine reported that after a routine physical examination she had had to take a special laboratory test which she then exaggerated into having a serious illness, and called her mother and father for reassurance. She then asked, "I wonder why I called." I suggested the call was to deal with her fear of abandonment by me by getting approval from her mother and father. She asked, "Why do I think I can't be independent?" I pointed out that thinking and actually being are quite different.

Interview #117

The transference acting out now came to the fore. After interview #116 Catherine called to say she would miss her next two interviews because of an unavoidable business trip, leaving a message so that I couldn't speak to her. When I discovered that one day was pleasure and one day was work, I told her I would charge her for the one interview and not make it up according to our agreement. She exploded and said she would lie in the future. I explained the reality of her responsibility for her sessions and suggested that her not telling me in advance was an effort to loosen her commitment to twice-a-week sessions; further her not telling me and expecting me to not charge her were an expression of her wish to be taken care of by me. In other words, this was transference acting out to avoid dealing with feelings about her parents. She then reported further acting out. She had met another man who was much older, much like her father, married and separated. She wasn't sexually attracted to him but was fantasizing being a lifelong companion to him. I again pointed this out as a defense against her involvement in treatment, another acting out of the wish for reunion related to her decision to come twice a week.

Interview #118

Catherine was blocking, had no thoughts, reported telling her mother she would not be home for Father's Day and feeling guilty about it. I pointed out that she was angry at her parents for not caring for her and wanted to punish them by staying away and blocking out her feelings, that blocking out was destructive to her objectives in treatment.

Interview #119

Catherine had a repeat laboratory test and was furious at what she considered the doctor's lack of concern, cried all through it, but in the interview blocked in trying to understand why she had cried.

Interview #120

She had figured out that the panic about the test was related to the doctor, that she was probably overly sensitive to male doctors. I pointed out that she was handling her wish to be taken care of with me as she did with her father—she blocked out. She replied this week she worried that I might take advantage of her. I interpreted "just like father." She replied that she told her mother that her parents don't help her unless she does what they want and the mother said, "What's wrong with that?" She told her mother that her father was a prick and could get his own Father's Day card. She's taking it out on the mother rather than on the father. She also reported having acted out with Harry, the older boyfriend. I again pointed out her acting out—her telling her father off through her mother, and then acting out the fantasy of being cared for with Harry.

The patient replied, "It's true, but now I'm becoming aware of what I'm doing." I pointed out that the acting out and the fantasy are defenses against depression. She then reported a memory of being suffocated with attention by both her mother and father between the ages of eight and nine. During this period she had gastrointestinal complaints for a year and was under a doctor's care.

Interview #121

Catherine had met a new man and was so anxious that she had headaches and almost vomited because he seemed like a realistic possibility rather than a fantasy. When she found out that he was just like Charles, that he wanted to be taken care of, she calmed down and became depressed.

She pointed out, "It's nice to be able to see what I don't want; I can't be myself with a man for fear of rejection. I'm so afraid of my father's wrath; I have no communication at all." I pointed out that she also blocked out communication with the father within her in her own thoughts and feelings. She replied, "I'm afraid of how much damage there is to correct." I questioned, "Do you have a choice? Why can't you draw some strength from your treatment so far?"

Interview #122

In the next interview the patient was resistant, wanted to get away, felt unloved and unwanted, and was planning a vacation. I pointed out that when she stopped acting out her fantasy of being cared for with Harry and came to the conflict with her father in the interview, her underlying feeling of being unloved came out with depression and that she wanted to avoid this by getting away from treatment by a vacation.

The patient replied, "It's hopeless. It's amazing I'm not gay."

I pointed out that her feeling of hopelessness about the father's love comes from the past and that she's projecting it on to the future. She then reported fantasies of the mother's and father's dying and her not going to the funeral, or Catherine's killing herself and the mother's and father's not coming to the funeral; also, she told of a fantasy of her telling the mother that the only time she was coming home was to bury them.

Interview #123

Catherine was feeling better and had decided against the vacation. She was ashamed at her hostility against her parents, as it's childish. She reported a "beauty and the beast" fairy story wherein the father won't let the daughter go unless he's threatened with death. I interpreted that the father won't let her go, and that she didn't want to give up the fantasy of her father.

Catherine replied, "I saw my father's not letting go as love. I was father's favorite early in my development. I think father is glad as well as sorry I left home because it means I took after him and my older brother didn't. Mother's attitude was the opposite. Brother was right to stay home and I was wrong to leave. I left because I was depressed, lonely and suffocated. I'm beginning to feel pleasure that I don't need them financially. I'm having positive fantasies about finding a new apartment, but depressed about problems and relationships. I will be an old maid." I said, "No, you'll have to give up the fantasy about your father."

"A girlfriend suggested that maybe my father had a sexual hangup on me and this made me anxious, and with me it's either sex or love—never both together. With Charles for two years it was to avoid involvement with men. Sex is to avoid love. I'm so aware now that I can't do what I used to do with men. I'm afraid of making mistakes." I pointed out that she needed to make mistakes to learn; the problem was not mistakes but not learning from mistakes.

Interview #124

Catherine reported that the father had called: She was much more perceptive about him, felt less helpless, felt her action had changed him, and that she did not play the game with him. She reported that after the last interview she felt much more optimistic about treatment, felt good and then acted out with Harry again.

I pointed out that she had played the game with Harry which she hadn't with her father on the phone to restore the fantasy and relieve the depression, which conflicts with what she's trying to do here. She replied with a dream: "I was stabbed and fell unconscious in the hands of a man I couldn't see and felt safe." Her free association was a fantasy over the weekend of killing her father. "A verbal fight, he tries to hit me and I kill him with a chair. It must mean I'm angry."

I pointed out that the patient's role as a placating, indulgent woman with a man and with her father was a defense against homicidal rage; she was afraid to be involved with a man as her only options were playing a submissive role or killing him— either way she couldn't win. The patient said, "Could I act out this fantasy and kill him?" I pointed out that there was a long distance from fantasy to action, that she was really afraid that if she went home her father would lose his temper and then she would want to kill him.

CONCLUSION

This report is concluded because its objective has been achieved —the demonstration of the therapeutic techniques necessary to deal with the initial defenses of the pathologic ego.

Catherine's therapy, however, continued for two more years twice a week. At the end of the four years she had progressed to the point where her fear of engulfment had so lessened that she was able to give up her acting out defenses and find an appropriate, suitable male partner. He seemed to fall in love with her and after a six-month period of intensive dating and experimentation they decided to live together. His capacity to love was always far greater than hers and he used it to teach her how to learn to love. Acutely aware of her own deficiencies in loving she became an eager and talented pupil. These events reinforced her therapy as it came to focus more and more on her problems in loving. Finally, she decided to stop therapy and continue the work on her own.

Once Catherine became fully engaged in therapy she turned around, asserted herself with her father, confronted the conflict directly, stopped acting out with men, began to assert herself at her job and to deal more directly with her anger and depression about her parents both in interviews and at home.

As the fear of abandonment by the father was worked through in psychotherapy, the patient's involvement in the therapeutic relationship deepened and this brought to the fore the more primary fear of being engulfed by the mother. As this fear and her distancing defenses against it were activated and pointed out in the therapeutic relationship she became progressively more aware of their profound influence in other relationships. This led to conscious control of her distancing behavior, which in turn enabled her to finally establish a viable close relationship. The fear was not resolved, but the destructive defenses against it had been removed and she was able to deal with it in more conscious constructive ways without it having such an overwhelmingly destructive effect on her life.

The four years had seen a total turnabout in her life. She had gone from being unable to love or work to a life situation containing a challenging, interesting job and a partner in love.

9

Life Begins to End at 40:

"My Life Is Going Nowhere"

The vague presenting complaints of the next two patients of a generalized discontent with their lives contrast markedly with the discrete symptoms of patients with a crystallized neurosis.

Deeper investigation is required to uncover the reasons for this discontent: the sacrifice of life structure to deal with emotional problems; lives half-lived to avoid depression; gratification in work blocked by the avoidance of individuation; and the satisfactions of a close relationship impaired by clinging and/or distancing defenses. Small wonder that in retrospect the patient should feel discontented with his or her "life."

NANCY: AGE 40—BUSINESS EXECUTIVE

Nancy, a tall attractive, 40-year-old woman, had a brash, flip manner. Her appearance, belying her age, seemed more like that of a woman of 30.

Chief Complaint

"In recent months I began to worry about my age and how my life was going. I began to feel depressed and lonely, had trouble concentrating and became indecisive. I began taking Valium up to three times a day and began to drink too much. I miss having a permanent relationship with a man."

Comment

Nancy complained about her "life," not a phobia, compulsion or some other specific, crystallized neurotic symptom. She said, "Life has caught up with me."

The 40-50 decade—"the epoch of last chance," the last period when effective changes can be made before one must come to terms with the fantasies and dreams of earlier years—had confronted Nancy with the destructiveness of her life-style and had produced a depression which finally brought her for treatment.

She complained that although she was very successful in her business career with a large company she found her work boring and stayed at the job because of the security it provided. She had enjoyed working as a photographer for a newspaper from age 22-30. She particularly enjoyed the photographer's role of objective observer. (Occupations that require this role, i.e., doctor, lawyer, photographer, writer, attract the borderline patient because they enable him or her to experience an illusion of closeness free from the anxiety and depression he or she feels when personally involved or committed.)

Nancy briefly reviewed the history of her relationships with men. She had had no sexual relationships until the last year of college when she had been engaged and had broken the engagement because of anxiety. In her late 20's she had had an affair in which she was the submissive partner to an older, narcissistic, domineering and married man.

When she was 30 her father died. Nancy, who was still living at home, suffered a depression, but she was even more concerned about the way in which her mother's clinging to her dramatically increased as the mother attempted to deal with the loss of the father. Alarmed about the consequences of this responsibility, Nancy quickly ended the affair and shortly afterward married "to get out of the house." Her husband, though sexually attractive to her, was a professional athlete who showed no interest in connubial bliss and spent long periods of time out of the home. She had married an illusion of closeness. The marriage ended in divorce a year later, at which point the patient was living in her own apartment away from her mother.

In the last six years she had had many "one-night stands," and complained that she tended to go out with ineligible men with whom she went to bed too soon. In contrast, when she was seeing a man whom she considered eligible—as she was when she began therapy—she had so much anxiety that she couldn't relax enough to think clearly or act appropriately. She was afraid her anxiety would cause her to do something that might ruin the relationship.

Her relationships with women were also conflictual. She had always had one older good girlfriend, who, like the present one, Rose, was strong and opinionated. Nancy said she put up with Rose's domineering ways because of the security she derived from the relationship. At this point she interjected, "However, I'm getting tired of being a little girl."

Her mother, in her 70's, still worked and still wanted to take an apartment with the patient. She phoned her mother every night because she felt guilty if she didn't. "Mother still wants to do everything for me." She described her dead father as soft-spoken and quiet, favoring her over her brother, but away working most of the time, often until 9 or 10 at night.

Landmarks of Past History

The patient's mother was sick for some months after the brother was born when the patient was 18 months old. During this period Nancy was taken care of by her aunt who became her "fairy godmother." Nancy always did well in school, but considered herself an ugly duckling. She graduated from college with a degree in business. She described her attitude towards life as, "I feel put upon; no one reaches me. I have to keep my chin up and keep fighting for what everyone else seems to get naturally. I never do get it."

This statement revealed the frustration inherent in this patient's relationships. She was acting out the wish for reunion with the mother by compliant behavior in order to receive approval. She denied the degree to which she suppressed self-expression and always ended up frustrated, since the approval she received was earned and not freely given. In other words, her basic wish for unconditional love went unfulfilled.

Impression

Her RORU consisted of an oversolicitous, smothering, infantilizing rewarding part-object representation and a self representation of the good little girl linked by the affect of feeling good, receiving supplies. The WORU consisted of an angry, withdrawing part-object representation, a self representation of being the ugly duckling who has to work for everything she "gets." These two representations were linked by the affect of abandonment depression. The defenses of the pathologic ego consisted of denial, projection and acting out of the wish for reunion, avoidance of individuation, and both clinging and distancing defenses against intimacy.

Nancy was defending herself against separation anxiety and abandonment depression by avoidance, denial, projection and acting out of the wish for reunion. She avoided self-assertion and substituted clinging for which she unconsciously demanded approval. The avoidance extended to her job, to which she clung for "security" although it was way below her real abilities. It extended to her relationships with women where she was partially aware that she was acting out a dependent relationship. She avoided the anxiety she felt about a real relationship with a man by acting out through one-night stands. She could not have a real relationship with a man because she could not leave her mother. Her awareness was primarily lip service because there was massive denial of the destructiveness of the very behavior that brought her for treatment. She had so superimposed the fantasy of the wish for reunion upon her work and her relationships as a defense against the feelings of hopelessness about receiving unconditional love from the mother—supplies for separation-individuation—that she was locked in and unaware of her destructive life-style. Vehemently she denied any feelings of inadequacy about this behavior.

We shall see that this acting out of the wish for reunion through dependent relationships becomes the first target of treatment as the patient's insatiable need for approval becomes frustrated in the interviews.

Confrontation of Transference Acting Out

The core of the patient's pathologic defenses was clearly revealed through transference acting out of the wish for reunion which became most apparent about the fifth interview after the history had been completed.

The patient became angry at my silence, my not asking questions. She expressed the anger by saying that she felt as if she were talking to a wall, a vacuum or a tape recorder. She elaborated, "Without a reaction from you I feel like a block sitting here, a non-entity, a nothing. I feel you're not interested in me and probably don't like me." When questioned as to why my doing my job—listening to her—evoked such feelings she described how much she oriented her behavior around other people's reactions. She explained that she sent out rays to other people and guided her responses by their reactions. When unable to send out rays she felt as she did in the interviews—left out.

This led her back to her feelings of being left out with her mother at the age of 18 months when her brother was born, then to feeling left out at school, which in turn led to the fact that she always established a dependent relationship with one woman friend and put up with the woman's bitchiness because of the security she received from the relationship. She concluded, "I need someone to lean on."

This need was an unconscious demand and when it was frustrated she became intensely angry. She then projected this anger on to the other person. She often suppressed her self-expression, as well as her anger, for fear of the other person's disapproval.

I pointed out the reality destructiveness of this behavior, i.e., she was coming here to understand herself, which required expression of feeling, but she was suppressing that expression in order to win my approval. She confessed that this pattern applied to all her relationships and wondered why she needed approval so much that it made her unable to express her feelings, particularly her anger. Her fear of loss of the object required her to handle her anger by splitting.

The confrontation set limits to the acting out of the transference and immediately posed for investigation the patient's principal defense—acting out the wish for reunion. She elaborates on the degree to which she had been indulging a mother-child relationship with both her mother and her friend. "I was the first grandchild on either side of my family and was quite overindulged. I probably never grew up. I'm an adult version of a two-year-old."

She elaborated further on how she slept in the fetal position, sucked her thumb and tended generally to suppress disturbing thoughts. She had always wanted to be a pampered spoiled little girl and had never wanted to marry except for money or security. She was afraid of pregnancy and had had a fantasy of marrying an old man who would die and leave her a lot of money. As a result of these wishes she has always resented working.

A second theme in these interviews (#5-15) was her reaction when she met a man who in her view was an appropriate partner. She felt so overwhelmed by anxiety that he might reject her that she went to bed with him as soon as possible, primarily to relieve the anxiety.

By the 15th interview she described a conflict between spending her weekend with a boyfriend versus having to check in by phone with her mother every night, feeling guilty if she did not call. Nancy did go away for the weekend, but felt guilty about not calling her mother. In the next interview she said, "I must tear apart from mother although I don't want to hurt her." Over the next two weeks, as she was talking about having to break free from her mother, the boyfriend did not call and she felt lonely and depressed. In the 18th interview she reported a dream which revealed the core of the problem.

Dream: "I was on a terrace wearing a nightgown, only the bottom was all dirty with what looked like candy stains. There was also a man there who was interested in me but my mother was there and kept saying to me to go put some clothes on. I said, 'No.' Then I woke up, perspiring and all wet. All my problems are there in the dream."

I made the following interpretation: "There is a conflict between your relationship with your mother and your relationship with a man. You hold on to mother because if you choose a man you will lose your mother. Therefore, you cannot get involved with a man and are neither a woman (the nightgown) nor a child (the candy) but actually both. However, you cannot be both; you have to resolve your tie to your mother to have a relationship with a man. Possibly you pick men who want a distant relationship in order to avoid this conflict."

Nancy replied: "Why am I so tied to my mother? It seems insidious and subtle. In the last year I have been very promiscuous, hopping into bed with men I knew I couldn't have a relationship with. But I've been in a panic all year, impulsive, restless, desperate, driving myself in the office and always cleaning up my apartment." I countered with a question, "Why do you feel you always need someone to lean on? Your first husband, your mother, your friend Rose, and myself?"

In the next interview—#19—Nancy told of feeling better than she had in some months, having worked well at the office and taken a firm stand with her mother which led to a fight. Nancy reported, "Mother said that she had no one, that I was her child, and that maybe she might die." The patient then mentioned that her mother had keys to her apartment. I countered with, "rather than a man." I asked why she had not made a stand with her mother before. Nancy replied, "I was afraid if I asserted myself she'd end the relationship." I asked, "Why?" Nancy answered, "Because I lost her attention for six months as a child." I replied, "This is too pat an answer to explain your holding on to the relationship with your mother." Nancy responded, "My earliest memory is of being sent away from home at three when my brother had scarlet fever. I've been scared most of my life. Scared of being incompetent at work." Here she reveals her fear of being on her own.

Interview #20

Nancy described a transference dream: "I was in a car with my girlfriend driving. Then I was in the driver's seat with another friend. We were swooping around mountain curves very fast with no one driving. I asked her if it was on automatic pilot and my girlfriend said 'Yes.' When I awoke I was trying to get out of bed. I knew I was not awake, I had a groggy, drugged feeling. I was out of control." She reported she had felt this way once before in college when she woke up to find a girl in a nightgown in the hall of her dorm sitting in a pool of blood from an attempted rape.

She could make no free associations to the sexual aspect of the dream. I therefore interpreted that the dream was about her treatment, that she had used dependency on mother, Rose and me as a defense against her fear of abandonment, but in the last interview she had asserted herself with mother and talked about her anxiety about being on her own with me. Therefore she had given up the old controls of her fear and felt terribly frightened about coming to grips with it on her own.

Nancy reiterated her need to have someone to lean on or take care of her, and I asked, "To deal with your fear?" She replied, "I take a lot of abuse for that security. It would really be something if I got myself in the driver's seat." Then she turned to ask me a question. I pointed out that the question was an attempt to get out of the driver's seat with me. She replied that she felt anxious in a position of independence. She asked, "What causes the dependency to build up? I often tried to break away but always came back. First in college, second when I was 25, and third when I was first married. I'm afraid you, my doctor, may become a crutch." She said, "People let me feed on them." I replied, "To use you."

Interview #21

Nancy continued to question why she was so dependent on her mother and reported feeling depressed, restless, empty, lonely and bored. She complained that she couldn't stop eating and had gained five pounds. She turned again to ask me why but I did not respond. Her abandonment depression was emerging as the acting out of the wish for reunion was being confronted.

Interview #22

Nancy reported a dream: "I'm getting off a boat and the customs inspector was going over my list, which my mother had made out. I was annoyed that mother didn't leave room for the purchases of liquor. I argued with the female customs inspector and got the liquor." I mentioned that as she stopped acting out the dependency on the mother she was depressed in the previous interview, felt helpless, attempted to act out the dependency with me and when this failed dreamed about returning to her mother. I linked the acting out of dependency as a defense against depression.

Comment

This patient had only been seen over a period of two and a half months and had begun to deal with her core defenses.

I pointed out further that the contact with the mother required her to act independent and responsible after which her mother would allow her to be emotionally dependent, but that the patient felt frustrated and used since she had to work to earn these supplies. I illustrated how she repeated this pattern in the transference, acting independent and then demanding supplies. Nancy responded, "This façade arose after my divorce; before that I had been mostly a scared kid. I was scared to death when I bought my apartment; my husband moved me and looked after me."

I pointed out that the dependency had persisted as a way of dealing with the anxiety and depression she felt about leaving her mother and becoming an independent responsible woman. I predicted that whenever she felt her dependency needs frustrated in interviews she would become angry at me.

Two interviews later (interview #25) Nancy reported a brief sexual interlude. She had spent the last two days with a male friend who had dropped in from South America. "He comes in every six months or so. He's great fun. I like the way he babies me. He makes very good sex but he's very transient."

She then reeled off a long list of similar relationships where she sought excitement and enjoyment for a few days. I attempted to confront her with the reality problems of transient relationships and to reinforce the ego-alien quality of her behavior by pointing out that a man seems to have to belong to the jet set and arrive by airplane to qualify for her bed. She replied, "I'm attracted to footloose men." I again asked, "Why?" She replied: "I like the glamour and the excitement." I challenged her statement by saying that she sought relationships with men which involved neither commitment nor consequences, that she seemed afraid of a permanent relationship with a man. I contrasted the satisfactions she reported from transient relationships with the anxiety about rejection she felt with eligible men.

I suggested that transient, distant relationships with men were defenses against separating from her mother. She confirmed that in these relationships she had intense romantic fantasies of being loved by a man (the wish for reunion). I pointed out that it was impossible for a man who saw her once a year to love her, that this was fantasy. She replied, "My commitment to mother is eating me up."

I pointed out that she must also come to terms with her wish to be a child which she's acting out in these relationships, that these men will gratify her wish to be a child by treating her like a baby as long as she does not ask them for commitment to the responsibility of a real relationship.

Interview #26

Nancy felt confused and in turmoil about herself. "I'm a shell, a whole part is missing. I feel like running away, escaping. I'm irritable, angry." I pointed out that she was angry at me for frustrating the fantasy satisfactions she got from these transient relationships.

Interview #27

Nancy returned to the theme of transient relationships, saying that she used to fantasize that each relationship would be permanent and that she was not interested in the sex without the fantasy of a permanent relationship. I asked why she hadn't tried for real relationships. She replied, "some kind of fear of involvement, exposure—I'm not worthy of a decent warm relationship. I'm afraid I'll bore them. When I married my husband he worked nights and we didn't spend more than one or two nights together a week." I pointed out that the marriage was another partial relationship. Nancy replied that the transient relationships were an expression of her feelings of hopelessness: "I'm afraid of being all alone and having nothing. I isolate myself in partial relationships to deal with this fear. Half a loaf is better than none. I feel I'm never quite good enough; I never quite measure up."

Interview #28

Nancy reported anger at me for having frustrated her fantasies of being taken care of by me. She not only had to do it herself in interviews but she also had to pay for it. This reminded her of her relationship with her mother. She always felt she had to work harder than the rest of the family to get any approval and gratification.

Comment

Confrontations with the patient's defenses led to a triggering of the WORU, which was then projected on me. In the next few interviews Nancy was angry, depressed and lonely. She was demanding, asking questions and becoming annoyed when I didn't answer. "I'm feeling depressed, all alone, I have no one. I'm eating too much, talking too much, feeling blue and sad."

After several subsequent interviews I pointed out that the transference acting out was a way of dealing with the feelings that arose—the abandonment depression—when her heterosexual acting out defense was confronted. I suggested that the confrontation made her angry and depressed and she wanted to go back to being dependent on me as she had been upon her mother in order to relieve the depression. However, the price of this kind of behavior was not having a permanent relationship with a man. A dependency relationship for her was like a drug. It gave her relief from pain with very little satisfaction.

Several interviews later (#33) Nancy reported that she was feeling better, that she had been very frustrated by her efforts to cope with her own dependency but that she had changed her relationship with her mother. She had ended her relationship with Rose and had stopped confiding in her mother so much. Both her mother and Rose were unhappy about this change.

She then related a dream the night before the interview. "I'm in a store; a beautiful salesgirl is trying on a nightgown. I asked her if it fits around the bust. What size? Three or four, but the sizes were 32, 34, 36."

Nancy then made this free association: "Three or four pounds is all I have to lose. It seemed like a pleasant conversation about something pretty." I pointed out that this was the patient's true femininity emerging underneath the dependency. I asked why her mother's and Rose's reactions to her self-assertion were the same. She replied, "They're both holding on and it annoys me." I pointed out that as she stops acting out her dependency needs with mother and Rose, she feels angry, tense, frustrated and depressed at having to handle these needs herself. She then changes her relationship with her mother and Rose and dreams about being a woman. The purpose of this interpretation was to reward the patient for handling her dependency needs herself, to reinforce her motivation to do so and give her some reason to put up with the discomfort of her frustration. The patient responded, "I'd like to test myself out with a new man, to go away this summer to a new place, to try myself out in other new areas." I reinforced this first sign of Nancy's emerging individuality.

Interview #40

The patient reported the following dream: "I rang a door bell and saw my mother on the other side of the door with her body coming through the door. I thought she was dead but then I woke up." Free association: "I felt nothing, no regret if she had died. I've had conscious wishes that she might die. Before the dream I felt a kind of tactile need in the morning that I felt was satisfied by mother's body in the dream. I though the need was for a man. Why do I need her so? It's sickening."

Interview #41

Nancy reported that she was furious with her mother. "She strangles me, invades my privacy." I pointed out that she resents her mother but does nothing about it because of her need for her mother, and often in interviews she intellectualizes rather than confronts her anger at her mother. Nancy replied, "She wants to live her life and my life too." She then reported that as she was acting more independent herself she observed that her girlfriends' behavior was immature and felt amazed at their behavior.

Comment

Borderline patients frequently socialize almost exclusively with other borderline patients where they can get a social reinforcement of their rationalizations.

The next four or five interviews were filled with depression, anger at the mother, and some reports of sexual acting out. There would be dramatic relief of depression and tension following the sexual acting out. For example, in interview #48 she continued to complain about her mother's behavior. I asked why she didn't do anything about it. Nancy responded that she loved her mother and was still vying for her attention by being a nice daughter. "Mother wants me to be a child but I don't want to be. In every phone conversation mother sticks a knife in me. She's there all the time and wants to be in on everything. I'm choked, strangled, suffocated. I've always been afraid of being a woman."

Following this outburst Nancy began to feel better and asked the mother to stop calling. She described herself as feeling more her own person. Her eating binge subsided and her sleeping improved. By interview #55 she was talking about doing things on her own without asking anybody's advice, about feeling better, about sleeping and "preparing herself for a change." Then she began to talk about the boredom of her work and the need for a new job. She had always feared trying to get a better job because she didn't want to give up the security of her present one. She planned a different vacation that summer. She wanted to go by herself to Europe for six weeks. Shortly before leaving she had a dream. "I wish to leave mother but if I do she'll die" (the tie that binds).

She then broke off with Rose and began to enjoy expanding her own individuality. "I feel like singing and skipping and jumping." This report brings to mind Mahler's description of the "love affair with life" of the young child in the practicing phase of separation-individuation. However, though she was only occasionally having a "one-night stand," she still had not been able to initiate or develop a realistic relationship with a man with any degree of continuity. She had that on the therapeutic agenda as her principle objective. Autonomy precedes intimacy and is simpler to achieve than intimacy since the latter involves the constant exposure to fears of abandonment and/or engulfment.

At the end of two and a half years of psychotherapy the patient had: 1) set appropriate behavioral limits to her relationship with her mother (she was not checking in by phone calls, not letting her mother visit her and keeping her mother away from intruding in her life); 2) discarded her inappropriate, immature girlfriends as well as her dependence on her relationship with Rose; 3) diminished her acting out with men through awareness of the wish for reunion fantasy behind her behavior; and 4) finally and most important, built up enough confidence to find a new job much more suited to her talents at a much higher level and at a much higher salary.

SUSAN: AGED 40—MINOR DEPARTMENT HEAD, WELFARE DEPARTMENT

Susan was a tall, slender brunette whose appearance belied her 40 years. She could have been 27. She had a strikingly flattened affect.

Chief Complaint

Susan said, "I'm getting older, my life is going nowhere, and I occasionally feel sad and alone." She complained of anxiety when she had to assert herself and of inability to express her anger except by withdrawing. "I used to be quite content when alone, but now it depresses me. There are no men in my life. Although I love my work I use it as an escape from my problems."

She had been in the department since graduation from college and, although she was now a minor executive, she had not advanced with her peers.

She introduced the problem in relationships with men as follows: "People say I am intimidating to men. Do I pass up eligible men for men with problems?" She began sexual relationships in her twenties. In her thirties she had a relationship for one year with a married man who was intending to separate from his wife when he died suddenly in an accident. Although she recalls having had orgasms with him she has been frigid ever since. This man lived many miles away, was married and ostensibly planning a divorce. He had to fly to New York City to see her about once a month. It is possible that the limits implied by the marriage and the distance allowed her a romantic fantasy about the relationship. Since his death, through a number of brief relationships (some for as long as nine months), she found that most of the men were either impotent or narcissistic or detached. Either they could not gratify her sexually or they could not gratify her emotionally. By this time she was convinced that all American men could not give either sexually or emotionally.

Susan had avoided her own anxiety about intimacy by picking men who themselves did not have that potential. She had many girlfriends but they were more on the level of early adolescence. She related to her closest girlfriend alternatively as the mother criticizing and putting the friend down or as the daughter being criticized and put down.

Family History

She described her mother as domineering and selfish. She couldn't be criticized and never admitted being wrong. Susan always submitted to her. The father was warm and loving. He supported her but was very passive with the mother and gave into her every need as Susan did.

Landmarks of Early History

Susan was the older of two children. Her brother was sick a great deal when he was born which required a lot of the mother's attention. She did well in school but felt left out of things because she was overweight. In high school her life took a turn for the better. She became more attractive and became interested in dancing. At this time she started to date though without sexual relationships. She attended college away from home but on graduation she returned home to work. Several years later, at the age of 27, she moved away from home to New York City and her present job. For the last 13 years she had been totally involved in her work and having transient, superficial relationships with men.

Comment

Susan's RORU consisted of a part-object representation that was demanding, self-centered, intolerant and provided supplies only for compliance. The part-self representation was that of a good little girl. The two were linked by the affect of feeling good or receiving supplies for compliance. The WORU consisted of a part-object representation that was angry, attacking, annihilating; the self representation was of an inadequate, passive ineffective blob; the two were linked by the affect of abandonment depression. The defenses of the pathologic ego consisted of denial, avoidance, passivity, isolation and detachment of affect and distancing in relationships.

Susan was defending herself against separation anxiety and abandonment depression by massive avoidance and denial, by distancing, by isolation, detachment and passive, dependent acting out. She could not assert herself and her job was beneath her talents.

In her relationships with men she used either distancing maneuvers or she picked men who could not form a close relationship and upon whom she could project her own anxiety about intimacy. In her relationships with women, she continued the role of the good child.

Susan's age—the epoch of last chance—confronted her with the destructive effects of her passive-dependent acting out and brought on a depression which brought her to treatment. She maintained massive denial of the destructiveness of her behavior and, rather than directly acting out the wish for reunion (as Nancy did), she adopted the stance of uninvolvement in anything but her work which limited her anxiety and depression at the cost of her life structure. The initial problem in treatment was to confront this patient with the detachment and the denial and isolation in order to mobilize the affect (anxiety and depression) necessary for motivation to change in treatment.

Susan's denial of reality, detachment of affect and passive-dependent acting out were confronted in the third and fourth interviews when she told the history of her relationships with men. I observed that the men seemed to have problems that made it difficult for them to get involved with women. I asked her what attracted her to this type of man. The question confronted her with her detachment and denial and started a current of curiosity which pierced the denial and detachment defenses and produced great anxiety, which she revealed in the fourth interview:

"It's hard for me to go into things deeply. I tend to pass them over. I don't think very deeply about why things are the way they are. I'm just like my father. He never fought for things; he put up with everything." Susan then elaborated on her passive-dependent wishes. "I wish I didn't have to do things for myself. I guess I don't want to grow up. I'm childlike. Usually, I don't face things. I never talk about anything with my mother. She always changes the subject."

I observed that evidently both her mother and father avoided conflict. Further, she avoided it quite strongly, but the cost of the avoidance was shown in the kind of life she had been leading. I suggested that perhaps the time had come for her to try to stop avoiding.

Interview #5

Susan reported that she had felt more confidence after interview #4, that she had faced her life situation and had already begun to do something about getting her long overdue promotion at school. This led to anxiety about being on her own.

Having temporarily given up the acting out of her dependency needs, she confronted the anxiety it had avoided as follows: She reported having once started a commercial career as a model and a dancer. "I was on my own. I was unsupported. Nobody was telling me I was fine. I felt so anxious I couldn't keep it up. I had been very coddled and felt very taken care of, particularly by my father with whom I am very close. I can commit myself to him because he's good and understanding and loyal. I worry about him dying and after my first session with you I wanted to call him."

I responded that perhaps she was still too close to her father, that she may have felt that the treatment threatened her relationship with him. Perhaps she called him to reassure herself that he was still there. I suggested the closeness with her father and the threat of treatment to that closeness might be related to her difficulties relating to men.

Interview #6

Susan reported her sexual immaturity, her constant feeling as a child that the genitals were dirty and that sex was dirty. At the end of the interview she emphasized the father theme by saying her father supported her and told her she was right, he confided in her more than in her mother and she and her father never argued.

Interview #7

Susan continued on the father theme by saying that the man whom she had the affair with for a year who was killed was very much like her father. He was kind, took good care of her and never argued. She added that all the men that she has been attracted to were of that type—gentle, sweet, coddling. At this point I interjected "and have trouble having erections" to confront her with the destructiveness. She replied that assertive men frightened her.

Susan then missed the next interview because she had overslept.

Interview #8

Susan reported a dream: "I was looking in the mirror, my face was filled with long hair, but mother told me it would be all OK, it could be removed." Free association: "Mother would take care of things, I shouldn't worry, she hid it from me." I pointed out that I thought she had missed the interview in order to reinstate her denial after I had suggested her difficulties with men were related to the closeness to her father, that she was acting out her dependency as a defense against facing her problems with her father and men. She replied by saying how she uses work to avoid or escape her emotional problems, how she wears herself out dancing every day and that most of the men she meets in the dance world are homosexual, that when other girls were thinking about boys between ages 12-15 she was thinking about horses.

Interviews #10 and #11

After a visit to her parents' home Susan talked about her conflict with her mother. "I get depressed when I visit my parents. I never get anywhere presenting myself as a person to my mother, it seems futile. I let her walk all over me. I can't stand the bickering, can't continue to put up with her attacks. She is constantly putting me down for not being married." Despite these observations Susan denied any anger at her mother.

However, in interview #11 she reported being depressed. She mentioned briefly that she thought her mother was a lovely lady who had needs that drained her and then she paused, stopped talking and asked me to direct her. I suggested she was turning to me to avoid the conflict with her mother.

Interview #12

Susan reported having asserted herself with her mother, which stopped the mother's demeaning behavior and made her feel better.

During the next six or seven interviews Susan reviewed the relationship with her father, her relationship with her mother and her own rigidity and sensitivity to criticism. This presented an opportunity to point out to her that, unlike most of my female patients, she did not seem to be bothered by not having an ongoing relationship with a man. This confronted her with her detachment of affect. I suggested that if she were really interested in a man she would have to find some way to stay in circulation. She repeated that she had used work as an escape from this reality problem. I questioned whether this was wise.

In the next several sessions she reported dates with several men of the usual type. I asked again why she picked this type. She replied, "in order to feel safe," which led to a consideration of her narcissism.

"I'm so used to being alone I have a difficult time subordinating my own wishes to others. I'm very self-indulgent." In describing her ideal day she didn't include men until five o'clock. I noted that the day ended up with her alone. She asked, "Why am I afraid of getting involved?" By interview #21 she reported having met a man with whom she had spent three days: "Feeling ecstatic. I felt close, could talk to him, tingling and could feel again. Making love rather than fucking." Susan's detachment of affect was beginning to dissolve.

Almost immediately, as she got involved with this man, Bill, her fear of abandonment rose; she felt demanding and possessive and wished to make demands in order to relieve the fear: "I'm afraid if I said something it would upset the applecart. Why am I so scared? Our relationship is so good I'm afraid of its ending." Whenever he would leave her without making a subsequent date she would feel the urge to demand. She became angry and jealous of his possibly having other relationships. I suggested that she control her angry and possessive demands and attempt to clarify with Bill whether their relationship was to be exclusive or not. In interview #26 she reported a memory of her father being very nice to her, protecting her, taking care of her, flattering her. She still called him when she was sick, still had a need for his verbal reassurance.

Interview #28

After a weekend visit home, Susan reported a change in her perception of her father. She was now able to see her need to take care of him as well as his need to take care of her and that they formed an alliance to deal with the mother. The father complained about the mother but did nothing and was a martyr. She felt sorry for him and could not be critical. She then reported a dream. "Mother and I were away together in a large house. I kept running away from her looking in all those rooms." Free associations: "I don't want to be caught up in my mother's grasp as father is. I woke up with a cramp in my leg. My mother is very strong. She's over 70 but she is still very active—a physical and mental powerhouse."

Interviews #28-33

Bill had not called and Susan reported feeling humiliated, cut off and put down; she was not getting the attention she wanted. She traced the feeling back to the second grade when her brother had gotten a lot of attention for not eating. She had great difficulty in admitting her feelings about her mother's behavior: "What good would it do?" She recalled that she had always been a good child but now seemed to have a nasty temper, that she had been dependent on her mother for love which caused her to suppress her anger for fear of losing that love. She had displaced the anger on others.

Interview #34

Susan described two changes in her response to a phone call from her mother: For the first time she perceived on the spot both the mother's need to be the center of attention and her own reaction of hostility and anger rather than depression. She then related that her brother was just like her mother. She put up with as much from him as she did from her mother in order to have him like her.

Interview #40

In the setting of conflict with her boyfriend, Bill, I pointed out how she denied her perception of Bill's difficulties—i.e., his periods of social withdrawal and sexual impotence—in order to use the good part of their relationship to build a fantasy of an exclusive relationship with him. Following this interview Susan became more anxious and depressed and broke up with Bill.

Interview #44

Susan reported that on a visit home her father had cautioned her not to argue with her mother despite her express wishes to do so. I underlined the conflict between her feeling of anger and the father's prohibition against expressing it.

Interview #45

Susan admitted that her mother's values offended her and that she can't take too much of her mother at one time. Despite the fact that she was "describing" anger there was still very little affect of anger present, indicating that her defense of detachment still held sway.

Interview #46

Susan noted that the fear of her mother had extended to fear of all authority figures. I pointed out that she programmed herself by control and suppression of affect to deal with this fear and that the rigidity and suppression of feeling were harmful to her emotional life. This led her to realize that she had so much invested in "being right" that the possibility of being wrong made her terribly anxious. She feared the withdrawal of the mother's approval. She reported that she was always the good girl and never argued with mother. In a later interview (#58) she added that she suppressed anger at me for fear of being disliked by me just as she did with her mother. She then began to act out the frustration of her dependency needs in interviews by saying that she felt as if she were talking to a machine. I didn't respond. She needed my direction. She felt my lack of response as disapproval, which roused her anger, which she then suppressed. I asked, "Why are you asking me to direct you when you complain so much about your mother's direction?" She responded, "It's very difficult to be on my own. My mother and father always told me what to do. I never had to decide for myself. I dislike change and being uncomfortable and whenever I make a decision I wonder if everybody will like it." I pointed out that her need for direction was a defense against her anxiety over autonomy.

After dating a man four or five times and having sexual intercourse with him Susan got annoyed that he did not focus all attention on her and expressed this by withdrawing from him sexually. I pointed out that either she's seeing no men or she's demanding an exclusive relationship, which then is followed by a break-up, after which she doesn't seem to be very bothered by the lack of a man in her life. I pointed out that both situations were reflections of her conflict over intimacy with men. Either she sees no men at all (distancing) or she hops into bed with the first man she sees (acting out and clinging), then demands an exclusive relationship with him to deal with her anxiety over rejection. I suggested that in reality it takes time and experience for a relationship to develop.

Susan reported that her mother reminded her on the phone to be sure to take rubbers and an umbrella when she went out in rain. Susan suddenly realized the degree to which her mother saw her as a child: "She still admonishes me like a two-year-old." After the phone call Susan had the following dream: "Mother asked me if I would take care of her baby. I got frightened, said I couldn't cope, that the baby would turn blue and die. Mother returned and asked me what had happened. I told her it died." Free association: "I'm afraid of bearing a child, taking responsibility for it." I interpreted that the child was the patient and that the anxiety was about taking care of herself.

Susan responded, "I operate like a 'good girl' to please others rather than be myself. The image of myself is of a much younger age; my work as a teacher keeps my figure trim so that I look much younger. My roommate is ten years younger, but looks ten years older. She's fat and droopy and she gets winded on the tennis court." "However," I said, repeating some information

Susan had already told me, "she manages to have· sexual intercourse regularly."

Susan's therapy had achieved the following in two and a half years: 1) Susan became more assertive with her mother and people in general. 2) Her acting out of the dependence on her father through relationships with men was clarified; the acting out was minimized but not stopped. 3) Much of the avoidance and denial, as well as the detachment of affect, were overcome. 4) Anxiety and depression were mobilized to provide further motivation for treatment. 5) Finally, by virtue of asserting herself at work, she managed to get herself promoted.

IMPRESSIONS

These two patients, Nancy and Susan, illustrate how quickly one can, indeed one must, initiate psychotherapy with the borderline adult. At the first possible moment reality confrontations are made of the core defenses of avoidance, denial, projection and acting out the wish for reunion. This mobilizes anxiety and depression and further motivates the patient for treatment.

To deal with sexual acting out it is often necessary to teach the borderline how normal relationships develop in order to highlight the patient's need for distance or "instant intimacy" to deal with conflicts over intimacy. Throughout the patient's therapy constructive efforts towards self-assertion, gratification through reality rather than fantasy, and the development of sublimation and of social skills are supported and encouraged.

It is quite clear that neither of these patients has gotten in touch with the affect associated with the original separation-individuation problem (abandonment depression). Nevertheless, the interruption of the pathologic ego's control—the alliance of the RORU and the pathologic ego—has begun the slow and tedious process of growth and development, whereby the patient's reality ego expands through identification with the therapist's ego to take control over more of the patient's behavior, and the therapist is introjected as a stable object.

Life structure is less and less sacrificed to deal with emotional problems, the patient's capacity to cope improves and the original presenting complaint of dissatisfaction with life fades into the background as the patient begins to obtain more satisfaction from both work and interpersonal relationships.

As Zetzel (244) has pointed out, this therapy can be slow, tedious and long-term business. Therefore the therapist should be prepared for slow progress and small results over long periods of time. This does not mean, however, that he can relax his vigilance at any time; if he does the pathologic ego will again reassert itself.

B. Reconstructive Psychotherapy

Case 1:
A Second Chance — Peter

The next five chapters describe the reconstructive psychotherapy of a 45-year-old business executive who came for therapy the first time at the age of 27 in what can now be called an abandonment panic. He was overwhelmed by the prospect of having to commit himself to living with his new wife and working for his father.

In retrospect it can be recognized that at that time a classic mistake was made in thinking that he had a probably hysterical psychoneurotic condition due to oedipal conflicts, which led to the use of inappropriate therapeutic technique. Under the notion that I was "allowing the transference to unfold," I did not at that time adequately confront his acting out in and out of the transference, nor was enough communicative matching employed. Confrontation and communicative matching are both vital tech-

niques to the success of psychotherapy with borderline patients.

Nonetheless, his symptoms subsided and some of his sexual inhibitions were reduced and he stopped treatment after three years. A year later, while planning to divorce his first wife after seven years of marriage and two sons, he again returned for psychotherapy three times a week. The same therapeutic technique was used, again with superficial success, and he again stopped after one year.

He came for the third and final time at age 45 when he was about to divorce his second wife in order to marry a third. However, much water had flowed over the dam in the intervening years, during which I had learned the art of psychotherapy of the borderline. When I had finally learned how to treat the borderline I had many regrets about this very patient, with regard to what I could have done had I but known. And then, as so rarely happens, life offered to the patient and to me this second chance. This time a different concept led to a different therapeutic technique and a better result.

The previous diagnostic mistake was classic because it is the most common diagnostic error made with borderline patients—i.e., the therapist is beguiled by the neurotic symptoms into overlooking the basic defects in the borderline's ego structure. This misunderstanding inevitably leads, like night follows day, to the use of inappropriate therapeutic techniques. It is not that psychotherapy is of no help, but the help is superficial, and neither the patient nor the therapist fully realizes it. It can be said in my defense that the first time the patient came for therapy I didn't know any better—knowledge in psychiatry about the borderline was scanty indeed, as has already been described. Although our knowledge about the borderline has undergone a recent explosion, it is still so new that it has not been disseminated widely enough to prevent this mistake from happening again. It remains a most common diagnostic error.

However, what began as a misfortune—for patient and therapist alike—ends as a piece of good luck from the perspective of this clinical research. The first experiences in therapy serve as a *control for the one reported here. In other words, one can compare and contrast the results in the same patient when his disorder is viewed as psychoneurotic and he is treated with techniques appropriate to the psychoneurotic and when his disorder is viewed as borderline and the techniques appropriate to that disorder are used. Only when the borderline concepts and therapeutic techniques were used did the patient's clinical condition begin to show dramatic improvement.*

Two parallel related threads weave their way through the five chapters that follow—the degree to which emotion or affect is invested (or cathected) in the part-self image and/or in the image of the part-object. These are the pathologic correlates of normal separation-individuation described in Chapter 3.

In Chapter 10—Acting Out the Wish for Reunion—the dominant emotional investment is in the part-object and the rage and depression at deprivation of the self are defended against by acting out. Thus impelled to act out the patient "feels good" and he is sublimely unaware of his lack of a self image.

In Chapter 11—A Therapeutic Impasse—the dominant investment continues in the part-object but, the acting out now controlled, the depression and rage begin to emerge in mood states and dreams as he begins the painful task of transferring the emotional investment from the part-object to the part-self. However, there is still little investment in the self. The patient can no longer act out, but he wishes to avoid working through his abandonment depression.

In Chapter 12—Abandonment Depression—the impasse has been resolved and the patient begins to work through the abandonment depression associated with transferring his dominant emotional investment from the part-object to the part-self. Throughout the emotional hurricane of the abandonment depression one begins to see the self emerge more and more clearly only to be swamped again and again by the associated abandonment depression.

In Chapter 13—Homicidal Rage—the patient slowly and reluctantly comes to face and work through the homicidal rage at the mother for the deprivation of self. The transfer of emotional investment from part-object to part-self image accelerates.

In Chapter 14—On the Way to Autonomy—the patient works through the homicidal rage and the self-image, establishing itself more clearly and definitely, finally takes charge of the patient's motivation. The balance of emotional investment has shifted from the object to the self, splitting has markedly decreased, a new whole self image—both good and bad—has been formed which derives satisfaction from coping rather than regression, and a new whole object image—both good and bad—has been formed based on introjection of the image of the therapist. Associated with these intrapsychic changes are continuous and stable changes in thoughts, mood states, and actions. The patient is now his own master—not yet without occasional anxiety or depression but without regressions to his former pathologic states.

10

Acting Out the Wish for Reunion:

"It Feels Good"

HISTORY AT FIRST COURSE OF TREATMENT

Chief Complaint

Peter listed the following complaints: panic when getting on the train to go to work in the morning; concentration difficulty; somatic symptoms, including grogginess, dizziness, nausea, sweating, chest pain and palpitations; terror that he might have hypertension and a heart attack.

History of Illness

Peter was discharged from the Army after service in Korea at the age 24 and returned to his home town against his will to enter his father's business and to live with his new wife whom he had married in college. He felt great conflict with his stern, rigid, disapproving father whom he felt he could never please.

Panic occurred on the train on the way to work every morning. "I though it was physical. I thought perhaps I had a brain tumor

192

or maybe I had heart trouble." As the pressure mounted he began to have chest pains. He recalled that when he was in the Army at age 22 after a particularly difficult period of physical exertion he had blacked out and had seen a doctor who misdiagnosed his symptoms as epilepsy, thereby reinforcing his tendency to somatize his feelings.

The panic on the train gradually increased. He worked from early morning until 7:30 at night, felt great need for his father's approval, and saw himself as very inadequate. One day the panic prevented him from getting on the train, and his internist, who had given him many ECG's to reassure himself that his patient was healthy, referred him for psychotherapy.

Past History

Peter was born in a large city, the oldest of three children, with a brother two years younger and a sister four years younger. He described his father as austere, forbidding, disapproving, stone-faced, but very successful, hard-working, never at home. He was compulsively neat, never expressed anger or other emotion and considered Peter to be inadequate and lightweight while favoring his younger brother.

The mother was described as attractive, vivacious, and "used to be a lot of fun." Peter had been very close to her as a child and a young man. However, he felt she had nothing to do when the children grew up and had become depressed. Peter felt he was more like the mother than the father in that he liked a good time. He recalled resenting his brother since the time of his birth and never getting along too well with him. The brother's personality was more like the father's.

His memories of his childhood were quite vague but he did recall spending a good deal of time with the mother and the father's working from early morning until late at night. While he enjoyed himself with his mother, when father came home the house was filled with an atmosphere of doom and gloom.

He vividly recalled the terror experienced at having his tonsils out at age four. Ever since he had hated doctors. When he was examined by school doctors he used to get palpitations and be afraid of being sent back to the hospital.

He always did well in school, had an attractive, easy going personality, made friends easily and was quite popular. Here he just got by in his marks but "had a good time" with dating and sports. He then attended college where he was an outstanding soccer player, and was active in the radio station and in his fraternity.

At the end of his junior year he became very much interested in a girl whom he viewed as intellectual and domineering—a combination of his mother and father. He was not sexually attracted to her. She was involved with another man but he decided to win her away which he proceeded to do, finally marrying her during his senior year against his parents' wishes. Following graduation he entered the Army as an officer to spend several years in Korea.

PRESENT COURSE OF TREATMENT

Peter returned to treatment as he was divorcing his second wife after she had a severe depression for which she had to be hospitalized. Peter had felt abandoned and started an affair with another woman. He was ambivalent about marrying this woman and when she pushed marriage he felt cornered. He could not afford a third wife. I reviewed the relationship of his past problems to present ones and suggested he come for therapy four times a week.

It quickly became apparent in the early sessions that Peter's anxiety about being on his own—i.e., separation anxiety—was defended against by acting out the wish for reunion through maintaining dependent relationships with women, by submitting to their wishes and manipulating them for their approval. In this opening phase of therapy it was important to confront the denial of the destructiveness of the RORU-pathological ego alliance, to confront him with his denial of feelings of inadequacy in order to change his view of this alliance from one that was ego-syntonic to one that was ego-alien.

He illustrated the dominant emotional investment in the part-object and the poverty of his self image: He felt that to be alone was like being dead, to be with people was being alive and gave him identity. These feelings were elaborated into the personality style of a supersalesman. He was an extremely successful salesman since there were literally no limits to the efforts he would make to please the customer. For example, he would not infrequently find himself in formal dress (which he hated), entertaining customers at the theater (which he also disliked) and then squiring them around town to various bars and nightclubs despite the fact that he didn't enjoy that kind of drinking. These efforts also extended to his personal relationships where he would go to any extreme to win the approval of almost everyone he came in contact with.

Whenever separation anxiety arose in interview he would run to his now separated second wife and sleep with her. A classic example: The night they signed the separation papers they went to bed together. Since this was his way of relieving anxiety it was impossible to do much about it in sessions—i.e., there was no anxiety in interviews. But I pointed out to him that whenever he felt apprehensive he would seek a connection with his wife in order to make himself feel better; on the other hand, after he did so he would feel great guilt and self-loathing and wonder why he had done it.

This confrontation interrupted his denial and confronted the patient with the separation anxiety and therefore stirred up resistance. In the next interview he externalized the source of the anxiety—i.e., it was in the treatment, not in him. He was angry, provocative and didn't want treatment. Why should he spend money on it?

I pointed out that he was angry at me for throwing a monkey-wrench in the works of his life-style, for undoing his acting out and denial and exposing him to separation anxiety and feelings of inadequacy.

The patient answered that he didn't want to be alone at all costs, that he had to establish a connection.

Following this interview the patient developed somatic symptoms of separation anxiety, such as chest pain, and a fear that he was going to have a heart attack, or pass out and lose control. Nevertheless, in the next interview the merest outline of the self image made its first appearance as he began to talk about self-expression—about things he wanted to do, such as cook, play tennis or go boating, and how he had allowed all self-expression to wither.

He began to look back on his life now from a realistic perspective, feeling guilt about how he had missed opportunities to make it worthwhile. He referred again to his feeling that being "on his own" meant being dead. I pointed out that he seemed to have only two alternatives: one, to establish a dependent connection with a woman (act out the RORU) in which his self image (which was denied) was that of a creep whom he loathed; or two, to try to be on his own and die (WORU). I pointed out that the latter was a feeling and not a reality and that perhaps he might use his treatment to learn to understand and master this fear rather than use therapy just to relieve it. Peter replied that the connection felt good (ego-syntonic), that he had lived his life that way, and that when he didn't have a connection he felt bad and he liked to feel good.

Comment

This was a good clinical description of the function of the alliance between the rewarding maternal part-object and the pathologic ego, resulting in a good feeling which made the whole operation ego-syntonic at the most of denial of reality—destructiveness. The patient activated the rewarding unit to avoid the affect associated with the withdrawing unit, all the while denying two things—the feelings of inadequacy at being a dependent child, and the destructiveness of it to his therapy and his growth. It is now necessary to take a closer look at the patient's intrapsychic structure—i.e., the split object relation units and the split ego. In this construction some clinical evidence will be summarized that came out only later in psychotherapy.

INTRAPSYCHIC STRUCTURE

Split Object Relations Unit

This patient's rewarding object relations part-unit consisted of an omnipotent, all good mother image who provided supplies and "kept him safe and protected" as long as he remained dependent on her, fulfilling her needs to cling. Beneath this mother image was another mother image whose attentions and demands were engulfing.

The mother's parents had died when she was an adolescent; she evidently had married her husband as a father figure. However, he was rarely at home so she utilized the patient as the object to whom she clung to deal with her own abandonment depression. The patient's affect was one of feeling good but the self representation was of being inadequate, unmasculine, a creep. This self image, however, was split off from awareness and projected on to others. The anxiety associated with it was relieved by compliant approval-seeking behavior.

The patient's WORU was much more complex and took more time to emerge. It consisted of an image of a mother who would not only abandon him but who would annihilate him or leave him to die if he expressed himself or attempted to separate from her. This withdrawing object relations part-unit of the mother —encouraged by her behavior—was handled by splitting it from the real mother and projecting it on to the father, whose part-image was that of a stern, cold, disapproving and punishing figure. The affect was one of intense rage and fear of abandonment which was equated with death and expressed in the somatic preoccupation with having a heart attack. The self image was a nothingness, a ghost without substance, an incompetent, a lightweight.

The part-image of the engulfing mother, linked with feelings of panic at being devoured or swallowed up, only emerged much later.

Relationship with Oedipal Conflict

The intrapsychic structure was further complicated by the patient's having, in addition, another image of the father as a punitive, castrating oedipal rival for the mother. The splitting and projection of the WORU of the mother on the father and the image of the father as a punitive, castrating rival became fused through the mother's projections. The tonsillectomy experience at age four dramatized this fear. The patient's guilt about individuative strivings, combined with his guilt about oedipal strivings, led to his interpretation of the experience as an abandonment and a castration, thus condensing his separation anxiety and castration anxiety, i.e., condensing the preoedipal and the oedipal.

Defense Mechanisms of the Pathologic Ego

The defense mechanisms of the pathologic ego consisted primarily of massive splitting, avoidance of self-expression or efforts towards individuation, denial of the reality destructiveness of this behavior, projection and acting out of the wish for reunion through clinging to mother and women. This massive acting out of the wish for reunion through dependency relationships with women, but also with others as a supersalesman, was so intense and so persistent that the withdrawing object relations unit rarely made its appearance and when it did it was of course greeted with great anger and resistance.

The patient's suppression of self (thoughts, feelings and actions) was extreme. His actions were motivated either by the need to please or because he felt he "ought" to act in a specific way. Thoughts or feelings arising from within that he *wanted* to act, rather than felt he *should* act, produced great anxiety which was fantasied in the form of preoccupations with a heart attack and fear of dying, thus reproducing intrapsychically the traumatic experience with the tonsillectomy. He was particularly anxious about free associations. His behavior under the domination of the RORU-pathologic ego alliance was extraordinarily motivated to please the object at the cost of suppressing the self.

PSYCHOTHERAPY

Let us now return to the report of the psychotherapy. For the next several interviews Peter gave up his pursuit of connection which triggered an increase in separation anxiety expressed in physical symptoms—heart palpitations, fears of a heart attack, feelings of unreality and thinking about death. The patient said, "I have to have that life preserver. If it's not there I get very frightened. I worry about my heart. I'm afraid I'm going to die. I never think of it as anxiety or depression; I can't give up the life preserver."

The separation anxiety expressed through cardiac symptoms was good evidence that the rewarding unit was not being activated to deal with the withdrawing unit. Peter now became aware of how he employed the rewarding unit to deal with the withdrawing unit. He talked about going on a trip and feeling terribly lonely and anxious; on his return he thought about calling his ex-wife, rejected the idea and then was unable to prevent himself from calling her.

This is a good example of externalization. The patient consciously conceives of his anxiety as coming from an external source—either therapy or physical distance from his ex-wife. He then uses external actions to relieve it: He acts out the wish for reunion, thereby seemingly confirming his original conception of the source of his discomfort.

I again reinforced the reality by saying that he wanted to separate from his wife legally but still use her as an emotional connection to deal with his anxiety.

Following this session, which bluntly confronted Peter with his defense against separation anxiety, he returned the next day and said he had blown it completely. He lost complete control and when drunk called his ex-wife. He hadn't cared about himself; nothing mattered except that he see her. The next morning he felt terrible—the splitting off of the guilt and inadequacy feelings had been overcome. He came in reporting that he hated himself and he hated the treatment and he couldn't make it. He could no longer act out the wish for reunion without feeling guilty and inadequate.

I pointed out that he got angry at me for taking away his connection and facing him with separation anxiety, which then activated the pathological ego, which sought the connection at the cost of reality destructiveness.

As Peter controlled his acting out, the WORU began to emerge. He began to talk more and more of hating the need for connection, of feeling alone, that no one cared. He had suicidal fantasies and feelings of depression and emptiness. He then mentioned how he saw me as a judge or god and it made it hard for him to talk, particularly about his need for a connection.

I pointed out that he denied his own conscience and projected it on me. He felt inadequate and guilty when acting out his dependent need for a connection but denied it and externalized it on me as a criticism and then manipulated me to get approval, thereby relieving the guilt and further adding to the pressure of the need for a connection.

Peter now began to report that he was able to be alone without feeling so awful; however, he felt that coming to treatment was a sign of weakness. I pointed this out as an externalization; he was projecting on the therapy his feeling of weakness about seeking the connection.

He then reported that the interpretation reinforced his ability to stop the acting out but then he fought awareness of the feeling that arose and found that when coming into the interview he was sleepy and angry. He then reported a dream of his girlfriend being in bed with another man, which roused his possessive feeling—since she belonged to him, how could she do it?

I pointed out his unconscious assumptions that he was very

well entitled to the connection, that it is the proper way of life, that it is ego-syntonic—and whenever I said that it was not he got furious at me. I also pointed out that if he controlled his behavior but then suppressed his feelings when he came to the interview he was working against himself. He again talked about his enormous need to be dependent on women, at the same time perceiving that he really didn't care about anyone else, only himself.

Before the next session he had a dream in which a doctor told him he had a terminal heart condition, and he woke up in a panic and went to see his ex-wife again and slept with her. I interpreted that it was better to hold on to a woman than to take a chance on being killed.

Peter now began to face his problem, asking why the huge void between what he wanted to be and what he was? Why the overwhelming childish need? He was sick of himself for not acting better. His anxiety and somatic symptoms increased. In addition, he reported turning down his ex-wife's overtures to act out his dependency needs, supporting the positive side of himself and battling the negative, which he had now come to call the creep or the connector (the RORU-pathologic ego alliance).

Confrontation with the destructiveness of the pathologic ego was changing it from ego-syntonic to ego-alien; it was becoming foreign. An alliance was forming between the therapist's ego and the patient's reality ego. Peter said he wanted to have a good image of himself and not let the sick part take over, that he was trying to control his behavior and not call his ex-wife.

He now became aware that even in business he needed people to tell him what to do rather than decide for himself. He recalled that the last time he was independent was in college. He asked why he got married the first time at 20; why didn't he go out on his own? It was my feeling that he married as a defense against separation and that graduating from college produced too much separation anxiety for him to handle on his own.

He then described that he left his second wife because she failed as a connection and he was not marrying the third girl because she was not an adequate connection either. He began to free associate and panicked. "If I let go, I'm afraid of these random thoughts. They make no sense. They will take over. I feel the lid has come off and they'll be like rats running around."

I think the patient panicked because the free associations were the self he had been squelching. He then reported that not only had he stopped seeking a connection with his ex-wife but he'd found that he didn't want to be the supersalesman he had been, that he was really doing it to get other's approval. He dramatically described his poorly invested self image: "I murdered myself to begin with. Today I decided to murder the supersalesman. I didn't get myself all geared up for the sales meeting." He now reported liking to be alone because he didn't have to put on an act.

In the next three interviews following this free association he became quite resistant since he was confronted again with his separation anxiety as he attempted to support his self image. Again he began to talk about stopping treatment until I pointed out the relationship—i.e., he was externalizing his separation anxiety on to the psychotherapy.

Peter had stopped calling his ex-wife but was permitting her to call him because he felt guilty and because he didn't want to let go of her. I asked him why he couldn't get mad at her and made the interpretation that he didn't want to give up the fantasy of the connection with her. He reported that with his mother he felt that if she loved him he wouldn't die—she would take care of everything for him. With his ex-wife he felt the same way. I pointed out that if he really had his ex-wife's welfare at heart he would leave her alone, but that he was holding on to her as a hedge against being on his own.

Peter responded with an analogy that his self-image was like a baby chicken inside the egg. The shell was the membrane or connection; his dependency on a woman was to prevent the chicken inside the shell from hatching. His anxiety rose after this interpretation and again he sought out his wife, reporting, "I have no backbone. I don't care about myself or anyone. I'm just destroying myself. I felt that I had no insides; I was an empty shell. I don't mind being alone if I know in the back of my mind there is a connection."

In the interim he and his wife had formally signed separation papers and he felt: "I'm on my own. What will I do? Who's going to take care of me? Who will be me?" He then elaborated on his lack of self image. "I am no one. I have no self image, I don't see myself as tall [though his height is 6']. Being on my own is being with no one, as though I'm a dead spirit, an empty shell, a shroud, and what gives me substance is the connection. I'm ectoplasm. Only a head. Externalization gives me a body. I'm like the invisible man who has to wrap himself in gauze to be seen. I feel I'm not alive if I don't externalize. I don't exist. I send radar signals into outer space and bounce them off people. Otherwise I'm empty." In other words, without the emotional investment in the part-object he will die.

He elaborated on his efforts to avoid self motivation: He kept himself busy all day, avoided thinking at all costs and never had insomnia at night. I pointed out the destructiveness of blocking out feelings between interviews.

His anxiety again rose as he started thinking on his own and talked about his self image as being negative, the connector, the masturbator. The positive image came from the approval of other people: "If my ex-wife could let me fuck her it would wipe out the bad image of myself." Peter again talked about the two alternatives of connection or death. He pursued the connection to feel better. It was the same with his first wife as with his mother. He recalled at age 10 going into a rage when his mother went out with his father and the father's beating him up for objecting. He thought she was his, there to take care of him. He felt the same way with his first wife and perhaps married her because she was so busy with another man; he wanted her all to himself: "She was mine."

I pointed out that he must feel my interpretations about the connection to be the same as his father's trying to take his mother away from him and he lets his anger out at me by going back to see his ex-wife. I asked how a 10-year-old could think his mother belonged to him? Despite or because of my interpretation, before the next interview he had seen his ex-wife and, although he had intercourse with her, unlike previous occasions he remained in touch with the feelings discussed in the interview and was able to see his actions as a means of dealing with them. In the next interview he continued with the same theme.

He described his belief that his mother could keep him from death but also could leave him. He said, "I have wanted to possess her since my brother was born when I was two. I remember at age three throwing gravel at his baby carriage and at four I had a tonsillectomy. Mother took me to the hospital without telling me why I was going there. She held my hand in the operating room and left me there to a fate I didn't know, people with masks with the light and the oxygen. I didn't want to be knocked out. I was terrified. I thought they were going to kill me. They held me down. I was helpless. I woke up in a room with my mother and later went home. I could still feel the terror. Always afraid of doctors, but I make them my friends. I'm afraid they will take my mother away from me." I said, "like me."

This experience at age four must be viewed in the light of the patient's relationship with his mother. He saw her as omnipotent and threatening him with death if he did not comply. However, the father was always used as the punitive agent. She reinforced this message with religious talk about how an impersonal God punished evil. It was revealed later in therapy that the patient felt the mother was taking him to the hospital to be "killed" or punished for his unconscious rage and guilt and the doctors were her agents—i.e., his father. This traumatic and terror-ridden experience gave the stamp of reality to the patient's combined anxiety about separation and castration.

It served to confirm in reality his worst, purely psychic and imaginary fears and thus reinforced his need to depend on the RORU-pathologic ego alliance. He must please his mother at all costs.

From this time on, all expressions of self would be severely burdened with the intrapsychic elaborations of this experience—i.e., fear of death. He would be compelled to avoid the self to avoid dying. The essential metaphor is the child abandoned by the omnipotent object (mother) to her agents (father) to be annihilated, and feeling helpless—the patient was bound and helpless during the operation.

Peter then had a dream which he related in the next interview. His father returned and told him he had to go to work. He was resentful and asked why he was the only one in the family who had to work. "Fuck him, I'm going to do something else." Then he talked about his mother. She can't leave him; no one else can have her. He has to be the only one. He expressed this with both his ex-wife and his girlfriend; the composite of the two of them made up his mother.

Peter's effort to face his feelings about his mother triggered the WORU and then the RORU and the pathological ego took over. He then complained of fatigue, blocking and resentment and talked more about the necessity to call his ex-wife. All was interpreted as resistance to the previous work about his mother. However, the resistance continued over the next several interviews as he played with the idea of getting in touch with his ex-wife. As his resistance persisted and mounted it became necessary to escalate the confrontations of his denial of the destructiveness of his behavior: The greater the resistance the greater the counterforce of the confrontation. I again pointed out that he denied his feelings of inadequacy about holding on to his ex-wife, that he was being destructive to himself and his treatment, and that the notion that he had a lot of time left to do the work of psychotherapy was an illusion. This was perhaps the last chance in his life.

Peter responded to this challenge with a dream in which I was attempting to call him and his secretary told him not to pick up the telephone. When he picked up the phone it was dead. Then I showed up in his life and he told me he had been seeing another psychiatrist three times a week and was paying him more money.

I interpreted to Peter that his personality was comprised of two parts—a reality ego and a pathologic ego and that the latter, whose objective was to fulfill the connection or act out the wish for reunion, was in charge of his motivation. However, in order to achieve this objective, the pathologic ego had to completely distort reality and therefore view the expressions of his real self (dreaming, free associations and spontaneous actions) as "being crazy." This perspective would cause him to avoid these activities so that he could devote himself to the wish for reunion. In other words, the pathologic ego required him to restructure reality in the light of his need for a connection. Consequently, when I confronted or challenged the pathologic ego's perspective on reality it produced great anger at this frustration of its objectives.

Peter then exerted more constructive control of his acting out behavior, his resistance decreased and he became more thoughtful. He had a dream about a connection with his wife, from which he waked with anxiety. Further, he reported that he was spending his time in much more expressive activity but still experiencing anxiety.

Peter now approached his behavior from the perspective of who's in charge: the creep (his pathological ego) or himself. The RORU-pathological ego alliance had now become ego-alien. Then he began to look at the destructiveness of his need for connection, saying that he spent $200,000 on his first wife in the last ten years and will have spent that much on his second, too. Despite this he again started thinking about seeing his second wife. I interpreted that when he feels anxious the creep comes back for the connection, uses all types of rationalizations to enable him to make the connection and deny the feeling of inadequacy.

11

A Therapeutic Impasse:

"Which Way to Go?"

Peter's increasing control of his acting out catapulted him into a dilemma. He no longer wanted to act out because he saw its destructiveness, but he was reluctant to work through because it required him to face the abandonment depression.

The therapeutic theme shifted from confrontation of the acting out to clarification of the above dilemma, as well as of the other defenses of the pathologic ego: avoidance of individuation, passivity, denial, externalization, the wish for reunion fantasy. This pressure brought the abandonment depression to the fore, as revealed in dreams, but Peter's resistance to working-through continued, as revealed by the denial of feelings, externalization of the dilemma on to the therapy, and sleepiness. After six months of firm confrontation his resistance gave way and working-through began in earnest.

Ten months into psychotherapy, at age 45, Peter now exerted more control over the pathologic ego and, as he did so, that which it was a defense against—the WORU with the abandonment depression—began to emerge more clearly. He began to dream and to be able to free associate. He now reported a dream which revealed the abandonment depression:

"I was alone at the airport an a business trip watching a plane crash on landing. Bodies were everywhere. It was a horrible mess. I didn't want to look. Then my ex-wife appeared. I felt better and we were to return to New York City together and I had an argument with her over keeping me waiting."

Free association: "I had that same old death feeling, the world going on and me not being part of it. My ex-wife was just screwing, not loving. She was a sex object. I had no feeling for her as a person." I interpreted the dream as a reaction to his interrupting the connection with his ex-wife and attempting to analyze it which brought on his feeling of abandonment. He replied: "The next step for me would have been to go find her and reassure myself that she wouldn't abandon me. A feeling goes with the fantasy. How could you do this to me? I must possess her, be the only one, otherwise death. I can be the only one inside you whom you have any feeling for. My mother used to feed me and I felt great competition with my father. With my first wife, rather than love her, I married her, I think, because she had another man."

Two interviews later Peter reported increasing control over the pathologic ego. He had turned down an overture on the phone by his ex-wife and then had the following dream: "I was with my two best friends, who were up to no good; something evil was going on. They were going to assassinate someone. They knew I knew about it and they were going to catch me, so I ran. I knew they'd kill me. A policeman was there so I told him, but an Army colonel was there and said that I was wrong and that he, the colonel, would take care of the situation. Then you came along with your wife and we ran through some smoke bombs and then the dream changed and you and your wife and I were at a party laughing and having a good time."

Free association: "There's no future. I feel trapped in an elevator and it's frightening." I interpreted that since he had turned down the connection offered by his ex-wife he again was faced with the other alternative—his feelings of abandonment—and that he sensed that he was trapped by this conflict. It was either be killed or have a connection and he was on a treadmill from one to the other. There was no future or no past, only the treadmill of these repetitive feelings. He replied, "I feel as if something awful is going to happen, like appendicitis or cancer or something unknown, maybe death." My interpretation further confronted him with his feelings of abandonment. In the next interview he linked the connection and the fear: "The connection is a shell to keep me safe from my fear of being on my own."

Eleventh Month

In the next interview, during the 11th month of therapy, Peter marshalled his defenses against the fear confronted in the previous interview, manifested as resistance; he brought up the possibility of cutting interviews down from four to three times a week because of finances. I interpreted that the problem was not financial but emotional and that his desire to cut down was a reaction to my confrontations with his resultant fear of abandonment in the prior two sessions. Then he reported the following dream: "I had a rattlesnake in a box and it was coming out. I was terrified. I couldn't keep it in. I knew if I let go of it, it would bite me. Almost better to get bitten than to go through the anxiety of holding the box down. I wanted someone to take the problem away and handle it for me."

Free association: "I wasn't thinking of ways to handle it. I refused to plan and look ahead or work it out." I interpreted that the dream was about his treatment, that this rattlesnake was his fear of abandonment—beneath which lay his rage, that without a connection he feels helpless and naked before a terrible threat. Peter replied, "I'm unwilling to face life on my own. I feel depressed; there's no future, no enjoyment. Without externalization all my games and toys are taken away."

The next three interviews were filled with depression and self-deprecation. Peter complained he didn't have the guts to assert himself. Since he now was in conflict about acting out to relieve his fear he began to somatize it in the form of symptoms of anxiety and cardiac pain. Peter said that he found himself wanting to externalize again but stopped himself. He could see no past or future, only death. Another line of defense appeared as he began to cut off feelings and talk about being angry, as my summer vacation approached: "I'm binding the hatches, getting myself ready for your leaving. You are the only connection I have anymore. I'm feeling that there's nothing to look forward to. I'm desperate. The whole world has dropped out. I've lost my sense of purpose."

In this setting his girlfriend Cindy laid down the law, telling him to either put up or shut up—i.e., marry her or stop seeing her. The patient reported the following dream: "All these men are in love with her; she treated me like a brother but they were all after her but I knew them. She had no romantic interest in me but I did in her and I knew I was losing."

Free association: "I realize I could lose Cindy, unlike my ex-wife. I love her for not making decisions for me, for assuming I'm a man, but I feel like a child with women. I don't want to feel controlled and captured by them. I gave up myself to get something from them." He continued, "I had a sick pattern with three women, my mother, my first wife and my second wife. I tried to make Cindy into a woman like the others but it didn't work, which created a crisis. That's why I came for treatment. I expected them to take care of me but I hated that, but I now see what's good and right in the last couple of days and I don't despair about the future. However, part of me doesn't want to stop my ex-wife from calling, doesn't want to be a man." I pointed out that one of the purposes of his intellectual control of his thoughts and behavior was to conceal from himself this wish to be a child with a woman.

After this interview I took three weeks of vacation and on my return the patient reported that in the interim he had been very cautious about acting out the connection but had gotten very little insight. He found that he didn't like being with his mother and couldn't put on the act of pleasing her anymore; he didn't like being a child but didn't like being independent either. He was afraid to do his own thing. His dreams had been either of a bad connection or of death. He was now caught between not wanting to act out the connection because he was aware of its destructiveness and still not wanting to face his feelings about the withdrawn image of his mother—in essence, fighting against the necessity to work through his abandonment depression.

Twelfth Month

This impasse was described in the next few interviews: "I feel stalled, the future is blank." On the other hand, he was considering his own wishes for the first time. "I have never thought about what I wanted to do in life. I rarely do anything on my own. I'm afraid of being independent."

He reported the following new type of dream: "I'm back on the soccer team but I don't want to play and I am dodging it. This is very unlike the old soccer dreams because it didn't make me feel good anymore."

Free association: "Doing better at work made me feel anxious rather than good. I saw the Cadillac under the tin lizzy." I reinforced the confrontation: "Therefore you don't have any more excuses." Peter answered, "One side of me is screaming 'don't make me be a child' while the other side screams 'don't make me do it on my own.' Who am I talking to? My mother? 'Please don't leave me in the door of the operating room?' "

This insight into his basic dilemma led in the next six interviews to depression and further resistance and cutting off of feelings. He complained about headaches. "I have a lid on my feelings. I don't like the fix I'm in. I would do anything to get out of it. I want to be made to feel good. I want it to come from you. I don't want to stand on my own two feet. I feel very depressed. I had a fantasy of seeing myself in a closed coffin but not dead and I began to panic. My past is shit; my future is nothing. I'd like to walk out of here."

Confrontation of the denial of the destructiveness of acting out the wish for reunion—the RORU-pathological ego alliance—had created conflict in the patient's basic system for "feeling good." He could no longer act out the wish for reunion and "feel good" without recognizing he also "felt bad." On the other hand, giving up acting out of the wish for reunion forced him to face the core abandonment depression which he was loathe to face. His struggle over which course to follow continued.

A key to the success of the confrontation was the patient's designation of the RORU-pathologic ego alliance as the "connector" or the "creep" which symbolized that for him what had been ego-syntonic and had made him "feel good" was now ego-alien and unacceptable. As a concrete shorthand symbol of this complex intrapsychic alliance it was dramatic evidence that the patient's denial of its destructive effects had been overcome.

The patient reported, "I woke up at 4 o'clock in the morning feeling I was dying, all alone. In the morning I'm angry at you." I interpreted that he was angry at the therapy for forcing him to give up the connection and face the feeling of death. This feeling angered and frightened him and he dealt with it by cutting off all feelings. I added that he could not face the fact that he felt he had no guts if he didn't deal with his fear so he externalized this feeling of inadequacy on to the psychotherapy. In other words, he was claiming that it was the therapy which made him feel bad and inadequate, not the fact that he had difficulty dealing with his fear.

The patient replied, "If I do it I will die; death is an excuse for not doing it. For example, I knew the head of one of my departments was no good but I did nothing about it." I interpreted this as an avoidance of action in order to deal with his anxiety. This interpretation was met by further resistance, the patient becoming sleepy and expressing no thoughts or feelings.

His girlfriend Cindy again laid down the law—either stop seeing her or marry her. I pointed out the reality of the situation to the patient: He had the best of both worlds; he was getting laid regularly but had to make no commitment to the girl. This might be fine for him but it obviously was not for her. In essence he was taking no more responsibility for himself in the relationship than he was for his feelings in therapy.

In the next interview the patient talked about how he wanted to possess a woman—a reference to the exclusivity of the wish for reunion—i.e., nobody exists for mother but me. He had married not only his first, but also his second wife to own her, to make sure no one else got her. "A woman's job is to eliminate conflict for me, not to create conflict. My mother always solved my conflicts at the cost of weakening me. My need is to be taken care of and to possess and not to be on my own."

I used this admission to point out to the patient that when I did not play the role of the mother and solve his problems for him he got furious at me and added that I didn't think that he was as unable as he thought to be on his own, again trying to dramatize and make ego-alien the RORU-pathologic ego alliance. I said I was tired of listening to how tough it was for him and that if he were going to be a man it was time he started acting like one now.

Thirteenth Month

This confrontation overcame Peter's denial as he said, "I have a hard time admitting my life has been a fantasy. I can't stand the need to be taken care of. I'm a liar and a phony. I am the devil and the exorcist both. The devil is in command and the exorcist doesn't fight too hard." Here the patient referred to the pathologic ego not as the creep but as the devil. Following these two interviews he reported the following dream: "I met a beautiful singer and in several days she fell in love with me. It felt good."

Free association: "Complete love from a gorgeous woman made me feel like a man. I created a world that would give me that feeling with everyone. I assume everybody feels about me what I think they're feeling about me—I'm a good guy and they like me but I'm discovering that people are individuals and differ and don't necessarily share my views."

I explained the dream as an effort to fulfill the fantasy of the wish for reunion that was being frustrated in reality; even in fantasy he denied the price of acting out this wish with women, although he was now paying each of his two ex-wives large sums of alimony.

In the next interview the patient reported the condensation of the preoedipal and the oedipal: "I'm more aware of the extent that I live in fantasy and that the need to possess is not love and it started with my mother. Why? My father was reality and negative. My mother was fantasy and fun. As an adolescent I didn't want to screw girls, I wanted to possess; it would be like fucking my mother. I chose my first wife on the same basis. I dated other girls for sex. Sex and a deep relationship were incompatible. When I was ten I got furious at my mother for going out with my father. I was able to listen to them having sexual intercourse on the other side of the wall. I could get anything out of my mother I wanted but I had to pay a price. I couldn't be forthright with her. I had to be a dependent, unhappy little boy. Why do achievements produce anxiety? Because I'm being on my own? Why am I afraid to do what I want to do?"

Peter had been projecting the RORU on to the board of directors of his company. His actions had been motivated by trying to get their approval, completely ignoring the reality of a president-board of directors relationship—that the purpose of the board was to advise and ratify his actions, not to tell him what to do. The patient now went against what he thought was the board's advice and hired a vice president on his own, had a panic attack, thought he was going to have a heart attack that night and took three Valium tablets to go to sleep. In the next interview I again confronted him, pointing out that three Valiums were not enough to help any panic, that he was taking them for psychologic not physiologic reasons, that it seemed to me that he exaggerated his fears as a way to avoid having to deal with them.

In the next interview I discussed the reality of the president-board relationship—that he ran the company and the board was there to approve his decisions, not to make them for him, and that if he did not assume that was so, they would run away with him, that perhaps his being timid and uncertain with them had prompted them to take advantage of him, to haggle over his decisions and frustrate his work. I suggested that the president's job was to educate the board to do what he wanted them to do, again underlining the reality limits of the president-board of directors relationship. The patient replied, "I'm acting like a child with them and I don't have any guts and I can't stand myself."

He was cut off and could express no thoughts in the next interview. I pointed this out as a way of expressing his anger at me for exposing him to anxiety. He replied, "I'm made up of two parts—a child who wants to be taken care of and an adult who wants to get well and grow up. I hate myself for what I have done to women and to my children. I can't stand myself for it."

In the next interview he reported a dream of spiders dying and reaching out to get him and his killing them. Free association: He had a fear of spiders as a child and when he had the tonsillectomy he had dreamed about them. He then reported that the board had approved his vice president after he asserted himself, which made him aware that he had related to them just as he had to women. "I expect them to take care of my problems and turned away from them when they didn't. I can induce anxiety by just thinking about being a man."

Then he became preoccupied that psychotherapy might brainwash him. I interpreted that underneath his fear of being brainwashed was his wish that I would take over his problem for him and brainwash him. I pointed out how his helplessness hampered his mastery of reality—he gives up and says he can't master reality without really trying.

He began the next interview with: "Why should I grow up when I have it so good?" I immediately countered with "That was 'the creep' talking." He replied, "Why isn't Cindy like my ex-wife? Why does she not take care of me the way my ex-wife did?"

Several interviews later he said, "If I'm neither 'the creep' nor the supersalesman, who am I?" He reported a dream. "My father dressed in black, spider-like, cold, came over to me, smothered me. I was helpless. I couldn't fight it. Only my mother could protect me."

Free association: His associations described the complete split between the RORU and the WORU—the omnipotent, all-loving mother and the fearsome, punitive father: "Mother protected me from father's put-downs. I was always afraid my father would throw me out. He could lower the guillotine any time. I dreamed about the spider during the tonsil operation. Dying, being buried, snuffed out. Why couldn't father be a nice guy? Only mother protected me from father."

In the next interview he told about holding on to his girlfriend. I confronted this as the creep's response to the fear he felt in the dream. The patient replied, "The creep was established to make me feel good when I couldn't cope with the reality of my father. Why don't I try to marshal my forces to exorcise the creep, the demon? The creep offers quick relief and I don't recognize the penalty." I pointed out that perhaps the mother encouraged the creep. The patient replied, "Mother said, even if I murdered she would feel the same, she would still love me. But after my father died and I disagreed with her over the running of the company she had me dismissed as president and cut me out of her will." In the 13th month this is the patient's first effort to link the withdrawing object relations unit with his mother—i.e. to undo the defensive splitting and projection of it on to the father.

In the next interview he continued: "My mother didn't talk to me for six to eight months after the incident. She could be vicious if you crossed her. If I told my mother how I felt she would be devastated." I asked why he must lie to his mother or she would be devastated. I pointed out how he had denied this side of her and had never mentioned it before. He continued, "My parents convinced me that they were always doing what was best for me, but made me feel inadequate and guilty. What do I owe them? If I look at the negative side of my mother I will fall apart. There was no love in my family but I denied its absence. I thought I was inadequate and had to pay the price to mother for her support."

Fourteenth Month

Peter then had a dream about being attacked and reported that he allowed the nameless fear to overcome him. I pointed out the relationship of the previous interview to the dream, saying that as he tells his mother and father off here in treatment he dreams of being attacked by the father.

The patient replied, "How would I express this rage I feel? I had this thought but I suppressed it." I pointed out that when he starts to investigate his relationship with his mother and father he gets angry, which leads to fear of being attacked by the father. He replied, "I also suppress my anger at you because I'm afraid you will kick me out."

This confrontation produced further resistance, Peter saying in the next interview, "I was reluctant to come today. I continue to think about my mother and father. I got very anxious and caught myself switching to thoughts about soccer. The anxiety went down; the creep took over. What am I afraid of?"

This led the patient to understand his splitting mechanisms further: He had given the mother the power to protect him from fear, and the father represented fear and death. He couldn't make it with the father; the mother was the only choice. Then he questioned, "Did mother love me?"

This led him to recognize that the only real love he had felt had come from his paternal grandfather who, however, had had a nervous breakdown when Peter was eight and died when he was 12 and who was looked down upon by his own son as being inadequate.

This led him to the awareness: "Home was a prison, love had to be paid for." This confrontation produced resistance: "That thought makes me anxious because I want to say that what I'm thinking isn't real. It's like looking into a dark room; it's frightening. I'd like to scream, 'I'm not going to be what you want me to be, fuck it!' to my father."

I pointed out that there was also mother and that he denied that the price he paid for mother's love was that of being a creep. This led to further exploration of acting out the dependency relationship with the mother, that brought on feelings of inadequacy which, however, were dealt with by getting other people's approval by being a supersalesman or superb soccer player. The patient replied: "There's a small voice inside saying, 'accept me for what I am.' I didn't get love from them then and I want it now from everyone; I want to make everyone into a loving mother and father." I pointed out that nonetheless he did not present his real self to anyone.

In the next two interviews the patient reported: "I bounce between being the creep and Jack Armstrong." He alternates between feelings of inadequacy and defense against them. Peter continued, "It's never me. I can't bolster my own feelings. When I don't have anyone to depend on I'm depressed. I'm furious at you." I said, "For not functioning for you like the mother did?"

He replied, "I don't have my heart in supporting myself." This led to an outburst of rage when the patient got home after the interview: "I got drunk and wanted to bash my face in the mirror. I had the urge to call my mother but I curbed it and I got drunker. I recognize that I'm so dependent on others to make myself feel good I don't even try to be myself. I felt guilty about not calling my mother."

I pointed out that he used guilt to serve the acting out of his dependency, that his real guilt was over why he did not want to call his mother. The patient replied, "I'm not really interested in her or my ex-wife, but I want to avoid the guilt feelings so I act like the good all-American boy with them. Mother and father both put me down but mother offered a way out. She was the only source of sunshine. In our family you got attention for being down and depressed and were put down for feeling good."

Following this interview the patient had an abandonment panic attack complete with chest pains and somatic preoccupation and did not want to come back to the next interview. He asked himself, "Why? Something's happening here and I don't like the trail we're going down. I'm having to get off my ass and give up my dependency. I get mad at thinking about it. Makes me feel inadequate." Then he switched and said, "Suppose I'm being brainwashed? Suppose you don't know what's best? Suppose I die?" I pointed out that this was the creep talking.

In the next interview he resumed analysis, talking about how he felt down and gloomy the way he always had felt at home when he was growing up. He recalled that mother was lighthearted during the day but gloomy when the father came home at night. "The whole family was serious, life was tough, awful things had happened. I got help for being down, not for fun or good ideas. There are now two alternatives: gloom, dependency and the creep or the new one of being myself. Now I feel as if I'm walking through molasses."

Following this interview he was obviously relieved, his self image emerged and he departed from his usual compulsive working habits, took the day off, went to see Cindy, had intercourse with her, which was followed by an anxiety attack, "because I was doing what I wanted. I wanted to stay overnight with her, not because I wanted to be with her but because I did not want to be alone. I was panicky but she confronted me. I decided to face it and went home with my heart racing. I sat down to watch television and saw the movie *In Cold Blood* and had another panic attack and when I went to sleep I had two dreams."

Dream 1: "I was visiting a state prison or a mental hospital as a VIP. I was fearful. I saw a huge Black being forced into a harness to be studied, to have an electroencephalogram, and I felt sorry for him and gave him a handshake. Then I saw some girls being undressed also to have an EEG. One of the guards was leering and wanted to rape one of the girls and I was repelled."

Dream 2: "I was asleep in my bed at home about 3 o'clock in the morning. Some tourists were walking all over my property.

They were lost. They started to take over my house and I erupted in a rage at them. You were there and allowed me to demonstrate the rage. I told them to get out. Then I saw blood on the bed and there was a cut at the root of my penis and I wanted to ask you if I could still use it."

Free association: "It all comes from the movie. I was afraid that what happened to those men might happen to me. There was as much fear of the executioner as of the murderer—the methodical way they executed the murderers just as methodically as the murderers killed their victims. They were placed in the harness which was in the dream and in this helpless condition they were hanged. If you resent someone you will kill them. The feeling of sexual arousal is close to the feeling of resentment. It's like rape; it's animalistic. My second wife wanted to be raped. It was a hostile act."

The dream links his association of sex with aggression and the condensing of separation anxiety and castration anxiety.

The patient continued to report fear in his next interview: "Makes me want to stand still." He recalled an incident in college when he had committed a prank at another school and had been chased by the students, caught by the cops and put in jail. He was afraid of being killed that time. He turned to me and said, "Why can't you tell me what the fear is about?" I suggested to him that he was asking me if he had to go all the way himself. The patient replied, "How could I let them do it to me? Why didn't I do something? They're not going to get me. When you're bound and gagged you are dead."

In the next interview the patient was reporting fear but said he was cut off and angry. I suggested the anger was at having to act on his own, but he expressed the anger by cutting off and arguing with me about money and time.

Peter's anger was a projection of the WORU on me—i.e., his father—which had always been his way of handling fear, but he split off and denied the feelings of inadequacy associated with the acting out.

At the next interview he reported further resistance, "I've been thinking again about seeing my ex-wife; anything is better than acting on my own. I'm infuriated by anything that shoves me in that direction." The patient then said, "OK, hang me and be done with it."

I again pointed out that there seemed to be three alternatives for him: either acting out the dependency on the mother; fighting me; or being hung. There has to be another alternative, which is analysis. The patient replied, "Letting go is like falling through the trap, like sitting in the executioner's chair. I have to go through it and I feel helpless. Save me! This interview is effeminate, like being with my mother, you want me to say certain things."

The resistance continued in the next session, the patient talking about how he didn't use his self for anything, took the path of least resistance.

In the following session the patient told about a dream of which all he remembered was feeling good and another dream: "I had to beat someone up and knock them out. I didn't want to but I did it."

He then reported an oedipal fantasy of undressing my secretary, feeling that the thoughts were childish. I pointed out that the thoughts were quite adult. He replied, "Sex was never discussed at home. When I was ten I told my mother that a boy told me that she fucked and that I came from that." He reacted to this information with a feeling of abandonment. "I couldn't handle it. Mother had always stressed closeness. It made me realize I didn't have mother's complete attention. I knew it was dirty. I couldn't understand why she let him do that to her."

Here again the two levels combine: the separation-individuation and the oedipal. The patient's rage at the mother not only for abandonment—i.e., their relationship was not exclusive—but also for choosing the father in preference to him.

Fifteenth Month

In the first interview of this month the patient again reported urges to call his ex-wife and inability to accept the idea of his mother giving herself to the father. He felt sexual thoughts were dirty. He mentioned seeing his mother for lunch. She had dangled money in front of him if he'd play the game and attacked his therapy. "I didn't respond except to say 'bullshit' to myself."

The next two interviews were filled with resistance, the patient saying he couldn't talk about sex feelings with me. He then told of a sexual fantasy of making love to several women, all of whom said they wanted only him, which I interpreted as "total possession." In the next interview the patient reported that for him sex represented being a man—possession as well as pleasure—that actually a man meant self control, not crying or screwing women, and not needing the mother. He then discussed his two sons, 15 and 13, who live with his first wife, and wondered if they were as anxious about their masculinity as he was.

To reinforce his capacity to cope with fear I pointed out that he had wanted to be a soccer player and had been willing to pay the price to do that; if he wanted to be a man in therapy he would have to learn to master his emotions here and accept the price, but part of him doesn't want to do that. In the next interview he discussed two homosexual mutual masturbation episodes at 10 and 16 which cast doubt on his masculinity, as well as two dreams:

Dream 1: "Boy dressed as a girl was giving me a blow job and it turned out to be my brother and repelled me. My mother lectured me and I got angry."

Dream 2: "My ex-wife wanted me to screw her on the old terms and I didn't want to."

Free association: "Leave me alone; my mother and ex-wife are trying to get me through sex." He continued with the sexual fantasy of "women wanting me to fuck them. It's not my initiative. They don't want it as much as I do and don't have the same need. I'm trying to prove myself to women but also to my self. If I really loved a woman, I couldn't fuck her. I was afraid of women I wanted to screw. Why do I feel sex is wrong? The only time I feel free is when I'm cooking or playing the saxophone." He continued, "I like to fuck women but I hate them."

I pointed out that he takes pleasure from women, feels guilty, then has to give them something to relieve the guilt. After this interview the patient's anxiety increased and he returned saying, "I can't believe my childhood was that bad. I tried to make wrong things right. There's an unwillingness to let go of the myth and the fantasy about the family." I pointed out "and about yourself as well." In the next interview the patient told how the mother had called him and objected to the way psychiatry was making a different man out of him. He later dreamed of the mother saying, "You can't let go of me like this" and then had the following dream: "Cindy's husband was angry at me for breaking up his family. I realized he had another wife and he was a bigamist; then the dream changed to my father who looked terrible and died."

Free association: "My father was silent for days when he was angry. He told me never to show emotion. He gave me the cold treatment." At this point the patient blocked out and then turned to ask me about taking a vacation to provoke a fight so he could express the anger at me rather than at his father. In the next interview he described another dream: "I was putting my son on a train. I felt sorry for him and for myself. I was both people. My son was trying to make believe everything was okay but I felt his anxiety and his rejection."

Free association: "My father rejected me completely when he was silent. The next morning my ex-wife called to tell me she was getting married and I had a sinking feeling and thought, 'How could she do this to me?' Rejecting, losing, being put out of her life. I worked so hard for my father's love but was always rejected. I thought, 'What do I have to do to please you?' If I leave mother all I have is myself, a weakness. I broke into tears and rage, felt maudlin and self-pitying." In the next three interviews resistance mounted. He had gotten a final divorce from his second wife: "I can't stand the freedom, I'm fighting with becoming myself. Even the creep is not as strong. Maybe I'm not ready. When do I feel good about being independent?"

In the next interview I reminded the patient that the mother and father had a compromise agreement of which he seemed to be a vital part; the family myth was that the father was a SOB but everyone tried to conceal this fact. Peter replied: "I got to thinking about it and felt it was true and then thought what was I doing? My father was going to get me for thinking this way when I get to heaven. If father deprived me of anything it was love."

Sixteenth Month

The patient remembered that the family system protected him from fear and again reported that Cindy had confronted him that he didn't care about her. At this point I defined the two levels of the relationship with Cindy: what went on between them and what went on in his head. I suggested that perhaps he did not love her since he wished to use her for defensive purposes. In the next interview he continued: "Why don't I feel about women and think only about self? It goes back to my relationship with mother."

I pointed out that the contract with the mother was based on meeting each other's needs, that feeling was irrelevant because it might screw up the contract, that rules were used instead of feelings. He replied, "I was deemed thoughtless by my mother and father. Thoughtfulness was doing what the other person wanted. It never came out of yourself."

I pointed out that in his family obligation was substituted for love and rationalized as being thoughtfulness. I gave an example of the behavior of a loving father by recalling a TV story he had mentioned previously, underlying those actions of the father that were expressions of love and then contrasted this model with the behavior of his father. The patient replied, "My parents were supposed to have this great love but when my father stayed home for one year after a heart attack my mother was driven up the wall. He was a burden to her." I pointed out how the parents concealed their inability to love behind obligation which was then rationalized as love.

I had to cancel the next two sessions because I was ill and

during this time the patient reported being more anxious and depressed and calling his mother who was very cool to him. "I'm afraid she could do something to me. I have no needs that she could satisfy now but the fear persists. She could love me or take me to a place where I was afraid. She could have my tonsils taken out. When I was 15 I lost my temper at my mother when she called a girl to cancel my date because I had a cold."

He then told about a dream of a very social interview with me which felt good and in the dream he called his mother to tell her to stop in to see me. I interpreted these as reactions to my interrupting the continuity of the sessions. He also reported having gotten drunk on one night.

In the next interview Peter admitted that he allowed a board member to push him into calling a meeting to re-evaluate a decision he'd already made. When the patient realized his mistake he called the meeting off: "I immediately felt something terrible would happen and I thought of having intercourse with my ex-wife and then that I might get a heart attack." He said in exasperation: "I have to realize nothing will happen."

I pointed out that the somatization of the separation anxiety in the form of the heart attack prevented him from mastering it. The patient replied, "I had the tonsillectomy after the time I was playing with the girl next door. Maybe I thought my mother had me operated on for that reason." I pointed out that this perhaps was another externalization. The patient replied, "I never had the feeling that mother and father cared about me. I had to negotiate and deal with them for love. I got it from soccer coaches and I broke my ass for them. My stomach is upset right now. I can't get that feeling from mother and father. I feel scared and pissed off at myself."

I pointed out that the deals he made with his mother and father were to avoid feelings of hopelessness about getting their love. He answered, "I don't face that I'm never going to get it and I feel both sad and angry."

By the next interview the patient told how the "connector" had taken over at a party and he had turned into supersalesman in order to get approval and relieve the sadness and anger he had felt in the interview: "I don't want to look under the surface of mother's behavior."

In the very next interview the patient reported the following nightmares: "I was in a room with roaches which were alive. I was supposed to carry them out but was horrified. I lay down and they came for me. I saw three spiders under the table and was petrified. The room was strewn with corpses. One of the corpses had hands around my throat. I woke up screaming. One of the corpses had the face of the board member whom I referred to the other day. Then I had a second dream. It was in a war, attacking through mine fields, walking over dead bodies, and then I was walking with my ex-wife's boyfriend and asked if they were married. He said, 'No.' "

Free association: "I'm afraid of looking under the table, of standing up to the people like the board members. They might strangle me." I interpreted that he looked beneath the surface of the mother's behavior and became afraid he would be strangled. The patient replied, "Fear is used to make the other things work. Fear makes the system go." I pointed out, "You mean the deal with mother." He answered, "Mother and father both used fear to establish the system. If I complied with their wishes it banished the fear. Why don't I want to look at the spiders under the table? Mother used emotional distress to get at me. She fainted once before I was to be married. Am I opening up a Pandora's Box? Before mother kicked me off the board I had stopped talking about her and excluded her from my feelings. This was her way of getting back at me. To look at mother means being independent. Mother's message is 'love me.' I wanted her to love me for what I am. But people don't cut off contact with their mothers even when they don't give love, do they?"

SUMMARY

Confrontations of the destructive effect of the pathologic ego-RORU alliance make it more and more alien and promote more and more control of the acting out. This activates the WORU with its abandonment depression and allows the patient to become aware of the former as a defense against the latter. This awareness reinforces the therapeutic need to control the acting out, which plunges the patient deeper into his abandonment depression (WORU), which again produces resistance (sleepiness, cutting off of feelings), but now these resistances are present in the interview and can be pointed out as defenses against the abandonment depression. While still struggling between resistance and working-through, Peter makes the first link between his abandonment depression and the negative image of the mother that had previously been projected on the father.

The patient is now poised between regressing and acting out and going forward and working-through. A key resistance is his projection of the abandonment depression on reality—i.e., if he goes forward in therapy (or separates and individuates) he will indeed die. It is essential for the therapist to set reality limits to the patient's fear at this point by pointing out that although the patient feels there are only two alternatives—the RORU-pathologic ego alliance or the WORU—the creep or death—there is in reality a third alternative—analysis of the WORU and growth through separation-individuation. This reassurance leads again to further working-through. There is continued shifting back and forth between growth and resistance (RORU), but the momentum has now slowly transferred from resistance to working-through.

12

Abandonment Depression:

"If She Dies, I Will Die"

Peter now works through the past over and over in his interviews, confronting his rage and depression, becoming afraid of being attacked and/or abandoned, but nevertheless working through more than acting out. He is undoing the split between the RORU and WORU. Resistance appears at each step and must be confronted constantly. In the next interview, in response to the previous dream (in which he was in a room full of roaches with three spiders under the table), the patient reported, "I'm afraid I'm going to have to confront my mother head on. Face the spider. Tell her I don't want her to stay.

"After the last interview I knew I'd have to take action in order to break the chain. Coming here today I thought about asking you for a cigar. If you say yes, you're my mother; if you say no, it's my father. I could get angry at you. After the interview I thought my mother might call and I would have to say something. Will I be honest or look for sympathy and play the game? Since my father died eight years ago mother has invited me to her house only three times. I'd like to cut the cord without pain but I feel panic and death, no one to love me."

Before the next interview he acted out the conflict with the mother with his girlfriend, demanding, "Love me as I am, accept me for what I am." The patient recognized this and continued by describing his need for the splitting defense, "Anger at my mother would wipe out the last connection. It's the last safe place. I can't cope with my mother. It's blasphemous. I expect to be struck down by lightning. Honor thy mother and father. I cut off all feeling with her in order to be able to play the game. I deny that she could be cold and calculating. If you don't play the game she can cut your balls off, wipe you out, exclude you."

Peter continued in the next session, "I called mother and she was absolutely cold, monosyllabic and annoyed. I didn't play the game. I told her communication was a two-way affair. Afterward I had the worst anxiety attack of my life and thought I might faint.

"My childhood was filled with darkness and gloom, being threatened with being left in an orphanage if I wasn't good. When I was nine I saw my grandfather in a state hospital crying; he had done something wrong. When I was ten, I saw a funeral of a girl who had died of tonsillitis; she'd done something wrong. With my mother if I don't perform, no love. She doesn't give a shit for me. If I don't conform I could die. Constantly lying, playing the game out of fear. Mother tells me that for the first time she takes my first wife's part and says she might be spiteful. Meaning if I don't play the game my mother might be spiteful with me. After the phone call I had a fantasy that Blacks may attack us on the beach. That something awful would happen and right now I feel like begging God for forgiveness. I live in fear. My mother was as bad as my father."

In the next interview the patient reported having asserted himself with the board and again feeling anxious that if he didn't play the game their way, they would wipe him out. Then he described the following dream:

"I was my present age. I was taking my son to a military school but it was my brother. I was also enrolled. I wanted to start life all over again but realized I couldn't."

I suggested that the dream was to get away from the conflict with my mother; he couldn't prevent externalizing the conflict with the mother on others because he didn't face it in his own head. When he worried about the board member being hurt or kicking him out he ignored the reality.

In the next interview the patient was blocked, had called his mother and brother and spoken to them—"the family's voice of doom"—and asked, "When will I accept that I am right and they are wrong and stop living just for the day?" Peter recognized that he was blocking out feeling.

The next interview was a truly prophetic one. He began by announcing that he was going to force the board members to resign and get a new board even if it took a proxy fight—a marked departure in the direction of self assertion from his prior compliant behavior with the board. He then reported having had the following two dreams.

Dream 1: "People are chasing me to murder me like in a movie but after it was over it started again from the beginning. Since I knew what was going to happen I changed the ending. I grabbed the people and threw them out the window."

Dream 2: "I was in your office but it was also my own home and Cindy was with us. I decided to talk out our problems with real love and wanted your approval of our relationship."

Free association: "I have to keep seeing you to recharge my efforts to be myself. I'm getting here what I didn't get from my mother and father. Approval for being myself. Don't want to keep coming here forever." At this point he cannot emotionally invest his self image but must use the transference instead.

I pointed out that he does not seem to be able to see the possibility of having a real ego autonomy and being able to express himself without the need for anyone else's approval. In the next interview the separation-individuation conflict was again re-enacted. The patient demonstrated more self assertion by doing well in his meeting with the board but again he woke up that night in a panic and reported that he felt flat and depressed after his victory over the board. Follow this episode he had thoughts about asking his mother over for dinner. He linked these feelings with his self assertion and said that he had wanted his mother over to dinner to stop the progress of his therapy. He underlined that he was changing and now wanted treatment but questioned how he would get independent from me. I questioned, "Why does self assertion bring on panic rather than gratification?"

Seventeenth Month

In the next two interviews the patient revealed that his self assertion was emerging more but that he tended to cut off feeling in order to deal with the anxiety involved, recalling two examples where he expressed himself, did not cut off feelings and held on to both feeling and anxiety. "I gave a talk to 320 employees. I felt myself getting panicky but I followed through, gave the speech and felt great and knew it was good. I had enjoyed being myself. However, that night I dreamed that an executive who had complimented me on the speech was actually putting me down. The next day Cindy told me my mother had called and I changed back into my old pattern of pleasing. That night I had several dreams."

Dream: "I was caught in a rose bush being attacked by spiders as I tried to go back to the doctor's office to get my 'juice.'"

Prior dream: "I'm 250 feet in the air after surging up through some water and I start down again towards a swimming pool. I'm afraid I will just keep going up and down. I thought if somebody would only put a net over the pool it would stop it."

Following dream: "I'm with my two best friends and my mother. My mother puts down what they are talking about. She's a real stoneface. I manage to please both my mother and the friends. Then a kid was there punching his mother in the face and I wandered away. I woke up with anxiety, chest pains, abdominal pains."

Free associations: "When I assert myself—when I change from other-motivated to self-motivated behavior—spiders attack me. I'm caught in a bind. If I express myself I get terribly anxious. If I don't I can't live with myself. Mother was a stoneface." In the next interview the patient reported another dream. "I'm in my house with Cindy. My ex-wife comes in and I feel guilty. I introduce them and sparks fly; my boys are there and feel uncomfortable. I put my arm around all of them saying we have to get along."

Free association: "I'm cut off today." I interpreted that the dream was an answer to the confrontation with the mother's stoneface—i.e., he was saying, "Let's all get along," attempting to deny the mother's stoneface. He replied: "I had been thinking about mother and money. I resent that I have to go down on my knees for her, that she is a whore and a bitch. I felt as if I were being suffocated after the tonsil operation. If I didn't like her, why didn't I like her? She's cruel, she lies, is devious, doesn't care for me and wants pity."

In the next interview the patient continued to be filled with rage, reported having had dreams about women, spiders and a dream about soccer. The previous night he had thought: "Why can't I have a girl who accepts me as I am?" He then related a story in which he was tempted to demand from his mother the money that he needed to pay for his divorce. I pointed out that he is attempting to act out with the mother the problem that arose here—i.e., his rage at having literally to get on his knees to have his needs met by her.

In the next interview the patient reported having called his mother and listened to her express her fear that he was moving away from her. He questioned: "Why did I call? The rage and resentment are eating me up, my stomach is very upset." I pointed out that I thought he had called to deal with the fear of his anger at his mother. He replied that if he ever expressed anger at home he got a strange look from his mother as if he were wrong or crazy; he had had a terrible temper but by the age of 13 he had it under control.

In the next interview he reported a dream.

Dream: "Mother was acting as my lover, not my mother. She was crying that I was leaving her. I felt it as a drag, a handle, a noose."

Free association: "Mother looked upon me as a lover, substituting for father when he wasn't there. I'm trapped, she has me on a rope. I'd like to say in anger 'I'm not your lover or confidant.' I don't want that role. My mother, however, treats my brother more like a son." He then reported a second dream.

Dream: "You were very upset and started to cry. You said you couldn't take all these pressures of residents not liking you and I commiserated with you and then you changed into a woman. I went over to comfort you-her, kissed her, didn't want to get involved. Wanted to get out."

In the dream he portrays me as expecting him to play the same role with me as he had with his mother—suppressing himself in order to fulfill her needs for support. I suggested further that his desire to not get involved was a defense against his feelings that if he got involved it meant either playing the role and consequent loss of self or abandonment by the other person if he didn't play the role. In other words, involvement could only lead to disaster— loss of self or loss of the object.

I suggested that he handled these feelings about involvement with people by keeping his emotions uninvolved while he at the same time manipulated the other person by his charming, eager to please, supersalesman behavior into fulfilling his needs. This created an illusion of a close relationship which in reality was based upon a manipulation.

In the next interview he had another dream to tell about:

Dream: "There was a woman who was a combination of my mother and my first and second wives. This woman was in bed with me and she had a stroke. I called our soccer doctor who said she hadn't had a stroke at all. I said, 'What is this?' The feeling was that she could have a stroke any time."

Free association: "My doctor had told me the day before that his wife had had a stroke. My second wife had hung on to me with threats of strokes or of leaving me. The idea of getting close really upsets me. I have to relive being a child, but don't want to. I'm afraid of your leaving me. I had great practice with mother finding out what button turned her on. Opening up is like going back to the operating room."

I pointed out that the patient today is cut off from feelings and tends to intellectualize rather than report feelings. He responded, "Why do I have to get close, why can't I stay at a safe distance? What do you want of me? Why don't I want to feel, cry, get angry, have true spontaneous emotions? I cut it off a long time ago and I was humiliated."

I pointed out to Peter that he expressed anger at his mother's demand for closeness by withholding feeling and playing a role. He replied, "When father beat me up at age ten I turned off all feeling. It was humiliating. You'd never catch me crying, feeling, getting mad—not since I turned into supersalesman, soccer player, bullshit artist."

In the next interview the theme of fear of closeness persisted: "To be close I have to give up my self completely, like death, drowning, infinity." I interpreted to the patient that he withheld feeling from his mother to preserve his self from engulfment. On the other hand, if he expressed himself he would be abandoned (loss of self vs. loss of the object). At the next interview the patient had experimented with expressing feelings, but this was followed by fear of loss of control, a fear of letting go, of being close, of having to get down on his knees and beg and give up his self.

In this interview the patient reported having confronted his mother for the first time. He called her to tell her he was going away on a trip. She was upset and said she felt she was dying, because he was leaving her: "I said I'd come over. When I got there she was OK. She asked me why I didn't call; I said I couldn't explain all that was going on. She attacked my treatment. I told her my difficulties had to do with the past and her; she didn't accept me as I was, was vindictive. She got very angry. I told her she used me to fill the void in her life. I wanted to be myself. She replied that I wanted to be thoughtless and cruel. She said that when she gets angry she withdraws, which to me meant leaving me. I got angry but was tentative about it. She said she felt abandoned. I didn't like her. I'm so different from the three of them. It's as if I didn't come from that family. I'm a piece of shit to fit her convenience and make her feel good. Today my stomach is very upset and I'm still fighting doing the job here."

In some respects the patient confronted his mother to avoid the rage expressed in therapy. In the next interview the patient was anxious, and following the confrontation with the mother he had become very doubtful of himself, worried about closing off feeling, worried that something bad would happen to him. This was symbolized by his saying to me that he was worried that something bad might happen on his vacation—his plane might crash or he might have a heart attack. I confronted him saying, "Yes, indeed, something bad may well happen, you might have a good time," making the point that he should not externalize his anxiety but should try and control it. He returned a week later with evidence of a stronger, more continuous self-maturation: "I had a ball. I recognized for the first time that all the fears were in my head which led to an awareness of how much my behavior was motivated by the need to please others; I tried to control it."

The patient became aware that he was projecting the WORU on people and trying to please them in order to relieve his feelings of inadequacy and anxiety about autonomy. He then had two dreams of my rejecting him which I interpreted as follows: If he tries to be independent I will reject and push him away and push my needs on him just as the mother had.

In the next interview he was again depressed, doubting his self assertion; either the vacation was unreal or the depression is unreal. I pointed out this example of his splitting—that both are real, that he individuates and on return feels an abandonment depression but his resistance to becoming aware of the relationship between the two—the tie that binds—increases because it means the recognition of the withdrawing mother and homicidal rage. The patient replied: "Feeling and self expression are unreal; not feeling and supersalesman are real."

I pointed out that he was angry at me for making it possible for him to be himself and enjoy it, thereby exposing him to separation anxiety. He expected me to disapprove of his being himself as his father and mother had, then got angry and anxious and handled these feelings by regressing to the supersalesman.

Eighteenth Month

The patient reported that when he called his mother she had been angry and withdrawn. He was not angry in return because he had expected it but he had turned off feeling, had made good business decisions, but started to put himself down. I pointed out that after self expression he puts himself down as his parents had put him down to deal with his anger and he would either have to get the anger out here or continue to put himself down. The patient replied, "You and Cindy accept me for what I am; that's love. I don't want to accept it. Why? Because I get angry?"

I pointed out that there are two parts to himself: 1) The reality ego is realistic and has to do with expression of himself. It was revealed on his vacation. 2) The other side is identification with his parents. This then takes over like the devil and exorcist and makes Cindy and myself the enemies, causing anger.

The patient replied: "The metamorphosis is incredible. Last week I was thinking positively about the future, this week I don't even want to think about it." I interpreted the splitting by pointing out that it was the real self which triggered the devil which in turn caused him to suppress the real self, and that he must become aware of the triggering mechanism.

In the next interview he talked about a repetition of the above events. He called his mother to invite her to dinner. She was angry and disapproving and the patient afterwards felt depressed and heard a voice saying, "Who am I trying to kid? I'd like to explode." The patient became aware that he cannot accept the fact that his mother didn't love him as he was and she will not change. "I can't stand my own need to be loved; I'm mad at it."

I interpreted that the patient defended himself against the feelings of abandonment by acting out the wish for reunion, thereby feeling good at the cost of destructive behavior, i.e., prostituting himself. The patient replied, "Today I'm having depressed fantasies about what's the point of living. Why live?"

In the next interview the patient reported the following dream:

Dream: "I was calling on a customer, a woman, who didn't like her boss and was going to get him fired. The more I supported him the angrier she got. I struggled to negotiate between the two. I went into the bathroom and my three fingers turned black and I began to worry about getting a heart attack and then blood gushed all over the floor out of my fingers. I cleaned it up. The scene shifts to a male customer and I'm late for an appointment. He wanted me to have lunch and then to return for dinner and I planned to spend the evening with Cindy. She told me to do what I wanted and I'm in conflict. Finally I tell him and he says OK, just like mother."

Free association: "The burden is my prostituting myself, by negotiating I give up my self and die." I pointed out he was now dreaming what he used to act out—the wish for reunion. I asked if his mother always idealized the father to him? He replied "No, she was fun loving, he was not. They disagreed." He questioned, "Was father the bastard I thought? At least he was honest. I knew where I stood. I knew he didn't like me. There must have been a time when I felt depressed as a kid. To overcome the depression was love.

"On airplane flights I fantasied romance with stewardesses to the music of 'This Time We Almost Made It' when actually I was seeking relief from depression."

He then delved deeper into his abandonment depression: "At some point I realized the dishonesty of the game between mother and father. Kids know when they are being lied to. The longing, the loneliness, the sadness were always there. I got angry at my mother for going out with my father or when my brother was born and I wasn't the only thing in the world. I had no love for father so I was dependent completely on mother. I was afraid of him from age four. No memories of playing with him except one of flying a kite. By age eight I was supersalesman. At five in the basement of an abandoned house next door I saw a couple having sexual intercourse. It could have been either my mother or father's sister who lived with us. The man was father's sister's date. I can remember details of the hospital when my brother was born."

In the next interview the patient reported having acted out with Cindy his rage at the mother for having to share his exclusive relationship with her with the father and brother. He provoked Cindy by telling her he would not take her children to a ball game with his children and later got drunk and flew into a rage at her for talking about her first husband and her interest in her children. He then had the following dream.

Dream: "I'm in your office with your daughter of 14. You were pleased about it, but I was inhibited. You suggested we play ping-pong. You were there with your sons and you had a good relationship with them." I interpreted the acting out with Cindy to be the rage at the frustration of the exclusive relationship with the mother.

In the next interview the patient told of having lost his erection when having sex, that he was pulling himself out of the act, feeling anxious and insecure, having thoughts about calling the mother. Then he reported the following dream.

Dream: "My mother attacked me for treating my brother badly."

Free association: "I'm confused about what I know about her and how society would view it. Why do I pull out of making love? It's related to the anger. The devil was the one who fucked. I gave up self to fuck my ex-wife." I suggested that perhaps he used sex to be a supersalesman in bed. He reported a dream in the next interview.

Dream: "I feel frustrated. I'm stuck at my old college, there's no plane out and no way out."

Free association: "The real bitch was the grandmother not the mother. I feel myself turning off. Thinking my first and second wives did like me."

Resistance continued in the next interview, the patient saying, "My father is dead, my mother will never accept me as I am. I'm all alone. Mother would never accept me for doing things myself. I don't feel. I don't want to see Cindy. I'd rather go to bed. As a kid, mother and God were there to take care of me."

I pointed out the two things that had triggered this response: 1) expressing himself; and 2) getting close to his anger at his mother. He replied, "Mother thinks I'm a SOB. She thrives on misery." I pointed out that he reacted to me in the same manner as to his mother—i.e., as if I could not accept anger. He replied, "I'm beginning to worry about your going away."

The next interview involved a long discussion of the patient's reluctance to change lawyers in order to alter an unfair divorce settlement, saying he didn't know his lawyer was only good for real estate but not for divorce work and he didn't fire him because he was afraid of the lawyer's disapproval. In actual fact his passivity allowed the lawyer to take advantage of him. The lawyer seemed more interested in getting the settlement concluded and out of the way than in pursuing his client's best interest. He even let the patient do the actual negotiations.

The next two interviews were taken up with how Peter again felt good in expressing himself and then became frightened that something awful might happen. In the next interview he recalled, "Mother took care of all my problems. She was omnipotent. The connection with mother saved me from death."

He saw the movie "Battle Ground" in which a soldier is shot, and the last word he screamed out was "mommy." I pointed out that he split the good mother from the bad mother and denied the latter and his resistance to treatment came from his need to deny the latter. He answered, "I couldn't stand mother's being depressed and complaining. My responsibility was to undo it for the whole family. I was to play the fool." I pointed out how he was assigned that role and at the same time put down for playing it. He replied, "I was called on to perform for visitors. Say something funny, had to do it to survive. Carrot and stick. She imposed a fear that something awful would happen if I didn't perform.

I was about to take off for a week's winter vacation. The patient cut off feeling in the next interview, saying, "I'm closing down the furnace, I'm scared, it's either connection or death. I feel helpless. If you leave me I will die. I'm not a man, I'm a baby. My first loss was my brother's birth at two. I wanted total love and dedication. When I expressed myself my mother turned against me. I stopped growing."

Nineteenth Month

When I returned a week later Peter said he had cut off feeling, had been depressed and had the following dream: "I'm stuck in the elevator and can't go up to the fourth floor to see my mother. I am glad I don't have to see her."

Free association: "It's where I am now. I'm cut off completely." I asked, "Did my trip affect this?" "Of course," the patient replied, "You let me down by going away. Dependency is awful. I can't stand these feelings so I block out all feelings. I'm angry, I don't want to repeat the dependency on my mother with you."

An encounter with the mother was described in the next interview: "I called my mother who said she was dying. She saw her doctor because she was dizzy and faint and he said she had high blood pressure. She came to see me and told me she had gone through hell since I last spoke to her. I told her my objections about some of the ways she's treated me in the past and I felt nothing for her right now. Mother told me she had cried, felt I was leaving her, abandoning her. I kept asserting myself in a matter-of-fact way. She offered me money and I turned it down but then she left, saying she felt better.

"I didn't play the game in action but I still felt like a child. Today I'm depressed, tired, feel lost and defeated. I didn't get that unconditional love and acceptance for myself but I denied that I was not getting it."

I pointed out that the patient substituted a fantasy for this reality: He denied the reality of a WORU and substituted a fantasy of the wish for reunion which he acted out with other women. He replied, "Mother's feeding me with that money and playing the game pissed me off after all I'd said."

The patient's ex-wife now demanded more money for the divorce settlement and he got furious, acting out on her the rage that he was unable to express to his mother: "I wish that mother and everyone, even my ex-wife, would accept me as I am. I'm mad that I was forced to play the game and mother still thinks I'm an idiot and will conform. The rage is of the worst order. You can't treat me this way. You can't force me. I'm not going to do it anymore. I really don't like my mother. She's so distant and shows no real concern."

When I pointed out the conflict, the rage and the need for total acceptance the patient blocked for a while and turned and asked me to give him a match for a cigar. This raised an issue we had discussed a number of times—I did not carry matches and if he wanted to smoke in interviews he should bring his own. Therefore, I refused, after which he acted out in the transference the rage at the mother. He returned to the next interview in a rage at me for not giving him the match. I pointed out that this was transference acting out, that he was acting out at me his rage at the mother's conditions. He should remember that we had several times discussed the need for him to bring his own matches if he wanted to smoke.

The patient replied, "I have been playing the game here with you about the matches." I underlined that he wanted from me what he wanted from his mother: unconditional acceptance. Since no matches are a condition he reenacted the battle with the mother with me; instead of being small, helpless, humiliated and dependent, he was strong and angry and wanted to hit me and walk out.

I questioned why he had never expressed that anger with the mother and he said, "I was afraid she'd leave me, abandon me. She loved my father and brother more than me."

In the meantime he'd contacted another lawyer and made arrangements to get a better settlement with his ex-wife. Before the next interview Peter had a dream that his mother had come into his room and had moved the nightstand around so that the two beds could be close together. In the dream he felt annoyed by her action.

Free association: "I ran to mother to avoid death and the infinity feeling. My lack of development was due to avoiding any feeling that wasn't good." He reported increasing depression and suicidal fantasies; he felt like an empty bag. A second dream was then described.

Dream: "I'm in a crummy hotel and a girl is trying to make me. I'm afraid to respond as my mother, my first wife, my second wife and Cindy are in there. Then it switches to beautiful scenes of Colorado but here in New York City. My first mother-in-law, whom I loved, is with me."

Free association: "My mother called to tell me that she still loved me but still had the blood pressure symptoms. I began to think that I'm not going to see you four times a week to infinity and death."

I pointed out that the patient was saying that if he continued with me the way he had been he would die. He did not distinguish between these feelings and reality and did not perceive that the need to avoid these feelings about dying caused his developmental disorder, that he cut off feeling, turned to the mother as an omnipotent person to relieve it and therefore didn't grow and remained dependent.

The patient responded with his first memory of the feeling of dying at age eight when he was running to play basketball, knew he was going to die, panicked and ran back to his mother for reassurance. Mother told him the story that the soul lives on, that it lived on with those left behind. He thought, "What happens to me?" He continued, "I was such a good kid and they didn't see it. All the good things in me were lost. They gave no muscle to my character. If I'm successful in treatment I will die."

Peter's way of dealing with his feelings of abandonment was

reported in the next interview: "Every morning I have to start filling the vacuum. By evening it's OK but I feel nothing. It's like filling a bucket with sand and there's a hole in the bottom. I was a good kid but had the image of myself as bad. I have a fear of being disconnected, of being nothing, not feeling, don't want to feel here."

I interpreted that he reacted to the therapeutic necessity to feel as a demand of the mother's that made him angry, which he expressed here as he did there by not feeling. He replied that he had a fear of all doctors ever since the tonsillectomy. They were the instrument of death.

He reported tales of minor acting out around age four, such as putting a caterpillar down a girl's neck, and setting a fire in the adjacent lot, which the mother condemned as mortal sins.

The patient reported in the next interview being in touch with his earliest feelings of abandonment: "I feel this! Please don't hurt me, I'll be a good boy, don't reject me, don't throw me into infinity. I'm afraid I could panic and be helpless. Tonsils was the first panic; I knew something bad would happen. I wasn't told anything about it beforehand. The cloth was put over my face. My mother was squeezing my hand, then she left, the cloth remained. I saw this huge light surrounded by people with masks. I sat up and said, 'Please don't hurt me.' They held me down under anesthesia. I dreamed about the spiders. I woke up feeling lied to. How could she do that to me? She had the power."

I pointed out that it seemed that without any knowledge about what the operation was all about the patient had felt it as a punishment by his mother for being a bad boy.

He returned to the next interview with two dreams.

Dream 1: Again it is a soccer dream where he recognizes that he's now 46 years old and can no longer play, i.e., can no longer act out the wish for reunion, and then he attempts to make me into a pal but is afraid that I will die.

Dream 2: "I need medical help but I won't ask you for fear of rejection."

Free associations: He expressed anger at his ex-wife for holding him to the divorce agreement, for not providing him with unconditional love.

First I pointed out the reality of his ex-wife's situation, that she certainly was entitled to demand all she could get, that he had left her, that his anger had to do with someone else which was his mother. However, his need to deny the WORU made him project it on his ex-wife and act it out with her. I further said that he made a pal out of me in the dream to relieve the fear of being killed by a doctor, the fear he had felt when he had the tonsillectomy.

He was resistant in the next interview and cut off, saying that it was a revelation to him that his supersalesmanship was due to fear: "If I please you, you won't hurt me."

Peter tentatively approached the WORU, his splitting defense, and the rock bottom of his self image problem in the next interview. "Father was all bad, mother was all good. I can't get angry at her. I do the same with all people. They're either all good or all bad. Mother used to say she could do whatever she wanted with me and I wouldn't cry. I would say 'screw you' to myself.

"Mother's bad side could punish, frighten, hurt me. At age seven mother gave a masturbation prohibition. I never stayed home. I was always out. If I didn't play the game she had the power to kill me. Her putting me in the hospital proved it."

I interpreted that he felt his mother had punished him, had made bad happen because of his wish to be himself and thereafter he associated self expression with annihilation. He replied, "Mother has the power to destroy me if I don't conform. I externalize this on to everyone."

His insight into his fear deepened in the next interview. "Every small expression of myself causes fear. The reason for my first marriage was to continue the framework of my mother after leaving college." I pointed out again the cycle of expressing himself and then acting out the fantasy of reunion as a defense against his fear.

At the next interview Peter had had a good weekend, during which he had expressed himself without anxiety.

In the next interview the patient told of being aware that he liked soccer because he was able to live by the rules rather than think for himself. At age eight he had panicked when he realized he was free and on his own. He then reported a phone call from his mother. "She blamed me for her condition, said she wouldn't go through it again, that she was dying but that she loved me and prayed for me every day."

Peter then asked: "Why can't I maintain the continuity of these sessions and reinforce my own growth?" (Why is the investment in his self image not continuous?) "Why do I cut off? It reduces treatment to a discussion of isolated episodes." I pointed out that his cutting off anxiety before externalizing and acting out interrupted the continuity of all his feelings and self expression. The equation seemed to be self expression producing anxiety which he handled by cutting off all feelings and then externalizing them. In so doing he cut off the connection of fear with his mother.

Peter replied, "I feel myself resisting. Mother said I had to have the operation. It would make me feel better. I had no say. I ran out of the hospital into the parking lot in a panic. I gave up. I was dead. Mother was there squeezing my hand, making it worse. Mother said to look what I did to her, not look what she did to me."

Peter continued, "After that I gave up and installed the monitor. Doctors were mother's instruments. Father was mother's instrument. Mother let me know that she was in control and could make me feel good or bad. She used fear to keep me in the game. Just like soccer coaches do."

Peter reported in the next interview having resisted the temptation to again act out these feelings on his ex-wife's demands and then continued: "Death was the ultimate weapon. Mother used it on me when I got married. She talked about death all the time, said she wouldn't always be around. She complained that father was never at home but idealized him. She had the same problem with father as I did with her. She couldn't admit he was a problem. She hated his mother but it was really him she hated. So much bullshit at home I had to cut it off. I couldn't tolerate it. I knew I was a bad boy growing up. I threw rocks at my mother, I put caterpillars down girls' backs, I pulled down their pants."

Having controlled his acting out, Peter continued to work through and in the next interview said: "I recall asking God in prayers every night to make me a good boy. I gave up hope of ever enjoying being a good boy and started to enjoy being a bad boy. It was the best I could do. There was no way out. I was expected to fuck up and I certainly did."

I asked, "Why did your mother make so much of your boyish pranks?" Peter replied, "Fear kept me from giving up and acting out the bad boy role completely. I was enraged at the injustice that molded me into the game." I persisted, "Why did your mother disapprove of your pranks?" Peter answered, "It was part of self expression. She always said, 'Do as I say. It's for your own good.' I scared them. I was curious, questioning, a maverick, a wild playboy."

Peter continued, "Mother had two personalities. She was one way with me alone, jovial and lively, but when father was coming home we made ritual preparations and she became solemn and serious. Implicit in the game with her was a pledge that she would protect me from him. They must have known I could split them. At age 13 I was humiliated when mother came down and kicked my friends out of the house. I never had another party in my home. Mother was afraid of losing me to a girl and today is afraid of losing me to you."

In the next interview he talked about a thought divorced from feeling: "I'm nothing without mother." Then he reported acting out a jealous rage at Cindy for dancing with another man. "I'll never let a woman hurt me again. Why was I afraid mother would leave me? Why was I jealous of my father and brother?"

He continued in the next session: "My parents were always right and I was wrong. They felt I had no value, lacked perseverance, was thoughtless and selfish. I felt deep down there was nothing in me. They were omnipotent and had the power to make life pleasant. I never grew in their eyes. I was treated like an invalid. Last night I had anxiety again about a heart attack. My parents' attitude was: 'In spite of how bad you are we'll take care of you.' When I was 15 my father sent his accountant to talk to me rather than talk to me himself. I felt like a freak."

I asked, "How did you get a sense of self value?" Peter replied, "By suppressing myself and being their way. By cutting off feeling and reality." I pointed out that his self image was derived from pleasing mother; he felt compelled to do it but hated it. The hate he handled by splitting and denial. Without complying he had no value or self image. Then I used as an example the story of the juggler in the monastery at Christmas who had only one thing he could offer up to God—his act. I said that he was afraid he would lose himself here in treatment if he confronted his rage at his mother and father.

Peter described in the next interview how "Mother used the fact that she was the conduit to father, to his approval." I pointed out that he denied that the mother whipsawed him with the father. He denied her WORU potential.

In the next interview Peter reported that right after the interview he again cut off, had a severe anxiety attack, was unable to function, went into a panic and wanted to call me or call his mother. I pointed this connection out and he replied, "You are omnipotent like mother and give me value." I said, "Part of you is like a baby without mother's approval. It develops tremendous anxiety and initiates a regression and the suppression of self to get the much needed approval." The patient replied, "I wanted father's approval too. Mother must have said I had to be a good boy to get it. I doubted self after that."

I pointed out that he looked at the WORU, got separation anxiety and then cut off. Peter replied, "Perception of mother is wrong. What is the grip she has on me? I denied she was the executioner. At the operation she gave the impression she couldn't do anything about it but I knew better."

At the next interview Peter told of not being able to enjoy his work. "Father was like that. He enjoyed it but felt guilty about it. Never wanted to be dependent on anyone. Can't show anyone you enjoy it. Father felt guilty about leaving mother at home and enjoying work, but couldn't show it. He had tension headaches."

I explained that the father's history suggested he was also deprived of the satisfaction of his dependency needs, had repressed them and developed reaction formations which were rationalized as virtues. Mother was allowed to be dependent on father but not sufficiently and the slack was filled in by her dependence on the patient, who felt guilty when the father came home.

The patient replied, "Father had to go to work when he was ten or twelve. His mother had a baby on which she lavished affection." I suggested that father resented the fact that his wife gratified the patient's dependent needs. Peter replied, "My father was closer to my brother because he was in the same boat and got nothing from mother. I don't like to be with my brother because he sees the same dependency in me that father did." I pointed out that his brother didn't want to be with him because the brother resented his getting from the mother what the brother didn't. He replied that the mother had given the brother full charge of the father's estate.

In the next interview the patient reported the splitting and projection of the WORU on to the father, "I transferred the image of anger and hurt to my father. Mother told me everything she did was for my good when she was really selfish and stupid. I'm angry at her because of the loss of her love. I couldn't disagree with either of them." He then reported the following dream.

Dream: "It was soccer again, the coach lying to me about giving me the wrong jersey number just like my mother did and the team practices and I'm not even dressed. I don't get to practice. I've admitted I can't play because I'm too old."

I felt this was an expression that the patient could no longer deny the WORU with his mother by being the supersalesman or the soccer player.

The patient replied to this interpretation: "Mother couldn't respect me without the bullshit." The next interview the patient talked about how the child part of him comes to the interview for comfort and the man part of him comes to get better, that he was feeling depressed and cut off. I pointed this out as a defense against his awareness that he had ceded his power to the mother, i.e., she was omnipotent. He had reported previously in the same interview that he had the power to change, to do it himself, but this feeling quickly dissipated.

He was furious at me in the next interview: "I'm madder than hell at you. I can't be dependent on you. I'd like to walk out. You said there was too much of a child in me." I pointed out that my comment had frustrated his wish for me to behave towards him like his mother had and that was why he was angry. Resistance continued in the next interview. "I don't want to face the fact that mother didn't care for me and manipulated me. I see myself doing the same thing. If mother doesn't love me who will? She was dependent on me to make her feel good. If I went along nothing bad would happen to me, if I didn't go along something bad could. She hated me, was nasty, vindictive, selfish. This is the point where I stop thinking."

In the next interview he reported anxiety about demanding the resignation of a board member—i.e., he was projecting the WORU on the board member. I pointed out his splitting defense: how he cuts off the connection between his feelings and his mother's withdrawal and then projects and acts out these feelings on others. Two interviews later he reported that he had told three of the board members to get off the board and was surprised that they went along with his demand without arguments. This concrete evidence of his emerging independence led me to point out how he had ceded his own powers and authority as president to the board, as a son to his mother and as a patient to me, his doctor. He then reported the following dreams:

Dream 1: "A woman is driving a car. I'm cleaning the snow from the front of it and she keeps driving on, taunting me. I get angry and throw the broom at the car and then realize I can't do that, maybe I should apologize."

Free association: "Mother's put-downs were done in a humorous way, done like a joke but it wasn't a joke." I pointed out the patient's denial of reality—i.e., the WORU side of mother, how she withdrew from him to force his compliance.

Dream 2: "I'm walking across the street with a small kid who has a hole in his stomach and only five minutes to live. I keep waiting for the kid to die. Then the scene changes and I wind up at a computer center which designs a woman any way you want her. Then I go on a ship and take the kid with me." I interpreted the dream as the patient's denial of his feeling that he will die if the mother puts him down. The patient replied, "I gave up myself to get mother's love. Mother always stressed I should be grateful to her for everything, being born, fed, taken to the park, clothed: 'Look at all I did for you.'"

Peter was now approaching the bottom of his abandonment depression where lay homicidal (destruction of the object) and suicidal (destruction of the self) feelings. If he confronted his anger at the mother she would die and he would die. At this dramatic point in his therapy Peter decided to marry Cindy.

SUMMARY

In this chapter there is even further movement towards working through though resistance persists. However, the greater control of the acting out brings the resistance into the interviews where it can be dealt with more effectively. Parallel with his greater commitment to therapy, rather than to acting out, Peter's depression and rage deepen but, outside interviews, his self begins to emerge more strongly.

As the tattered and tangled threads of his chaotic life begin to assume some organization and coherence through his increased awareness of his intrapsychic state—split object relations units and split ego—and its relationship with his external life, Peter's motivation also deepens.

13

Homicidal Rage:

"I Want to Kill Her"

The material in this chapter differs from the material in Chapter 12 mainly in intensity, so the division into two chapters is somewhat arbitrary.

Peter's decision to marry Cindy presented a very difficult therapeutic problem. To be sure, Cindy's personality was quite different from either his mother's or his two ex-wives'. She supported his individuation and confronted his regressive acting out, not permitting him to act out the wish for reunion on her. In these respects she seemed a good, healthy object choice. However, now that he was well into the working-through phase it could not be overlooked that his desire to marry her at this time might be motivated by a need to defend himself against the painful feelings associated with the separation and emergence of his new-found self. This process, though well under way, was still tenuous

251

and not fully consolidated. Was he marrying her as an expression of his self and in the interest of further growth and development or was he marrying in order to reinstitute the ancient and time honored defense of the wish for reunion? I finally decided to present both sides of this issue for him to consider in making his final decision.

In the next interview he presented the following dream, which underlined the tentative quality of the separation from his mother and illustrated exactly how far he had progressed in therapy: "I was playing basketball with a good team and doing well but I thought I didn't belong and my playing got worse. I told them I couldn't stay and I left, giving the excuse that my mother needed me. I felt if I continued playing something bad would happen. I talked with my father, who was interested and not critical, and one of the players asked me why I left the game as I was doing OK."

Free association: "After your comments about Cindy and marriage I began getting my house ready to welcome her. I had an anxiety attack and I didn't want to get married. I wanted to crawl into bed and do nothing. I was afraid of mother, too. I recalled the fear I had when I married my first wife. Afraid of mother's other side—I still deny it. I haven't called her in two weeks. Marrying Cindy requires me to be a man, which frightens me. If I do anything, express myself in any way, my life is in jeopardy. To admit the truth outside of the interviews is sacrilegious. The creep hears it and says, 'You'd better watch out.' "

I said, "Making the truth your own is sacrilegious." The patient replied, "Yes, it's dangerous. Denial of mother's black side and reluctance to make the truth my own are the same."

In the next interview he reported another dream: "I was a spy in Germany in World War II, was caught, shot several Germans and they shot me."

Free association: "I was a spy, a phony with mother. Now I'm shooting her." Finally linking the image of the part-object to the image of the part-self of the wish for reunion, he said, "Looking at her dark side and at the same side of me. Dependency and helplessness. After the last interview I could see my mother's vindictive face. I dreamed of feeling helpless, no way out, no one to save me. I was dying. I could recall my mother's disgust at toilet training. Urinating was called making tension, defecating was called making a mouse. Mother was vindictive, she didn't care about me. Her silence was disapproval. Her talk was doing me a favor. She only talked about feeling badly. Telling me as a kid, you'll be sorry when I'm gone. Threat, a guillotine. You need me. If you're not a good boy I'll take me away from you. I deny that she was a bad person." At this point the patient slipped by saying he had to marry to be a man, meaning to say he wanted to be a man to marry. When I pointed out the slip he replied, "I'm nothing without my mother. She didn't want me to grow."

Twenty-first Month

The confrontation with the WORU activated resistance and Peter became sleepy in the next interview, defending against his anger at the mother, saying, "What is it in me that won't let me admit she's a shit? In the following interview he reported having called the mother to tell her that he was getting married, that her response was cold. She said she could not come to the wedding. He told her that he felt she was cold, didn't understand him, she was full of shit, etc. But afterwards he cut off his feelings. I felt he cut off feelings in order to deal with his feeling that without the mother he is nothing. Peter said, "Huge fear, absolute panic causes me to cut off feeling."

In the next interview, after a dream in which he was obviously going back to the old game with the mother, the patient questioned, "What is the huge investment in this game? It's safe, self expression is not." I pointed out that he played the game, the wish for reunion, to defend against fear, as if there were no other way to cope with it. The patient replied, "I'm afraid I will have no resistance."

He then acted out the wish in the transference by throwing the ball back to me by asking questions. He got angry when I didn't answer and said, "That's what I'm paying you for." I interpreted that he was now trying to act out the wish for reunion with me. This confrontation led to the tie that binds—that he will die without the mother. Peter replied, "I'm nothing without mother. I'm a vacuum. I'm afraid of not being, of evaporating. My existence is totally tied to mother. If I stayed inside what mother wanted I was safe. If I stepped out there was trouble. I gave mother's power to destroy to father. I denied anything good about him."

This confrontation brought on the separation anxiety and by the next interview the patient reported having awakened in the morning with physical symptoms of sweating and chest pains and having wanted to go back to the dependent state and have his needs met. He had been thinking about the fact that his mother had called. She is waiting for him to call and he isn't going to do it. He reported several dreams whose theme was that he was controlled by his mother for his own existence. He decided he would never be in that situation again. In other words, he would control others to gratify their needs for his own purposes.

Resistance and symptoms continued in the next session and he talked about waking up at three in the morning with the thought, "I'm brainwashed. It's not my mother; it's what she did to me. Mother was the first and last authority, the omnipotent one. If I give up that I'm committed to being on my own. Being on my own equals awful things could happen." I again pointed out that the patient acted this out in the transference, ceded to me the power he had ceded to mother to deal with the feelings about being on his own. He replied, "Like with mother I have to keep returning to you for reinforcement."

In the next interview the patient reported that he left the previous interview feeling committed to giving up the emotional investment in his mother. He became terribly sleepy and fatigued and while driving the car home almost fell asleep. However, this time he asserted himself, supported his self image, took charge and the fatigue went away. I pointed out that the first defense was sleepiness and the second intellectualization.

The patient told how as a child he used to crawl into bed with mother when he was anxious rather than stick it out and that now when he gets anxious from an interview the first thing he does is find a way to dump it. "As I talk courage and strength here, the other side, the creep, is attacking me. When I stand up and am a man the other side puts me down. A little repetition of what mother did when I expressed myself." In the next interview, he related a dream.

Dream: "Mother handed me a sick baby which urinated and shitted all over me. I didn't know what to do with this baby, awful. Three murderers came into the room and tried to shoot me but I escaped."

Free association: "I think the baby is the voice that puts me down." I interpreted also, "If you challenge the voice you get shot." At the next interview he reported that after a weekend, "I tried to control the voice of the baby. I awoke on Saturday morning on the verge of panic with heart symptoms but I maintained the continuity of feeling until today." This led to the awareness of the structure of the WORU part-unit. "The voice, the baby, the creep are my mother and her voice, and as I'm saying this now fatigue overcomes me. It's almost a physical battle. Sleep is an agent of the baby voice, the creep, the mother. Both are part of me. Like a barnacle on a ship. I'm looking on the voice as an enemy, a foreign body. It has to be fought." He illustrates the growing strength and continuity of his self image. "I felt good all weekend; then the creep started to question it. How do I get rid of the baby voice, creep, barnacle. Something bad will happen." I questioned, "What?" "The voice wants me to put an ether mask over myself, to put me to sleep. Mother wants me passive."

I pointed out that doubting and passivity as well as intellectualization and cutting off are other operations of the creep. At the next interview the patient told of having acted out this rage at his mother for the first time in an overt way with one of his vice presidents who reminded him of the mother and expected him to sign letters which were not right.

I again pointed out that he avoids fear of his present rage at his mother by neglecting her but he needs money and approval from her for his marriage. I asked, if he doesn't confront her out there how can he do it in the interview? I said his fear of being abandoned caused the monitor to go into action to control his rage. His not dealing with his mother directly in life makes him unable to deal with her in interviews.

In the next interview he said he had called his mother who again told him about her illness, saying her blood pressure was up and she had to avoid anything upsetting. She accused him of changing, but now at least she could see him as he is. The patient complained about the garbage he gets from her, saying she neither cared or understood. "She's not going to change and I'm not going to play the game so the relationship is hopeless." However, he pointed out that the creep had control today and was trying to put him to sleep. "I'm angry; the creep is saying I need my mother. It's a draw; I feel shitty, don't want to do anything. You make me feel better."

The next interview was on the day before the wedding. He had called his mother again to ask her to come to the wedding but she was too busy to talk. His response was to feel anxiety, want to run away, be hospitalized, do nothing: Something awful was about to happen. "I had a fantasy of mother ready to put the javelin through my gut, my saying 'go ahead and do it.' Venom in mother's eyes strikes me down. My destiny, the electric chair or back to mother, the viper snake. I'll have to go to the chair, take a full jolt and hope there is a God. Chair is the operating room, but I've been a good boy, don't hurt me. Always ran from the chair to mother. Helplessness, what will I do, see only the mother and the electric chair." I again raised the possibility that his marriage was a hedge against separation-individuation and treatment.

Before the next interview the patient had been married and reported he awoke that day in a panic, with pains in his chest which he couldn't control. His mother didn't come to the wedding. "I have to cut her off, I'm desperate, the creep is taking over." He reported a fantasy: "I'm dead at 46, I've given up, I can't cope with the fear. Fear is the creep's ultimate weapon. Can't fight the sleepiness and externalization." However, the strength of the self image increases: "Had a good two days, enjoyed being married." I asked, "Why can't you cope with the fear?" Patient: "I'm convinced to the point that I'm dying." I pointed out that he can't cope because this feeling of helplessness goes with the fear. The patient replied, "Fear of death, I'll have nothing to say about it. Go to the hospital. Doctor says I will die. Doctor is the executioner, being dragged bodily from the chair. I fear because I got married and mother didn't show up. Dying, alone, helpless. Mother was the only one who could save me. Cut her off. Age four the tonsil operation, the electric chair is the tonsil operation."

Over the next two interviews the patient discussed the signing of a settlement with his ex-wife and finding out that his mother had told the ex-wife that he was getting married, probably to cause difficulty for his marriage. He was unable to believe it. I point out that this is his life's problem, denial of the WORU. Patient says, "I'm astonished, it's like revealing the villain at the end of a murder mystery." I pointed out that it seems that way only because of the degree to which he splits the positive and negative.

Twenty-second Month

At the start of this month the patient said he was using therapy as a hedge, ceding the power to me instead of to his mother in order to deal with the fear. Part of him didn't want to get well. "I'm trying to establish a connection here to keep from doing my own thing. My symptoms go up when I realize I will be alone with feelings for three days without seeing you."

I pointed out that cutting off the connection with feelings is one of the mechanisms to turn power over to me. I pointed out also that in turning himself over to me to deal with his fear he loses himself. I confronted him: "What good is having balls if you don't have a self?"

In the next interview he told how, in a setting of a dream about a group taking over the company, he woke up with anxiety and heart symptoms, feelings of helplessness, but this time he attempted to control them, realized that he wasn't dying, felt better and went back to sleep. The patient then reported, "I felt love for you, things are beginning to bloom but I doubt them. Feeling good makes me feel bad, doomed. Nothing I do can be real. Doomed for being myself. Mother said don't do this or that or something will happen. What I wanted to do could only result in failure at best or death at worst. Father chastized me for normal adolescent sloppiness; he said I was self centered and thoughtless. If I did something wrong I would be punished by an impersonal authority, not by my mother or father. God would smite me with a ball of lightning. Added to the terror of the operation was this executioner. I used to pray, 'Dear God, please make me a good boy, help me. Father will kill me.'"

This theme continued in the next interview where I pointed out that he expresses himself, develops anxiety, cuts off and externalizes. There must be something in his feelings he hasn't picked up between separation anxiety and the externalization.

In the next interview he reported three dreams.

Dream 1: The mother's withdrawal: "Mother and father were at my house. Mother took a check out and said it could have been mine; then she ripped it up."

Dream 2: "A big dog has my hand in his teeth, not vicious but more than playful—no way I could get rid of the damn thing." This is the treatment which has him by the hand and is dangerous, dangerous in the amount of rage he feels toward the mother.

Dream 3: About a doctor who did what he wanted, got the most out of life and then died.

All the patient's associations had to do with being tired, helpless and hopeless. I interpreted that fear of death was grafted on to the wish to be himself and that he had to get rid of it before he could be free to express himself. He reported being himself at a big business meeting and not trying to be supersalesman and then waking up in the middle of the night with fear of a heart attack. He tried to identify and understand the feelings that were associated with the fear. I pointed out that this was a somatic externalization of his defense against perception of the WORU. He replied that he had a fantasy that the mother was dead. I asked, "Why?" He replied, "She said, 'If you don't play the game with mother you will die,'" and continued "In a panic I thought I would go see mother. Thank God I'm sane, and I thought, 'Thank God, I am seeing Dr. Masterson today.'" I pointed out, however, that the affect appropriate for these thoughts was not there, it had been isolated. A dream was reported in the next interview.

Dream: "I was working for my father, who was furious at how I had treated my mother. My mother called and said she knew I was annoyed at her, that she really loved me. Father was the trouble. I was furious at her for the way she played one of us against the other. Father should be mad at her, not me. I wished I could explain to him how mother is."

Free association: "It's the trap I was in as a child wanting to express the injustice but knowing father wouldn't believe me. I had feelings of helplessness, rage, injustice, no one on my side. I was feeling sleepy, lost, lonely. I had dreamed the story of my life—mother, father, brother against me. I got angry at my mother for putting down my father in a dream as I never did in life." I pointed out again to the patient his detachment of feelings —a defense against his homicidal rage.

In the next interview the homicidal rage came out in a dream of a father hitting a son who asked him to buy him a drink. "The father hits him again and I feel sorry for the son." The scene changes to Vietnam. He saw another father in a family—father, mother and son—the mother had a gun with one bullet and tried to shoot him. He shot both mother and father, but took the son home with him and told him he wouldn't hurt him.

Free association: "I woke up in a panic with heart symptoms. I'd killed my mother and father. Always felt guilty about father's death—I had pressed him to expand the business and then he died of a coronary. Being myself would kill my mother and father, a fear I wanted to switch off. If I kill them I'll be killed, have a heart attack and die. My executioners are the doctors. If she had a gun she would have used it but not him. I didn't want to kill them. I killed him first, don't know why, knew she was going to kill me. I felt no remorse then, but I was sorry for the old man who was defenseless, sorry for what I'd done to the kid. No remorse when father died but panic. Thought I'd die every day but then I'd turn to Norman Vincent Peale. I expected to be killed by them. Can't get away with murder except in Vietnam. Why did I do it? Saw on TV last night *The Dowager Empress* who drove her son crazy the same way my mother manipulated me. Evil, corrupt power. Really think I am going to die. The bridge between these feelings and my mother is my desire to kill her. The Dowager Empress died in her sleep so she never paid for what she did. I got no personal revenge and the anxiety was always to kill to get revenge.

He explored his homicidal rage further in the next interview, saying, "Anger was blocked off all those years to deal with the wish to kill mother for revenge, to run away from it. Even today I've cut off feeling. Why did I kill father? He wasn't doing anything." I said, "Perhaps that's why you did it. He didn't intercede with mother for you." Peter continued, "I never complained to father about mother. The child in the dream was me. He was the one I felt most sorry for; I was longing to be a child also. Don't like to admit to myself that I seek revenge. I threw rocks at my brother as a child. She made constant threats that she would tell my father and that he would punish me if I crossed her. She probably told father about me but told him not to tell me. He wouldn't speak to me nor I to him. Why?"

Peter continued, "Mother split father and me to maintain power, to possess me and father. My discussions with father were about his attachment to his own mother. These discussions, however, made my mother jealous. Mother didn't try this with my father; she only needed one lover, me. Part of me wants to throw off what I know to be true. Father's mother was another bitch.

Mother wanted to own me, couldn't have father, had me. Something to hang on to for stability. She lost her mother and father at 12. Did she deliberately keep father and me apart? Then I get a feeling that I'll get a call that mother is dead." Then the patient cut off.

He continued, "Why didn't they like me for me? They used me. I feel as if they were talking back to me, talking down God, gloom, doom-like when I was a child."

The patient continued in the next interview, "How could mother cut me off so completely? Why did she want to own me? I gave her life meaning, viability. She depended on me more than on father. He wouldn't permit it. She always stressed, 'I only have one dress, your father has only one suit.' We had to eat only soup. I've succumbed to becoming what she made me. Frightened, dependent, gloom, doom. Mother's acts were deliberate, without love, to make her feel good at my expense. Why not my father? He was a father to her and might leave her. She didn't question his long absences and when he stayed home she couldn't stand it. She used physical complaints to get sympathy: 'I don't feel right.' In my last phone conversation she talked about high blood pressure and dying and I didn't respond and wasn't sympathetic. When I was a kid I put a funny look on myself when I sat at the table because I had to feel badly to get attention. When I felt good I was put down."

At the next interview Peter still continued, "When I was independent I got abused; when I was dependent and down I got along."

At this point the patient raised the question of cutting down the frequency of interviews in the fall because he had to spend more time with his work. I confronted this move as resistance. In the next interview Peter continued, "Mother has the power to make something bad happen. I feel helpless, passive, tired, sleepy. If I express myself and feel good, then I feel bad with anxiety and depression. Something bad will happen." I pointed out how he split his feeling of self expression and depression from his feeling that his mother withdraws from him, doesn't like him. By splitting the two he managed to keep the connection alive; perhaps his resistance was an effort to get me to step in and take over as his mother did.

At the next interview the patient overcame the splitting without further interpretation. "The link was the putting down for being myself by my mother and father which produced frustration and resentment." I pointed out that this conflict is now re-enacted. Patient: "It's in my head, not out there." I pointed out that it's both in his head and out there, that he said it's in his head to avoid facing the fact that the mother didn't like him if he expressed himself. Peter replied, "My tuning fork is on all the time and responds to others being put down as well as myself. Is my anxiety from recognizing the link with my mother or from expecting punishment for recognizing it?"

Twenty-third Month

Peter in the next interview acted out in the transference by asking me why I charged him when he could not keep an appointment because of work. After I reviewed our initial understanding on this issue he ignored my remarks to talk about therapy as a one-way street, unjust, not giving what he wanted. I pointed out that he was acting out his anger, the frustration of his wish that I be his mother. Later he talked again about getting his strength and confidence from the attachment to mother. He never said to his mother and father, "I don't want to do it." He always went along to be loved. He had been away for a week on vacation at the beach, had enjoyed himself and then had the thought that he would have to pay for it. He never thought, "What's happening to mother?" I pointed out how these latter thoughts were an externalization of his separation-individuation conflict.

In the next session he told me an anecdote that the firing of a vice president went OK, which I used to point out that his failure to challenge the mother causes him to be unable to see the reality of everyday life, that he projected the feeling that something bad might happen from his relationship with his mother on to everyday life events. The patient replied, "My reality success is constantly negated, by expecting something bad to happen." I pointed out that this was a projection, that he had to 1) strip the projection from reality and hold on to the feeling; and 2) trace it back to his relationship with his mother.

The patient replied, "I played my ability down to get my parents' and my brother's approval. How does mother get the power? It seems like going against God." The patient then reported a dream: "My father came back into the business. I had a sinking feeling I couldn't run it as I wanted to. He was excluding me from meetings. I thought I should tell him off but I didn't."

Free association: "I'm giving up my balls by not standing up for what I am because it means conflict with my mother, father and brother." To this I made no comment.

Peter was now defending himself against the suicidal depression and homicidal rage about his mother (his feelings of abandonment) by his pathological defense mechanisms of splitting, avoidance and passive-aggressive acting out in the transference, which were expressed by silence.

SUMMARY

Under the onslaught of his feelings of abandonment the patient loses the capacity for self observation and denies the reality of the therapeutic situation but projects into it the distortion of his relationship with his mother. In other words, if he expresses rage he will be abandoned. He reveals this in comments about being a fool to let his feelings out and further expresses his resistance by silence or by talking in circles about his parents, rather than expressing his rage.

The therapist's first job is to clarify the reality, i.e., the destructiveness of the patient's behavior which the patient is unable to perceive because of the intensity of his affect and because of his projection, i.e., he is unable to differentiate between transference and reality. The therapist first confronts reality, saying this is not the same situation, the same thing will not occur. Next he interprets the destructiveness of the patient's behavior. I asked Peter if he realizes what he's doing with his family. He says, yes, he would be a fool to do anything else. I then differentiate the feeling state from the reality and attempt to get him to express his feelings in the interview. This increases his resistance and his silence. I then interpret his anger at my behavior, at my therapeutic focus, which deprives him of his fantasy that I am the mother who would take care of him. This makes him angry, which he demonstrates by silence. The reality destructiveness of this silence is then confronted.

In other words, his silence is destructive to what he's attempting to achieve in therapy. As his silence persists I increase the confrontation by saying, "You're terribly stubborn. How long is this going to go on?" He avoids this issue further by saying he doesn't know what direction to take to express his feelings. I again point out that he persists in avoiding the reality of which he is now aware. He confirms this by saying he feels if he gets angry he will be cut off by me as he was by his parents whenever he tried to grow up. Again I confront the transference distortion in this attitude. I reinterpret the reality of the transference situation to clarify the distortion, which puts him back on the spot. Again he retreats to silence and then I interpret and finally he breaks through with his homicidal rage at the mother.

At the heart of the working-through phase the abandonment depression is most intense and is expressed in the feeling that if Peter separates and individuates he will die and his mother will die. Suicidal depression and homicidal rage emerge in tandem. This emergence in therapy triggers the original cardiac symptoms that brought him to therapy and links them as a somatic expression of the abandonment depression—i.e., if he allowed his homicidal rage to be expressed he, in turn, would be killed.

14

On the Way to Autonomy:

"I No Longer Feel Responsible to Her"

As the working-through of the abandonment depression and WORU continued, Peter began to reevaluate his self image and resistance developed against the feeling of hopelessness about ever getting unconditional love from the mother. "I believe I'm bad. What is so bad about me?" I pointed out what he thinks is bad about him is what's good about him, his self image and drive for individuation. The patient continued: "The only way to make it in the family was to play the game. The frustration drove me nuts. I knew underneath they were afraid of me as a maverick no matter what I did. I was odd, strange, way out. They used fear to keep me in line. If you bite your nails you get cancer. Treatment is making new rules about life that go against every tenet that I was taught."

In the next interview the patient described a weekend of looking for approval and he came in with feelings cut off and wanting to stop treatment. I pointed out how over the weekend he had been wanting to act out his wish for reunion to defend against his feelings of hopelessness. The patient answered: "I don't want to be the hopeless child who wants to be loved just for himself. Not getting the love leads to hopelessness, emptiness, black void, death. I got it for being a baby but when I started to grow up I didn't get it. Mother's love couldn't adjust to growth. I went from adoration to nothing. I got love in proportion to dependency."

Again, however, the working-through leads into resistance. In the next interview the patient comes in depressed but not working on it. "I deny or forget the reason for the depression." I point out that he disconnects the feeling of depression from its content or source.

In the next interview the hopelessness comes out in a dream.

Dream: "My son was crying and sobbing, but he had my face, saying, 'How could you do this to me?' I was trying to console him but there was no way. Mother was indifferent. You gave a kid a new sail for a sailboat. The sailboat was missing. I found it and gave it to him and he sailed it off."

Free association: "Mother and father squeezed my balls with a smile on their faces, saying they were doing it for my own good. They'd let up if I were a good boy. Best I could expect was I wouldn't be tossed out and emasculated. That's death."

Twenty-fourth Month

The patient returned to the next interview with the results of having confronted the WORU—a dream in which a group having a reunion breaks into open warfare, at the end of which the patient saw that one of the machine guns they were using was real, tried to get away and was killed. The self image of the withdrawing unit is revealed in the second dream in which he sees a malnourished kid who wants to join a football game but thinks that he is too sick, and he decides to take him to a doctor.

The transference theme is illustrated in the third dream the next night in which "I'm jogging with a psychiatrist friend talking about another psychiatrist who is a phony. We ended up in a house where my friend caught the looks going on between me and a girl. I knew I could show him that I could make her but didn't do it and this was followed by a Civil War movie in which I'm playing a Northern soldier about to be shot and I say, 'You're not going to shoot me, this is only a movie.'"

In this dream the patient's perception of the psychiatrist as phony, i.e., one who confronts him, led to anxiety, which he attempted to relieve by acting out the wish for reunion, but he checked this and then felt that he would be shot and killed. He triggered the WORU and finally his reality perception took over and said it was only a movie.

In the next three interviews the self image part of the WORU emerged and the patient now split this from the object image: "I'm weak, lazy, nothing; I can't do it. The fantasy of my wife going to my mother and saying 'Look what you did to him' after I'm dead. Mother won't be moved by that. She won't realize how good I am until I'm dead." I pointed out that the game —acting out the RORU—was to avoid this feeling of depression and hopelessness at facing the WORU, i.e., the fact that it was hopeless to get his mother's love for being himself. I pointed out also that he splits this feeling of hopelessness from his interactions with his mother.

The patient in the next interview showed great difficulty in accepting the object image of the WORU—"I can't get it into my head that mother treated me that way, that she was malicious, malevolent—she always seemed supportive." I interpreted the splitting and his acting out of his behavior at the mother by saying that he has no trouble getting furious at the injustices of others—for example, when his ex-wife's lawyer subpoenaed him —but he never gets angry at the mother. The patient responded: "I was aware of this difference and since yesterday I've had fantasies about dying and what would happen if I died in an accident. I felt sorry for mother. She dumped on me but she did it with positive statements. It was all for my best. She was omnipotent like a god. Father was against me. He was the devil."

In the very next interview the patient said, "I'm cut off. I can't believe it. I found myself counting the days until you go away on your trip [about two weeks hence]. Being on my own to me means death." Next he reported having cried deeply and bitterly at a movie where the major theme was loss of love. I related this to his inability to face his feelings about the loss of love on the part of his mother, i.e., looking at the WORU. The patient replied: "I must have had love at one time. I had to keep it." I pointed out that he had it and he lost it and spent the rest of his life trying to deny the loss and avoid the feeling about it by playing the game. I suggested that possibly he was experiencing my leaving as a repetition of the loss. I asked him, "How did you lose it?" The patient said by growing up, by being myself and was now crying with tears flowing down his cheeks: "They gave up on me." I pointed out that he denied the WORU and suppressed these feelings of self to avoid these feelings of loss.

In the next two interviews the patient expressed his shock at recognizing how early in life his difficulties started, at realizing that the mother today is the mother of so long ago which destroyed his notion of a loving mother. He questioned if he could get over this anger at the mother. Why did she pick him?

In the next interview he continued to work through the WORU—"My relationship with mother was phony, unplanned, spontaneous. When I was four I was left at the kindergarten by mother. I was frightened and upset but adjusted because I had a girlfriend. Whenever I did something wrong I told mother and she relieved the guilt. My candor was used against me. How long will this treatment take? I'm feeling desperate. If I had incurable cancer would I continue treatment? I was always afraid I'd die before I'd get better. Now I know it was to get the love I lost. The more I get into this treatment the further away I get from the old goal of getting love. It never was and it never will be there. I feel like I'm drowning. Going down the whirlpool alone. Nobody cares."

In the next interview the patient reports a dream: "If I hold on to my disguise as a German for two more days I'll be free." I point this out as reaction to my leaving. He looks at the WORU, feels fear and anger, and then cuts off his inner self and acts out the RORU to avoid his feelings of abandonment, telling me if he maintains his disguise he'll be free of confrontation by me.

Twenty-sixth Month

On my return from a two-week vacation the patient reported for the first time that he had stayed in touch with his feelings, had not acted out or played the game, had done his own thing, but had been very nervous. He is now establishing continuity of the self image. This was confirmed by his report of a dream that his mother was going to tell his father something he'd done wrong and he would be punished.

Free association: "You were going to punish me like father for a wrongdoing." He also reported a fantasy that his wife had called to tell him that his mother had died. For this the patient reports feeling cut off, that he's giving up and doesn't want to be himself. But at the very next interview he reports the burgeoning self image: "I had a great board meeting at which I was quite assertive and in control of the board rather than looking for their approval to make me feel better." In the next interview he goes into a rage at his wife's ex-husband for his unjust treatment of the wife and children—acting out his rage at the mother's withdrawal which is externalized.

This confrontation leads to a dream related in the next interview. "The old babysitter who used to wash out my mouth with soap when I was a kid was going to tell my mother that I was bad. Then the scene shifts to the present. I'm back in the old house and want to get away and masturbate. I drive to my mother's house where my grandmother says I'm putting her to sleep. I'm not Jack Armstrong, the All-American Boy. My mother appears and makes a big fuss upon my return. I'm filled with rage and disgust. The scene shifts again to your office, I tell you the dream and you say I'm all finished with treatment. I wake up realizing I'm not through." However, his free associations to this dream revolve around acting out the anger of the WORU on his wife by provoking her by failing to give her a valentine.

The patient now went on a long-planned two-week vacation to Jamaica—a unique expression of his self image and individuation—where he consolidated much of his previous work. "I stayed in touch with my feelings on the trip. I saw how I project the feelings about my mother and father on other people. I caught it and stopped it. This allowed the further emergence of the self. I was myself. I had dreams of being myself and taking action and supporting myself. A total switch. I know the difference of what goes on inside and outside. I didn't want to go back to treatment because I felt it was like going home again." He then talked about cutting down treatment, which I interpreted as resistance to continuing to face and work through the WORU. The patient said: "I don't feel good about the treatment. I can see my mother, a constant reminder of my mother, connection, the electric chair." Then he goes back to the working-through. "I have the same bad qualities as my mother. She was a supersaleswoman, a cold, selfish person. A lousy mother. The closer I look at her the more I see myself."

In the next interview he said, "The bad feelings about my home and here remind me of my own lack of worth. It's just like going home to mother and father. I want to cut down to avoid this bad feeling. With my parents I had to suppress me but I don't have to here. I make you into the one who puts me down." He then complained bitterly about my having charged him for his vacation. I interpreted that he was cut off from feeling, that his facing the WORU in the last interview had made him feel bad about himself and angry, that he cut off and externalized his anger at my charging, i.e., my not playing the role of the mother, that this kind of externalization is part of his dependence.

He projected the WORU on the therapy to externalize it and blocked out the reality of the therapy. If he accepted the reality of therapy and didn't project the WORU he would feel bad and have to manage his anger himself.

The patient now entered a phase of resistance, saying, "The realization that I have to be on my own makes me cut off feelings. I'm having dreams of loneliness, of being alone, and fantasies of calling my mother to re-establish the connection. My reality experiences or achievements don't seem real, they're not put into the computer. I discount the achievements and deny the cost of acting out my dependency." I pointed out he denies both the cost of acting out and his capacity for individuation.

His resistance to facing his anger at his dependency on the mother continues with cut off feelings. Independence is no love or being alone, frightened. He reported a dream of a woman like his mother coming to see him. As he saw her he was very depressed, felt he wanted to get out, couldn't stand it. He then talked about wanting to start a fight with me, about being angry at me. I said he was angry at me for confronting his playing the game and breaking the connection with the mother. I'm exposing him to anxiety. He expresses the anger at me by cutting off. Peter replied: "Coming here is like seeing my parents. I used to tell them what they wanted to hear." I pointed out that he wanted to resolve his dependency on me as he had with his parents, i.e., move away physically rather than work it through. The anger is at having to do it himself. The patient replied: "You have to provide something." I pointed out that his anger was at losing his dependency here, right now, and at having to pay me money for it. Who needs that?

This interpretation resolved the resistance and the patient talked about being dependent on the need for love. Independence and being himself meant no love. He was paying me a fee to get love. I pointed out that he was denying that he only had one mother and father. No one else could be his mother and father. "As an infant I had love from my mother and it was taken away in my development. At some point I lost the feeling."

At this point the patient is denying the fact that it was self expression that induced the mother's withdrawal.

Twenty-seventh Month

The patient was then away for a trip, returned and continued the working-through of his anger, depression and need for love, as well as his wish for his mother, brother and father to have seen him as he was. He reported the new strength of his self image. "Now it's easy to stay connected with feelings." He realized that he was looking for recognition for himself, but playing the game does not get self recognition because it's based on suppression of self. He then reported the following dream: "I was on a lake with a man, a woman and a child in a boat. Shapes started to come out of the water. I said they're alligators. The man insisted they were whales. They were alligators. Then a huge form came out of the water—an alligator with a trunk like an elephant. I was frightened and thought, 'Do I run or stay?' I decided to stay. I wanted to see what happened. Would they devour me?" The patient is now beginning to confront his fear of being engulfed by the withdrawn object.

In the next interview the patient reported that he felt that the dream had made him feel anxious and depressed. I reinforced this, saying that he expressed himself and monsters in the dream came after him and he ran away to avoid facing them. "I try to face it and think about good feelings and then I'm confronted with the abyss or void. I have dreams of masquerading like a gun man and of having to live as they lived—my parents. These are signs of the abyss: the tonsils operation, being put in an orphanage, my seeing a girl in a casket who died when I was about eight. If I didn't conform, that's what would happen to me."

At the next interview he followed through, saying he did not connect this threat, however, with his parents. I pointed out this part was split and externalized in his feeling about death. The patient said, "I recall my brother's birth when I was between two and three and the feeling of being left out." I interpreted that he denied the loss of an exclusive relationship with his mother when his brother was born and had been acting out the fantasy of reunion ever since. Peter said, "The game started there. I wanted to be the only one. I wanted her devotion to me. It supplied a little motivation to the game, the longing, the search. I externalized the threat, the tonsils. The alternatives were to feel anxious and depressed or suppress myself." I pointed out that he knows a third alternative, that he could put the pieces together in treatment. He could do it himself, heal the split and allow conflict to subside into the past.

This led to several interviews of anger at the mother and bad feelings about the self. "I'm bad, wrong; my only salvation is through mother. I feel great guilt for being myself." He described the badness that he was born with, that came with the package. "It was innate." I reinforced, saying "like part of your bones and muscles." Patient said, "Right! There's nothing I could even do about it. There's no way out." The patient continued in the next interview with the theme about his badness and his guilt about it. The anger and guilt about being himself and the WORU response were revealed in the following dream:

Dream: "When I was snorkeling, a fish with a body of a shark and a mouth of a hippopotamus tried to swallow me. I woke up and screamed."

Free association: "Kill me, wipe me out, destroy me. My son and I wanted to go snorkeling where I could be myself and this thing got me. The monster was the retribution for the badness, what would happen to me. The only out was the game. I was bad. Mother knew it, tried to help me overcome it. Doing what you want is bad." I suggested that mother and father both had systems to suppress the self and the patient's desire to be himself threatened them.

This theme of the badness of the self and being annihilated for being the self continued in the next several sessions, as reflected in the following dream: "I am involved with the CIA and some people are coming after me. These people are going to get me and I see you and throw you a document knowing they won't kill me if I don't have the goods." I pointed out that he throws his self to me to keep the self from being killed. This led to several interviews of cutting off and blocking: "I'm right on top of it but I keep on blocking. I'm afraid I will be eaten up if I'm myself. I'm so angry at mother's bullshit. Reading the Bible, morning meditation. How much she loved me. Mother was the shark, the hippopotamus, had the gun and wouldn't let up. She had to change and mold me. I ran away from the hatred. Struck down. I was her possession. Both times I got married mother had physical problems but was OK when I divorced. The third time she was going to die. I was gambling with my own salvation."

The retribution theme for being himself continued, exampled by the following dreams: "I was going to sleep with my second wife. She had two male accomplices who sat on me and stuck a needle in my finger to kill me. I was furious. I wanted revenge. Then I saw my mother saying, 'I told you this would happen but I will still help you.' Two men were trying to shoot at me. I ran over them with a car."

The patient continued to feel he was running away from his anger, looking for an external stimulus to discharge it on to avoid the fear of being abandoned or engulfed. Dream: "I will get you; it's just what you are doing. Both mother and the grandmother in the dream. I was angry and helpless and mother comes in to help. I was wrong to get mad at mother and father as they sacrificed everything for me." Then the next night he woke up sweating and screaming but as soon as he woke up he cut off feeling completely. Next was a dream of trying to get father's and brother's approval for being a supersalesman. Free association: "Father put me down so I was super-sensitive. I never stood up to him. I made myself a doormat. Anger was a crime."

Twenty-eighth Month

Peter reported having been in absolute control of his board meeting and immediately afterwards having severe symptoms of a coronary and reporting that he recognized and kept in touch with a feeling of anger. This was a great change. He was no longer cutting off his feelings. "My anger causes great fear. It scares me to death and that's what produces the symptoms. Anger is desecrating the altar. Something awful has to happen to me. I might be put in an orphanage or have to have another operation."

After 20 odd years of recurrent severe disability due to this perplexing and frightening symptom, Peter had finally seen the connections between his feeling state and the physical symptoms. His patient and persistent struggle to face his feelings had done for him what 40 ECG's could not.

Dream: "Mother was superselling and I wanted her to shut up." Free association: "I recall being embarrassed, annoyed, upset at mother's dominating salesmanlike behavior. I would always dismiss those thoughts. I did it again after the dream and went back to sleep. I resented not getting her love and admitting it scares the hell out of me. I give up and don't fight it."

I pointed out that he was projecting the feeling of hopelessness that he had in the past about ever getting his mother's love on to the present possibility of getting over his condition—i.e., he would no more be able to get over his condition now than he was able in the past to obtain her love. Peter replied: "It's unfair, unjust. I want it; I can't do it. I don't believe it will ever come. I hate my mother and father; it's not fair." Instead of acting out the wish for reunion it now appeared in dreams of longing for his mother's and father's love. Helplessness is expressed by, "I don't care about loving. Nothing to look forward to, feel terrible about myself. Hopeless and desperate. I'm hit by the realization that I've been angry all my life. I paid a terrible cost for suppressing it. I have to do it myself but I have terrible shame and guilt about being myself. I have given up. I'm tired of being put down and doing nothing about it."

In the next interview he was depressed and guilty. He thought it was time to stop therapy and manage his feelings on his own. He felt depressed and hopeless. I pointed out that he was externalizing the depression and guilt on therapy and wanted to stop it by running away. "I've been waiting for punishment all my life. Death, hospitals, heart attacks. I don't stand up for myself and don't expect anyone else to do it. I feel helpless."

In the next interview he attempted transference acting out, demanding that he was not doing something right and I had to tell him. He asked me a direct question: "Why is it so difficult for me to do it myself?" I pointed out that he was externalizing his anger at the mother's and father's lack of support on me. He responded, "I can't give myself any value. I give their value more credence than myself." He described two dreams, one "a frustrating drive up a long hill. Construction blocked the hill, I had to turn around and try another way." Second dream: "My father advising me about a trip I had to take but doing it based on his values, not mine."

I interpreted that he was angry at me for not permitting him to manipulate me to take care of him. The manipulator part of him did not believe there was a human being that he could not manipulate. Nevertheless he was denying that both guilt and feelings of inadequacy sprang from his efforts to manipulate. This brought the divided guilt and low self-esteem into awareness, and he talked about how he had manipulated his mother as much as she had him, which led to the following dream.

Dream: "I was in combat and dependent on others to tell me when a mortar shell was coming in. I was shown how to get down in the hole. The round came in. I buried myself in the ground and wasn't hurt. The scene shifted and I was singing every word of a song. Normally, I can't do that. The scene changed again. I met army generals explaining that their system was best but I said they weren't free and I wanted to be free. I wanted to tell them they were wrong but I was afraid they would imprison me."

I responded that these dreams were a reaction to my interpretation that he had no image of a relationship in which a therapist helps a patient to be his own self to find his own system. It's always a repetition of the past, i.e., I'm the authority trying to indoctrinate him into my system.

Peter replied: "I had to earn father's respect; I had to be worthwhile. It was a yoke but I feel the same here with you. I have to work to earn your respect and I want to run away. I feel helpless."

I interpreted that having to earn love defeats the wish because conditions destroy the wish that it be unconditional. Peter then said, "Every time evidence of my independence comes up and you confront me with it I feel that you are just like my father, saying that I have to grow up to earn your love."

The next interview the patient reported, "I'm looking for unconditional love. I was the only one for two years before my brother came along. By age five or six I was supposed to take care of him." He talked about the origins of his fears of hospitals. His first experience in a hospital was when his father took him to the hospital to see his mother when his brother was born. The second was the tonsillectomy when he was separated again from his mother. The hospital equals death, losing connection with mother. The patient then reported the following dream: "There was a gorgeous baby who loved me and clung to me and didn't like it when I handed it off to someone else. Then the scene changed. My ex-wife wanted to see me. I had a conflict between going to bed with her and not wanting to." Free association: "My ex-wife was finding the exclusive love I had lost. She wouldn't leave me and I didn't want to be responsible for the baby."

In the next interview the patient reported thoughts of his own death and his mother's death and dreams about his former acting out behavior of making love to his ex-wife but then feeling disgusted afterwards. I interpreted this feeling—the tie that binds—that if he doesn't get supplies of love and approval, he will die and the mother will die. In seeking love and approval he loses himself, but if he asserts himself he loses love and dies.

Twenty-ninth Month

At the next interview, in a setting of fantasies and dreams about the wish for unconditional love, the patient talked about wanting to cut down the number of weekly therapy sessions, which I interpreted as an effort to lessen the pressure for individuation, as well as to act out the anger in the transference for not receiving maternal supplies.

The patient then continued to report his efforts to be himself, feeling guilt, anxiety or punishment which was overwhelming. He was still talking about wanting to cut down, which I interpreted as a cop-out due to anger at the weak and dependent side of himself which resists autonomy. He wished to cut it off, to exorcise it. I pointed out that he tried to get rid of that side by externalizing it on therapy and decreasing the therapy. He complained of losing the ideal of the omnipotent doctor. In the next interview he reported feeling sleepy and had great difficulty in letting go of the myth of love and devotion about his parents and realizing that they were "phony and imposed their values on me to make me feel bad about myself and I did nothing about it." Here we see both the WORU object and self images with the affect connected. He talked about having both a child and a parent in him but no adult.

In the next interview he reported a dream in which both of his ex-wives were in a room putting him down. He felt guilty but mad and woke up feeling sad and guilty. "I deserve their wrath, but I don't like it." I pointed out that guilt and depression were associated with individuation and that he did not connect these two nor pursue the connection, nor assert that the WORU fantasy was not true. Peter responded: "The adult in me allows the parent and child to run me."

The patient now brought up money as a reason for cutting down. I raised the question as to why, when his self is emerging and he is reevaluating his relationship with his parents, he would want to cut down to three times a week. Patient: "You're like my parents, saying I can't do it except four times a week, and

I'm saying, 'Screw you, I'll show you and do it my way.'" I pointed out that he was externalizing and acting out his parents' emotional withdrawal for separation-individuation in the transference.

In the next interview the patient talked about his feeling that he would rather fight me than face them. He did not want to admit they were bad because they were so bad. "I must have hated them an awful lot—why didn't I ever tell them?" He acted out on his wife his anger at his mother's demands which he recognized as similar to acting out his parents' put-downs with me. He continued for the next several interviews to want to cut down, acting out the parents' put-downs on the therapist. "Believe me, I'm bad, but it's unjust, I don't deserve it." This led back to overt fury and rage at the mother and brother over the next several interviews followed by hopelessness and depression. I pointed out how the adult in him gives up to deal with the anger. The next interview the patient responded, "I have no choice but to do it." He had several dreams during the weekend of not asserting himself, not expressing his anger, "letting people shit on me. I feel trapped, no place to go, no alternative but to go forward, but hopeless. I can't do it. Have no choice. I had coronary symptoms over the weekend. The more I looked inside the more anxious I get. I feel panic like I did when I went in for the tonsillectomy. The adult has to emerge; I have to give up the fantasy that theirs was the only road to salvation and it scares me to death. As a kid I ran back to mother when I had this feeling. My fantasy is that I can still do it. I felt so bad and guilty about being different from my parents."

This led to the following dreams: "I was running away from an evil force. I escaped to a cabin with my wife. As a man entered I bashed him over the head. I felt I'd hit the wrong man or he wasn't that evil." Second dream: "Two Germans were shooting at me, pigeons, they were really bombs. I shot live pigeons back. I killed one and my partner shot the other."

Third dream: "My neighbors, angry at a family for digging up its yard, were going to attack them. I supported the family and was furious at the neighbors. They turned on me to beat me up. I felt hopeless, furious at the injustice."

Free association: "My parents used me to give them ego support. I felt good in the last dream because I expressed the anger and decided that I would take them with me as I went down. Fuck them, I'm going to be me."

The patient again became resistant and cut off. He told me he couldn't pay the bill. I pointed out that this was another replay, to act out in the transference to avoid working through his anger at his parents. He placed me in an impossible position—i.e., as expressed in his free association "to take them with me"—either I do it for him (RORU) and allow him not to pay or tell him to pay up (WORU) and he can replay by telling me to go to hell and leave. I said it was his responsibility to pay—to which he agreed, but he insisted that he cut down to twice a week. I replied that I thought his motivation for cutting down was an expression of his anger but that I would have to go along with his decision.

Thirtieth Month

The first twice-a-week interview he talked about cutting off his preoccupation with what he was working on in therapy. I pointed out that the cutting down was an effort to avoid individuation. This made him angry until he finally realized, "Maybe I'm saying either you do it for me or fuck you." I said I thought that was exactly what he was doing. At the next interview he reported a dream about the mother saying she was institutionalized and couldn't cope because of him. "Anger and depression—why do I have to deal with myself? Mother treated me like a dope and I acted like one. When you don't take over I get angry and sleepy. I can't do it and give up. I don't want to do it, it means death. Totally alone without my mother and father." Then he talked about being sexually attracted to his wife's sister but doing nothing about it (an example of oedipal guilt about sexual feelings reinforcing guilt about self expression). The patient then defended by regression and denial "having to do it myself or having someone else take it off my hands. I feel beaten and haven't even fought. Wanting to be the parent or the child, not me. Twice a week convinces me it's up to me. I had used treatment to relieve my anxiety. I'm having coronary symptoms at night, but I'm not trying to work out. Why? No one to depend on but me and I don't like it."

Then a dream: "Two cops were beating up a vagrant, kicking him in the face. Two kids were saying the police were rotten and I thought there were no police to call. I spoke to them. They said, "Shut up or you'll get it.' I backed off and offered them a cigarette."

Free association: "Authorities are brutal. They speak up and threaten by saying back off and I try to ingratiate myself. At least I was me and I spoke up. The cops were my parents. Supposed to be a benevolent authority, who else do you call? Maybe I was the vagrant too." Here the patient connects the harsh parent with the guilty self and the search for the benevolent parent to relieve it. By the end of the month the patient had not paid his bill, which I brought up. I pointed out that he was programing himself to fail, that he was putting brakes on himself by acting out an instant replay on the therapist as he tried to work through in the interview, externalizing both the RORU and the WORU, i.e., if I don't allow him to pay I'm the WORU and if I let him off I'm the RORU; further, he was acting out his hopelessness by making treatment hopeless, i.e., money was causing him to cut down which made the present a repetition of the past. He could no longer act this out with his parents. The present is different: He is older and he has help.

The treatment was now stopped for a month for my vacation.

Thirty-first and Thirty-second Months

On my return Peter reported that he hadn't externalized but was still feeling hopeless. As he worked through this feeling in the next two months two new themes emerged: 1) anxiety and feelings of hopelessness about his capacity for individuation; and

2) fear of separation from the therapist. The former was revealed in dreams as in the following. Dream 1: "I hit a golf ball and killed a five-year-old child who was me." Dream 2: "Took a test, couldn't come up with the answers although I knew I had them." The fear of separation is seen in the following dream: "You're telling me I only have six months of treatment left."

Resistance now developed at doing it himself because it meant leaving me. "I know I can do it but I'm afraid of leaving you. When I assert myself I can see the negative voice and fight it but I can't seem to exorcise it. I am still too guilty about being myself."

Thirty-third Month

Peter began to get the upper hand on "the voice" and he worked through his guilt about individuation: "I beat the voice. I worked well, saw the anxiety, overcame it. A great feeling of victory. But I was anxious coming here today. Part of me doesn't want to leave you."

The analysis shifted to working through his separation anxiety as he got greater and greater control over "the voice." His resistance to separation again manifested itself in helplessness and hopelessness which had to be confronted—i.e., "I have a huge block to doing it. I would rather lie down and go to sleep. It is as if I were giving up something."

Thirty-fourth Month

Peter saw his mother for the first time in 18 months and his perception had undergone a drastic change—the self image was now in charge. "I felt free, not responsible for her anymore. I saw that her life was based on bullshit, not reality. I felt calm, peace, that I was right. I began to have thoughts about stopping therapy. I've been doing what I wanted. I'm coming out of therapy as *me* with insecurities I have to live with."

Thirty-fifth Month

"The more I do for myself, the less I need her. I am anticipating giving up a security here, the last connection. Makes me sad. Time for the boy to be a man. The final wrench. I'm not anxious, but sad." At this point Peter was tearful. "I guess I'm missing the chance to be a child." Peter continued to work through his feelings of loss at the termination of therapy. He went on a two-week vacation, planning one final interview on his return.

The final consolidation and continuity of his self image were confirmed. He reported it as the best vacation of his life. He had fully asserted himself and enjoyed it, had maintained his connection with his feelings and had not regressed. He felt he had now had a long sustained period of being in charge of himself and being connected with his feelings so that he wanted to stop therapy and do it on his own. He still had feelings of loss about the separation but could manage them.

I was confronted with a final therapeutic dilemma. Peter's functioning and intrapsychic state had improved dramatically. The splitting had been overcome and he now saw the mother, the father and himself as whole objects, both good and bad. The RORU-pathologic ego alliance had greatly diminished, as seen in the decrease of his defensive acting out. He had a new object relations unit, consisting of myself as a new positive object that approved of separation-individuation and a self image of a worthy, competent self with an affect of feeling good based on coping and mastery of reality. He had worked through the abandonment depression and homicidal rage. He was able to be motivated by his own thoughts and feelings (to individuate) without having to cut off feeling to deal with the substantial anxiety still present.

These intrapsychic changes were reflected in his life structure. He functioned efficiently now as the president of his company with the result that the whole structure of the company had changed. He revamped the board of directors to obtain his own men, fired subordinates who interfered with his company policy, and in general took over the reins of the company with consequent improvement in the company's financial operation. His relationship with his new wife was also dramatically different from his previous relationships with women. He was assertive and supportive with her without leaning on her or expecting her to take care of him. Incidentally, she had such little need for him to play this role that she had been a useful aid to the psychotherapy in helping him to change. Whenever he would regress a bit and begin to play the ancient role with her she would sense that something was wrong and confront him. Much of the time his days had been filled with compulsive activity which gave little breathing room to the inner self. He was now able to reorient his daily activity to give equal time to that voice—in order to further explore his individuation.

Despite all this change both intrapsychic and extrapsychic, and despite the fact that I thought Peter actually was in the last or separation phase of therapy, I was concerned that his decision to stop at this moment might be an effort to resolve his feelings about separation by acting out rather than working through. He would deal with the pain of leaving me by leaving me to avoid working through those very feelings in the interviews. On the other hand, when I presented these issues to him he remained adamant about his decision so that I reluctantly agreed to stop with the reservation that if his later condition indicated that the work of separation had not been completed he would return.

DISCUSSION

Having been given the proper therapeutic support—through the addition of confrontation and communicative matching to interpretation—Peter regained his long buried persistence, gallantry and courage, joined battle with those ancient twin specters —the WORU and the pathologic ego—and struggled valiantly and painfully for three years to exorcise their malevolent influence and allow final and full development of his true self.

The misery and agony of this lonely struggle can ultimately be known only by the patient. The psychiatrist's technical, abstract terms, while useful to him, fall woefully short in conveying the depth of emotion the patient must endure and survive. The therapist, his partner, can only sit on the sidelines and marvel once again at the extraordinary recuperative power of the self when it is given half a chance.

The final comment on his therapy must come from Peter. In his next to last hour I spoke briefly on the phone to give a new patient my standard directions to my office. Peter immediately picked up what was happening and said, "He thinks he's coming for help with a problem but he's going to change his whole life. It's hell, but it's worth it." As a therapist I could only add, "Amen."

Case 2:
A Daughter's Legacy

So far in this book the borderline mother had been described by history through reports of memories, dreams and free associations. The next four chapters, presenting a direct report on six years of intensive reconstructive psychotherapy of a borderline mother of a five-year-old girl, will serve to refine the focus on this problem.

Chapter 15—The Tie That Binds—presents a study of the clinging defense mechanism from two perspectives—its defensive function in protecting the mother against feelings of abandonment and its destructiveness to the child's efforts to separate and individuate. When the mother clung she "felt better"—that is, less anxious—but the child developed symptoms of separation anxiety. When I confronted the mother with the destructiveness of her clinging to her child she would curb it and then experi-

ence and describe in the next interview her resultant feelings of abandonment. The child, on the other hand, would not only feel better but also, relieved of her own fears of being abandoned, would take further steps to assert herself and develop. In the course of these sessions there was an uncanny one-to-one relationship in the interaction between parent and child: the patient's presentation of her clinging in interviews, my confrontation of the destructiveness of the clinging and the patient's efforts to curb the clinging, followed by feelings of abandonment on her part while the child improved and was able to separate and individuate.

In Chapter 16—Tragedy—the mother now turned to do for herself what she had helped her daughter to do—individuate— and the struggle focused on the transference relationship with the emergence of two new themes—anxiety about autonomy, and fears of engulfment or abandonment if she might have a close relationship with a man. However, in the midst of this struggle her daughter developed a malignancy and died within two years. The mother's efforts to manage both her own feelings and her daughter during the long terminal phase of the illness are related in detail.

In Chapter 17—Mourning—the effectiveness of the psychotherapy is demonstrated in changing the patient's reaction to object loss from pathological acting out of the wish for reunion through clinging with all its destructiveness, to the healthy mourning of the loss with subsequent ego growth and achievement of some object constancy.

Chapter 18—Triumph—confirms the change by the mother, describing how the patient's newfound capacity for object constancy equipped her to find and relate to a more appropriate man with whom there seemed—for the first time in her life—some realistic chance of a close gratifying relationship.

By this ironic, tragic twist of fate the daughter's final legacy fulfilled her mother's earliest and deepest wishes to become herself. In psychotherapy the patient's mourning the loss of the only true relationship in her life enabled her to grow, to in-

dividuate and to achieve enough capacity for object constancy to relate to a man without clinging and acting out the wish for reunion. What she had been unable to do with her own mother as a child, i.e., cope with the feelings of loss involved in separation-individuation, she now was forced to resolve by the death of her daughter.

In this strange, poignant way the daughter, through her love and her death, did for her mother what her mother had done for her—enabled the mother to free herself from the bondage of the tie that binds with her own mother—to separate, individuate and find her true self.

15

The Tie that Binds

Lynn, a slender, attractive, 33-year-old brunette, was married and taught at a local college. Her chief complaints were depression, dissatisfaction with her work, and conflict with her husband, whom she described as cold, insensitive, stingy, ungiving and depriving. He objected to her working, but demanded that she pay more than her share of the family expenses. She could not respond to him sexually, though she was able to have an orgasm with her lover. (A good example of object splitting with projection of the negative image of the mother on the husband and acting out of resentment at deprivation through an extramarital affair.) Although she functioned compulsively well at her job, she derived little satisfaction from it. Her chief satisfactions were found in her relationship with her five-and-a-half-year-old daughter Margaret and in the affair she was having with a male teacher.

289

FAMILY HISTORY

The patient described her mother as being cold and without feeling, but said, "I bought her line." She described her father as an irresponsible Don Juan, who was hospitalized for a suicidal attempt when the patient was 26, at which time the mother divorced him. A younger brother, now aged 26, the mother's favorite, has been chronically ill with asthma since the age of three. His illness always required much of the mother's attention, and finally impelled him to move away from her to the West.

Past History

Lynn was born in a large Eastern city, the oldest of two children. A compliant, compulsive child, she was subtly terrorized by her mother's threat of abandonment. If she did not obey, the mother would withdraw. The mother, whose lifelong ambition to be a professional woman had been frustrated, coerced the patient to fulfill this goal for her. The patient complied, spent much time studying, and did well throughout her schooling. Her first abandonment experience came at age eight when she was sent to summer camp for the first time. She became panicky and depressed, instigated a call by the camp authorities to her mother to take her home. However, the mother's obvious rage at what she viewed as the patient's unruly behavior created an even greater threat, and the patient reluctantly agreed to stay, having "the most miserable summer in my life."

In high school the patient was quite aware that she had difficulty in getting involved with boys. Her boyfriends had to be approved by her mother, and since very few of them were, dating was infrequent. She graduated from a local college, left home for the first time to attend graduate school, and had her second clinical episode of abandonment depression: "I completely fell apart. I was depressed and afraid, spent all my time in my room, and was unable to study." After six months she transferred to a college from which she could commute to her home on weekends and began an affair with one of her professors which lasted for three years until the end of her graduate studies. At this point the professor suddenly died, her father attempted suicide, and she had to leave college to take a teaching job. She left home again, this time going far away to teach. Here she had her third clinical episode of abandonment depression. She described herself as "totally coming apart," depressed, lonely, and frightened—exactly as she had felt the first year at graduate school. At this time she met and married her husband quite consciously in order to "not be alone." Thus she clung to the husband to defend herself against the feelings of abandonment. The marriage was filled with conflict from the beginning, since her husband, a replica of her mother, was demanding, obsessive, rigid, cold, ungiving, and rejecting.

PSYCHOTHERAPY

In the first year of psychotherapy the relationship with the daughter, Margaret, remained at the periphery while the problems with her husband and her lover were worked through. During this time I made little reference to the patient's reports of her clinging and her daughter's obvious separation anxiety. However, after about a year of therapy, when the patient decided to divorce her husband, her clinging to Margaret increased, and I began confronting its destructiveness to the daughter. As we worked on this problem, I asked how it had begun—that is, what was the origin of the tie that binds?

Feelings About the Birth of Her Child

The patient reported: "When Margaret was born I felt like a woman fulfilled. I loved the stage when I had to be up with her at night—even though I was tired. I resented others' efforts to take care of her. I loved her needing me, I thrived on it. I never let her cry, I always picked her up. It reached monstrous proportions. I hated to leave her . . . that is, to go out at night. I hated having someone else take care of her. She ended up crying all the time and if she didn't get picked up she'd throw up. I used to rock her to sleep on the theory that you can't spoil infants. All a child needs is to have love poured in endlessly. Obviously I was satisfying myself." Here the patient described her identification with and use of the child to repair her own feelings of deprivation at the hands of her own mother. "The physical experience of holding Margaret was like plasma to me. It got so bad my pediatrician raised hell with me—told me to stop picking her up. I stopped, but I was very upset. I couldn't bear to hear her cry and leave her there. I felt as if it were murdering her. I did it though and it worked."

I asked, "What happened when Margaret learned to walk?" She answered, "She walked at 14 months. It occurred coincidentally with a lot of other things. Those two weeks saw the worst depression I was ever in. Margaret was born in May, I returned to teaching in September. I had wanted a summer vacation but my husband said 'No,' so I had done some summer teaching. Then the next summer the in-laws invited us and we went. I was annoyed because I wanted to go away with my husband and Margaret. When we arrived company was there for the night. I was in no shape to be up around the clock. I was upset the whole time, angry at my husband and myself. I remember that was the time Margaret first walked on her own. I still recall it. On the drive back she climbed out of the crib and I knew she was not able to do that on the trip up. I felt she had 'moved on.' I was not happy about her advancing out of babyhood. But to my surprise I have enjoyed later stages of development. I knew infancy would be great, but didn't expect to enjoy other stages of her growth. I had never faced the reality of her growing up.

"I wanted the infancy state to last forever, never thought of her growing up. I saw myself surrounded by a large family—I had the fantasy of not crying anymore if I had children. I would age with them, but they wouldn't grow up—I never thought of that. Having Margaret was like heaven, the greatest thing I ever dreamed. Nothing I've ever done has made me feel as good as the love and affection I poured into her. It is only clear now that she is going to move on and I have to do something about myself."

Comment

Three aspects of this report require emphasis: 1) Lynn's use of her daughter as an object to make up for her own feelings of deprivation from the past, to the exclusion of the child's needs; 2) the fantasy that the child would be her possession or object forever—strong enough to replace reality; 3) the gratification she felt during her child's infancy.

Although every mother feels special gratification during her child's infancy, the gratification of the borderline mother has a special quality to it; it is in great contrast to the frustration later when she desperately struggles to ignore the reality of her child's growth and development.

This has given rise to a clinical observation of the so-called "symbiotic smile," which is almost diagnostic of a separation-individuation problem. When the mother of a borderline child or adolescent is giving the evaluation history her facies is usually angry, depressed, guilty, and withdrawn as she describes the various transgressions. When the therapist then changes the subject and asks the mother what kind of an infant the patient was, this depressed, withdrawn facies breaks into a beatific smile as the mother recalls and reports the pleasure of the symbiotic stage.

Let us now return to the interviews. Prior to this point in psychotherapy Margaret had had school phobic symptoms, occasionally not going to school because of getting "sick" in the morning, occasionally requiring the mother to go to school with her. Mrs. Brown reported, "Margaret's behavior made me further aware of how I cling to her and how I treat her like my mother did me. She sounded off at me and I was so mad I could have killed her. She is the only person I have a total attachment to. When she walks out of the apartment I'm never sure she will be back. Since she was born I haven't moved without her. I can't see our relationship through her eyes. I don't know what it's like to have a mother who loves you. With Margaret I'm being good to her so she'll love me. I was so afraid of my husband's taking her away from me that I gave him anything he wanted in the divorce settlement."

At this point Margaret was to start attending day camp and was complaining to her mother that she did not want to go—clearly testing her mother to see if she would let her go. Under some pressure from her mother Margaret went off to camp in tears. Lynn, in a quandary over sending her to camp, but unconsciously wanting to cling by keeping her at home, did not think of asking the camp officials whether Margaret's behavior indicated that she liked camp. I interpreted to the patient that she was holding on to Margaret to defend herself against her fear of being abandoned—these fears by now being an old topic in therapy. I said, "Margaret must feel that she cannot grow up without losing her mother's support." I then interpreted that she was sacrificing her daughter's welfare to the demands of her neurosis. Lynn checked with the camp officials and found that Margaret was enjoying herself immensely. Consequently, she insisted that Margaret continue.

Lynn reminisced in the next interview: "When Margaret was to leave for camp I felt like I did when I left my mother and went to camp: I was going to die, but mother insisted I had to go. I cried my way through the whole summer." Her clinging defense interrupted, further memories of being abandoned returned. For example, she continued talking about her year at graduate school where she felt abandoned, was unable to work, flunked her exams, was suicidal and paralyzed, and was finally rescued by her affair with one of the teachers. She also reported having fantasies of starving herself to death, as this was probably the only thing that would make her mother sorry.

In the next interview Lynn went further into her conflict with her own mother. If she expressed anger, she said, her mother would withdraw completely, would "cut off her oxygen supply." The madder she got the more she was afraid of dying. Several interviews later Lynn returned to the subject of her daughter:

"I am in a bind about Margaret since she has never been away from me for more than a day. My mother never listened to me; she always made me stick things out and I never functioned when I was away at college. When Margaret gives me flack about going to camp. I can only see myself and I don't want to do to her what my mother did to me; I don't want to force her to do things." I interpreted this as a rationalization for holding on to Margaret. The patient then recalled the memories of how her husband and her mother both withdrew from her at the time of Margaret's birth and that Margaret was the object to replace them.

Two themes side by side dominated the content of Lynn's interviews: Margaret's difficulties with day camp and the patient's reliving in psychotherapy the period of abandonment at age 21 when she went away to college. She dreamed about it at night, felt afraid of being alone during the day, recalled that she got through those years only by working compulsively. Following this, she reviewed her next abandonment experience when her father was hospitalized and she left graduate school to go South to teach.

During this time, whenever her former husband came to take Margaret out for the day, Lynn would report that she was furious at him for taking Margaret and at Margaret for going with him. "I think I'm never going to see her again. If I let her go I will drown. When she goes away I'm in a vacuum. She's my reason for living. A whole part of me goes with Margaret almost physically."

At the end of the summer, when plans had been made for Margaret to spend two weeks with her father, Lynn reported that her daughter was fearful about going, had nightmares of being kidnapped. This time, however, Lynn, in better control of her feelings of abandonment, instead of clinging to Margaret reassured her about her fears and encouraged her to go. Margaret went and enjoyed her holiday. I reinforced Lynn's efforts by saying that she had responded to the message implicit in Margaret's behavior in an appropriate and constructive way, which was proven by Margaret's response. She had reassured Margaret that she need not fear for her mother's continued love and devotion (i.e., emotional supplies) and should go with her father. When Margaret returned, however, Lynn said: "I was fearful that I had lost her, but our relationship was never better. We are both happy and this is the first time she has returned without being cranky."

In the fall, when it came time for Margaret to resume school, Lynn, with better control of her impulses to cling, said: "For the first time I can't wait for Margaret to start school." She later reported that Margaret went off to school happier than she had ever been. In November, when Lynn was finally beginning to have a relationship with a man, Bruce, she complained for the very first time of being "bugged" by her daughter. "Margaret asks if I'm coming to a school meeting when I've never missed a single one since she was two; I'd tear myself inside out for her schedule. Now I need time to collect myself before teaching and I can't put up with all of her demands." I mentioned that having clung to Margaret to deal with her fear of abandonment she had had no independent existence and had probably encouraged Margaret's demandingness, and, because of her guilt about using Margaret for her own support, was not able to assert her own independence. Lynn responded, "From the day Margaret was born I wanted to do the opposite of what my mother did with me, but I'm not getting total gratification out of Margaret anymore. It used to be a total plasma injection. Seriously, I couldn't have spent more time with her."

As Lynn began to get more involved with Bruce, Margaret became anxious. The worm now turned. Lynn reported, "Margaret is testing me about my going out and being on my own. Today the plans were for her to go to stay with a friend after school and then come home. This morning she threw a temper tantrum about going to school. She was in tears, said she didn't feel well, didn't want to go. I said she had to go. She went into the bathroom and slammed the door; I got furious. She came out, slammed the door, threw herself on the floor, kicked her heels, hysterically shouting that I was a terrible mommy if I made her go to school. For the first time I was able to look at her as something other than myself. Not a thing the matter with her—I knew I was right. I could listen to her and could hear her as myself talking to my mother. I let her get away with murder. Mother always had candy in the house for company but was furious if I had a piece. I finally realized that it was important for me to win and I forced her to go to school."

In the next interview Lynn described Margaret's response to this seemingly drastic maneuver. "The change in Margaret is fantastic. She's cheerful, happy, a changed child." I interpreted that Margaret felt her mother had neither overindulged nor used her but loved her—she had recognized Margaret's need to have limits set and had had the strength and confidence to set them. In the next interview the patient told that she left Margaret at home with a babysitter for the first time to come to the interview.

Several weeks later Lynn reported, "Margaret threw another temper tantrum on a Friday night when I was going out and wanted her to stay with her friends, but I handled it and went along and later she was in a great mood.

"However, I'm still afraid to completely let go of Margaret. If my relationship with this man doesn't work out I'll be left alone, even though I can see it's good for Margaret. I can only let go a little because I have Bruce. I need more from Margaret than I do from Bruce."

During the next interview Lynn reported further separation-individuation on Margaret's part: "The change in Margaret is fantastic. I didn't see her all day and she was cheerful and relaxed. I can't get over it. She's blossoming. Her inner tranquility astounds me. She's capable of handling things herself. I'm caught in the middle between wanting my freedom and feeling abandoned if I get it." Several interviews later Lynn said: "Sometimes I'm so pleased about Margaret I can't get over it. I was able to spend the whole weekend away from her without being lonely or depressed. Christmas will be the acid test. I couldn't have done this last August. I feel separated from Margaret's life but not left out."

After Christmas vacation when Margaret had spent time with her father, the mother reported: "Deep down I'm mad at Margaret for visiting her father. I'm upset at seeing her again. I'm mad at her because she doesn't need me anymore. I'm the world's biggest Jewish mother and can't stand it. I could have killed her this morning." I interpreted that she was angry at her daughter because she is more on her own. Lynn responded, "She's more mature than I am."

Two weeks later Lynn reported that she excluded Bruce from her relationship with Margaret: "I'm ambivalent about letting Bruce in on my relationship with Margaret. I would just as soon keep him outside, but on the other hand it's beginning to look funny." I interpreted that she wanted Margaret exclusively to herself and questioned whether this was good for either of them.

Again, two weeks later, as Lynn began to make inroads on the exclusivity of her relationship with Margaret, she said, "I'm having difficulty with Margaret. I'm not spending 24 hours a day with her. She's no longer the exclusive center of my attention and she gets cranky and irritable before Bruce comes to visit. I have difficulty disciplining her because I wait until I get furious. Feelings of abandonment are always just under the surface —a piece of baggage I carry." The very next day, she remarked: "I'm upset at not seeing enough of Margaret; I can't handle my feelings of abandonment. Can't stand being alone. I'm so mad at myself for signing the visitation agreement with my ex-husband. Either I'm working or Margaret is off with him. I'm in a state of terror that she's going to leave me."

A few sessions later the patient said: "I'm realizing that having Margaret around is not helping anymore, maybe because I'm letting go. I never before faced the reality of her growing up and having interests of her own." Margaret then got a severe cold and her mother almost cried out: "When Margaret coughs I'm afraid she will die! As Margaret grows I feel I'm losing my last support. I am digging my own grave."

A little later Lynn finally asserted herself with her ex-husband, telling him that Margaret wanted to change the visiting agreement. Lynn had been unable to do this previously because of fear that if she asserted herself he would take the daughter away from her. I again reinforced her efforts, saying she was acting as a mother interested in Margaret's welfare and not using her. These efforts again brought her feelings of abandonment to the fore and the very next interview she said: "I feel as if I'm at a funeral all the time, yet I deserve it. The fear is almost physical; I get sick to my stomach, totally frightened. My motivation for standing up to my ex-husband is so that Margaret won't think I'm a cream puff. I realize that it may be good for my character someday; however, when I assert myself I do it for her."

By this time, a year of psychotherapy had passed; it was summer again, and Lynn reported: "Unlike last summer Margaret is excited about camp. At her age I did nothing happily; I was miserable at camp. I was scared to go and scared to come home. I almost wish that Margaret didn't want to go."

Lynn now had conflict between her desire to be with Bruce and her feelings of guilt about leaving Margaret, as well as fears that Margaret might abandon her. "I feel guilty and fearful every time I go out. I can't put my feelings about Margaret in perspective." I interpreted that she did not want to put her feelings in perspective. The situation itself was clear: Margaret was testing her and the problem was not Margaret but her guilt about being on her own. She must set limits to Margaret's testing for Margaret's own good. Lynn said, "Margaret is my last mooring; giving it up is painful."

When Lynn was able to set limits to Margaret's testing and discussed the situation with her, Margaret told her mother that she was afraid she would marry and had had a nightmare that someone would kidnap her and take her away. Lynn continued: "Margaret said finally that she didn't want me to stop seeing Bruce because of her, because it would make her feel bad and I would bitch at her about it and she didn't want that. I told her, 'No one can take you away from me.'" I asked Lynn if that's all she should have said to Margaret and she replied, "Margaret just needs to be reassured that I'm not going to leave her." I interpreted that Margaret's questions aroused the patient's fears that Margaret would abandon her if she should go out on her own and because of her wish to cling to Margaret the patient failed to meet Margaret's need—that is, to point out that her relationship with Bruce could not exclude Margaret, that there was room for both, and that someday Margaret would have a relationship with a man of her own. I pointed out: "That's what it's all about."

Several weeks later Lynn reported and reflected on the change in herself and her daughter in the last year: "Last year on Margaret's birthday I felt like committing suicide. My ex-husband had just called me to tell me that he was going to remarry. This year I had an absolutely marvelous time; I couldn't believe it was either me or Margaret. Margaret said, 'Mommy helped me get the party ready but then I didn't need her.' Then I went off for the afternoon with my boyfriend. Margaret knows and I know when she needs more freedom. I keep pinching myself. It can't be true."

The treatment of Lynn and Margaret clearly illustrates the extraordinary tenacity of the defense mechanism of clinging. It envelopes the personality like the roots of a tree that have deeply burrowed their winding and tortuous way to the very core of the personality. I can only be extirpated by the kind of slow, painful, tedious work that Lynn undertook in her psychotherapy with such great courage and at such great cost to herself.

16

Tragedy

It took approximately two years to achieve the objectives described in Chapter 15. The psychotherapy resumes in this chapter with the twenty-fifth month.

Twenty-fifth and Twenty-sixth Months

As Lynn's defensive clinging subsided Margaret's development literally mushroomed. Lynn then intensified her clinging both in the transference at interviews and in a relationship with a very self-centered man whom she was dating. Confrontation of her clinging in the transference and the break-up of the relationship with the man led to the two major themes that began to replace the clinging theme: anxiety and anger about being on her own, and fear of being engulfed or abandoned if she should allow a real close relationship with a man to develop.

301

When the transference clinging was confronted the patient began to individuate, i.e., operate according to her own thoughts, feelings and wishes. At the same time she reported: "I'm furious at you because I have to be on my own without any advice. It's totally irrational. For the first few days I was depressed and angry but I've gone back to working on my book" (a textbook she had been having great difficulty in writing).

She continued, "I'm going to take a trip to Europe. Doing this on my own is so painful. When does it get easier? I don't know what I want to do. I never lived without having a schedule or a plan." Comment: For the borderline patient the systematic schedule avoids the anxiety about individuation evoked by constant choices.

Lynn elaborated, "I'm doing it but I'm so anxious I can't eat. I vomited once. I'm so nervous. I can't stay in my apartment alone. I don't want to leave you or ever finish treatment but the more I do on my own the closer it comes. I need a reservoir of confidence in myself which I guess I won't get until I succeed in being myself."

After days of painful indecision Lynn decided suddenly—a marked departure from her usual style—to visit Europe alone for 11 days. On her return she then visited her daughter at camp for a day. She reported being pleased as punch with herself: "I feel terribly pleased that I could finally tolerate being on my own without panic and that terrible feeling of being alone. I was proud, pleased and scared to death. I think that trip for me meant a crossing of the Rubicon—I've done it alone." It seemed that she had introjected enough from therapy to begin to feel some degree of object constancy in order to function on her own without fear of abandonment (loss of the object).

She now reported increasing individuation and autonomy, which led again to fears of engulfment or abandonment if a close relationship with a man were to develop: "For the first time in my life I got my menstrual period without being depressed. I'm now satisfied with my life and don't mind being alone in my apartment. I don't miss my daughter being away at camp and I'm enjoying work on my book."

She continued, "However, being close with my boyfriend makes me terribly anxious, a nervous wreck. Part of me wants to deal with this anxiety by leaving him." Lynn's thoughts about marrying this man led to guilt, which she projected on her daughter: "I felt guilty about telling Margaret but it is really my mother I felt most guilty toward about marriage. It's the last step in becoming a woman. I'm afraid I will fail. I also have another impulse to be promiscuous to pay my mother back. I'm afraid she will be angry and descend on me if I get married. I feel sure it will happen."

Twenty-seventh Month

In the next interview, Lynn continued: "I'd like to see my mother again. My physical image of her is of someone who is very together, very attractive, never a slip showing, but also very angry. No one could be as dehumanized, imposing and perfect as I remember her. Her image is frozen in my mind. I haven't seen her in five years. She was lethal. When she hears I'm getting married she'll do something."

When it came down to the wire, the man she was going with was unable to follow through on his intention to marry Lynn because of his own anxiety about intimacy. The break-up led to an analysis of her acting out defense against her fears of engulfment and/or abandonment if an intimate relationship should evolve—i.e., picking inappropriate partners with whom a real relationship was not possible. She said, "I never expected a man to love me and I fulfilled this by the kind of men I chose. I'd rather be taken to dinner at the Plaza than have a real relationship with a man. My father was charming but I could never rely upon him. I've always been attracted to that type of man and I never expected more than words."

I pointed out that her actions seemed to indicate a wish to fulfill her gloomy prophecy: She carried out her expectation of not being loved by picking men who were unable to love—i.e., she settled for arrangements rather than relationships.

Twenty-eighth Month

The patient's continuing individuation was challenged by her decision to get a haircut, which threw her into a panic: "I don't know whether it's positive or negative." I pointed out that the haircut as an expression of her desire to be an attractive woman was positive but that from her mother's perspective it was negative and this conflict produced the panic. She continued, "I never saw myself in relationship to a man. I never thought about the future. I never thought I had one. Being successful at work has not made me feel more like a woman." This interview led to the following dream: "I was being mugged and assaulted by my ex-husband and my last boyfriend." Free association: "I realized that I was enjoying the misery of those two relationships. I expected to be rejected and I picked men who would." I interpreted to Lynn that she had been an injustice collector, i.e., she had acted out her mother's prophecy of being rejected by picking men who would reject her. She consciously thought of a man who would love her but unconsciously picked men who would reject her. I elaborated that she was unwilling to face the fact that her wish for her mother to love her was hopeless and she was using herself as a vehicle to carry on a vendetta against her mother.

She replied: "I would murder her in cold blood except I don't want to go to jail. Mother functioned so well in all areas that it's hard for me to accept that she was wrong about me. I knew it was hopeless when my brother was born. She acted differently with him because he was so beautiful. I still think she didn't love me because of the way I looked. She was a perfect, unattainable object." I pointed out that she had never subjected this childhood image of her mother to the later test of adult reality.

Lynn complained, "I'm tired of being on my own, of working, teaching and making decisions. I want a man to support me." I pointed out that she would have to "be on her own"—be independent—even if she were married, that her wish for a man to support her was her wish to be taken care of as a child, which would cause as much difficulty in a marriage as it did now.

Lynn replied, "You want me to be alone just like mother. It's not worth it for me to grow up. I'm too petrified. I get up at 5 o'clock in the morning in terror." I pointed out that actually she had been functioning very well. "I'm frightened about being on my own, by every decision." I pointed out that her failure to set reality limits to her anxiety, to tell herself that it was not real, was dramatizing and perpetuating it. She answered, "Every step ahead means I will stop treatment." I responded, "If you don't need treatment, you don't need it." She replied, "I mix you up with my mother. I almost didn't sleep with a man I had a date with because I would have to tell you. I feel you'll be mad at me if I make my own decisions." She then reported a dream.

Dream: "I went to the office this morning and found it filled with my old clothes that I had gotten rid of and I was upset and shocked. I asked my new secretary how they got there and she said the Salvation Army returned them."

Free association: "I woke up very unhappy, feeling I'm being swallowed up by my past. I thought you would be angry." I interpreted that the old clothes were her projections of the mother image on me which she had to put behind her in order to perceive me as I am: a psychiatrist. She replied, "It makes me feel sad and bereaved as if I'm losing rather than gaining."

Twenty-ninth Month

This led in the next interview to further discussion of her projection of the mother image on men. "I don't feel good about a man unless he finds me inadequate but overlooks it and is nice to me. I feel the same with you." These assertions illustrate how Lynn defended herself against the hopelessness of her wish for unconditional love from the mother by acting out the relationship with the mother with men. If the man disapproved of her she had regained in fantasy the mother's love. However, this was at the cost of any real relationship with a man. I pointed out that she had to give up this wish for reunion and face the hopelessness in order to have a real relationship. Lynn replied: "I still see you as a mother and expect that you will not be pleased even though I know it's not true." I responded that she could use me to either act out the relationship with the mother or to get over it.

This confrontation led to a dream: "I was lost in the subway, called mother and she was angry and wouldn't come," which led to a discussion of her "lifelong search for a mother." The patient continued, "I thought I'd solve the problem with my mother by not seeing her." I pointed out that nonetheless the wish for reunion persisted. She continued, "When I confronted my mother she thought my perceptions were crazy. I was never sure. It seemed unreal. I wanted my mother-in-law to be my mother. She liked me." I pointed this out as the Cinderella solution—i.e., the mother-in-law is the good mother, and the real mother is the bad mother. She replied, "If mother would only tell me she cared."

Lynn then became angry and depressed, dreamed of telling both her mother and her former husband off, had insomnia and headaches. She was furious at everyone. I pointed out that she was externalizing the anger at giving up the wish for mother's love on to the former husband and myself. She replied: "The only thing that would give me satisfaction is to hurt my mother, tell her off. I'd do anything to hurt her. I can't stand to face the fact that she just didn't care. If I accept that, I feel no one will care."

I pointed out that the opposite was more likely to be true. Not until she faced the hopelessness about the mother would she stop pursuing men to fulfill the fantasy of the mother loving her. She replied, "The only motivation I've had was to please my mother. When I date a nice considerate man he doesn't turn me on." I suggested that she needed a narcissistic man in order to be able to replay the relationship with the mother and the father. I repeated that this male fairy godmother was her fantasy way of dealing with her feelings of hopelessness about her mother's love.

She then reported two dreams of memories of real events that took place in her childhood: first, being lost in the subway and her mother being angry; and second, going out on her first date and seeing her mother scrubbing the floor on her return.

I pointed out that the mother's message seemed to be: "You can't have a man and me." She replied, "Mother attacked any date I ever had. She made me miserable in advance by talking about how fat I was, how awful my nose looked. At my Ph.D. graduation mother took a picture of my head from the rear and had it framed." She then reported a dream.

Dream: "Mother died and the family was angry that I didn't go to the funeral. I fought with my brother over mother's clothes."

Free association: "Mother gave my things to my brother. I woke up wondering, 'What would it feel like to not feel entitled to the clothes?' Why do I care? If mother didn't love me no one will."

Thirtieth Month

In the next interview Lynn reported: "Every time I do something I get panicky and my plumbing backs up. Also I feel guilty. I'm not entitled." I pointed out that she used to deal with the anxiety and guilt by avoidance of individuation and she felt better but her life was worse.

A new man now entered the scene, "He's considerate, he likes me. I keep trying to find things wrong with him. It unsettles me that he makes no demands. He thinks I'm pretty. In the past I would have ended this type of relationship right away. I recognize objectively that it's a good thing but I'm terribly anxious. I used to go to bed with a man instantly because it was the only way I was sure he liked me—my way of holding on to him."

Lynn now reported that her daughter Margaret had begun to show symptoms of an upper respiratory infection. She also told of having finished the first section of her book with which she was very pleased. She reported a dream: "I was helping the prisoners to escape. I knew how to do it." Free association: "I woke up and was still in the prison. Felt angry, frustrated. Still staying there even though I knew how to get out. Embarrassing. Felt I was being a martyr with a smile on my face. Stayed but didn't mind it. I was furious at myself."

I interpreted her denial of her own urge for separation-individuation. She replied, "I feel hopeless, I have no future. I was furious with my mother for causing such trouble and pain."

Seven months had now passed and Lynn was making excellent progress when Margaret suddenly fell acutely ill, with severe shortness of breath due to fluid in both pleural cavities, and had to be hospitalized. Emergency drainage was immediately begun and, astonishingly, an X-ray 24 hours after admission revealed large masses in both lungs, probably due to acute leukemia. The prognosis was guarded and she would have to have chemotherapy which would cause her to lose her hair.

In the next interview, Lynn described these grave developments and seemed to be in a panic, not only about the illness but about the loss of hair. Lynn projected that Margaret would feel about the loss of hair the same as she would—i.e., it would take away her only shred of femininity. I clarified that Margaret had more sense of her own femininity and would probably not react that way and the panic subsided. Margaret was hospitalized for two weeks, responded to drug therapy and was discharged.

The psychotherapy now took on a grave and urgent air. The impending tragedy posed as great a threat to the integrity of Lynn's newfound self as it did to her daughter's health. She would be under severe pressure to regress and to provoke me into the role of the care-taking mother to deal with her feelings of loss as she always had in the past—at the cost of the loss of her autonomous self. It was necessary to empathize with and support Lynn in her time of trial without infantilizing her or permitting her to pressure me into the care-taking role. It was no easy task to keep my own empathy for this terrible tragedy under close scrutiny and control so that I could meet this therapeutic challenge. She needed realistic not regressive support.

Thirty-first Month

Lynn reported that Margaret was extremely weak, was throwing up constantly from the drug, and could hold nothing in her stomach. Lynn was frightened and depressed. "I will commit suicide if Margaret dies; I can't bear it," she sobbed.

I challenged this assertion by saying that there still were other alternatives. Lynn continued, "I feel so guilty about being alive, wanting to stay alive. It should be me. I never used to feel entitled to a life of my own. I feel like I'm being punished for existing."

Lynn's individuation had been progressing well at the time that Margaret became ill and it seemed likely that she would feel Margaret's illness as a punishment—i.e., mother's withdrawal for individuation. Lynn phoned her own mother and told her that she didn't want to hear from her and didn't want the mother to have anything to do with Margaret.

Margaret had been home a month and was starting back to school one or two hours a day. Lynn was determined to invalid her as little as possible. She got a wig to replace the hair that fell out. She said, "I don't know if I should open up feelings here. I am coping by keeping myself busy and not thinking." I did not encourage her to open up her feelings at this time as I felt she had to suppress them in order to cope with the many daily problems of Margaret's illness. There would be ample time later to deal with her feelings of loss. When the wig was found to be a big help Lynn recalled that at age eight she had been hospitalized for a mastoidectomy and her head had been shaved, leaving her without hair for six months.

She reported, "Margaret is doing better. I'm resentful of the burden. It horrifies me. I feel too guilty to do anything myself." I said that it was natural and human to feel resentful of such an extraordinary burden but that she must take care of herself in order to be able to take care of her daughter.

The enormous realistic demands on Lynn's care-taking capacity caused her to regress and she acted out in the transference by expressing her anger at my not playing the RORU role. "I'm annoyed that psychotherapy hasn't done more for me. I need more help from you. I'm exhausted, drained all the time." I listened without comment.

In the next interview she continued, "I'm angry all the time. I'm angry at you." I now confronted her that her anger was at the possible loss of Margaret, at the demands of Margaret's care, and at me for not agreeing that life without Margaret was unsupportable. I went further, saying that although she had separated from Margaret in her behavior, and was an appropriate mother with her, she still clung to the image of Margaret as mother in her head. In succeeding interviews I offered reassurance about her anger over the burden, and interpretations about her guilt about leaving Margaret.

In the next interview Lynn reported that she was able to do nothing. I suggested that she was inhibiting her own actions to avoid her feelings of guilt about Margaret's illness as a punishment for individuation. She responded, "Right, but I've decided to go ahead. I'm going to move into a new apartment and I had the first date with a man since she got ill."

She reported spending a weekend with the boyfriend away from Margaret: "I felt isolated and depressed. I literally feel I can't live without her; she is the only one who has loved me." I countered with "Baloney! You're still reacting to Margaret as mother." I again interpreted that she had gotten rid of Margaret as mother in her behavior but not in her head.

Her life was now dominated by the need to manage Margaret's daily symptomatic episodes. One day Margaret, feeling better, went shopping for the day by herself. Lynn said, "It's amazing to me that she can operate on her own." I replied, "It's not amazing. What is amazing is how you refuse to learn to live as independently as your daughter does because this would interfere with your clinging to your own mother in your head."

Margaret continued to have nausea, vomiting, depression.

Lynn reported, "My efforts in her behalf are driving me to hysterics. I have no social life. Mother said I'd make a fool of myself and nobody would take me out. History has proven her right. I'm afraid of a relationship with a man; I'm doomed. It's mother's fault but I agree with her, although I'm furious with her. I don't expect positive results. Mother made me feel not a desirable woman."

Margaret was now hysterical, did not sleep, cried all night, was frightened and worried. Lynn reported, "I'm depressed and angry and I get fed up with myself and start to make some plans, but I get anxious, have headaches, my plumbing backs up and then I screw up the plans. I have to have a life of my own, I feel guilty and Margaret's illness reinforces the guilt. I punish myself all the time. I feel so guilty about what I do that I undo it." Nevertheless, Lynn went out with a new man and liked him but felt guilty. At the next interview she reported, "I'm obeying your golden rule. I felt awful but I'm making progress. I'm going away for 12 days with this new man."

Thirty-fourth Month

She returned from the trip saying that she had had a good time but was made anxious because the man did not make demands. Demands make her feel secure. She reported a dream of a memory that she'd forgotten: Her mother had made her wear a covering on her hair throughout high school so that her mother wouldn't have to look at it.

In the next interview Lynn reported, "My need for an exclusive relationship used to be due to the fear of being alone, which is now gone. Now it's due to the feeling that I can't make it in a competitive market. I dream about my mother's comments that I would never make it. I'm angry at her for not giving me approval for what I want to do. She assaulted how I looked. The more I do the worse I feel. I need oceans of approval. I'm not getting it from anyone. If I don't get it I fail."

I pointed out that her "track record" proved this was not true.

As the relationship with the new man improved, Lynn's anxiety increased. "I'm afraid of something awful happening. I feel guilty. Part of me wants to run away by not seeing him. Doing what I want to do is the problem. I expect disaster. Margaret's illness is a punishment. My appearance displeased my mother. I would have gotten my nose fixed at 18 if a doctor would have agreed to do it. I thought mother would kill me if I tried to get away. Every time I got a job she spoke to my employer and quit for me."

I interpreted that she seemed to feel she was a possession or object of the mother's that the mother did not like. She replied, "If I took mother on I would kill her or she'd kill me. If she was crazy I'm crazy."

As the relationship with the man got closer the anxiety mounted: "He's very thoughtful but I can't accept the fact that he likes me the way I am and doesn't expect me to do anything. I find myself thinking I shouldn't get involved with him."

I pointed out this was her mother talking and her refusal to recognize it impelled a temptation to act on it. In other words, her failure to face and put to rest the wish for her mother's love and face her feelings of hopelessness caused her to be unable to deal realistically with men in her life.

Lynn replied, "I'm afraid she will kill me." I reinforced, "The wish is hopeless." She answered in her old refrain: "If mother doesn't love me no one will." I again emphasized that her refusal to face the hopelessness with her mother was linked to her difficulties with men.

She responded to this confrontation by reporting a dream in the next interview: "A wicked witch from the Wizard of Oz shrivelled up and disappeared except for her shoes." Free association: "My mother. Hilarious! What I would like to happen. I feel much better today. Finally accepting that my mother will never be the good fairy. I can tell when she's bothering me by how I feel when I look in the mirror. When I *feel* that I look good, rather than have to tell myself that I look good, she will be gone. I had a fantasy of revenge. I died from starvation and mother felt sorry

and wept over my coffin. Does she have any notion of what she's done? I'd think she'd want to see me to yell at me but she doesn't. I knew she hated me for being a woman. It would have been better if she'd been physically violent. I'm ruining my life.

"My image of a woman is ugly: awful hair, terrible nose, fat. Mother told me I'd end up like father, a street walker. Mother was preoccupied with body functions but had no body functions. She was purified, never perspired. She was interested in other people's sex lives." I suggested the possibility that the patient had had a good sexual endowment, which threatened her mother.

Thirty-fifty Month

Lynn reported that she was allowing her daughter to climb into her bed every night. I pointed out that she was infantilizing her daughter to deal with her own feelings of guilt and blaming it on the daughter. She was tempted to regress Margaret for her own symbolic gratification. Lynn then talked about her anxiety about intimacy with the man she had been dating. She wished to break up the relationship and was convinced no man could like her. "You don't know what I'm like. No self image at all. I was a gray mole one year ago."

In the next interview Lynn began, "I can see my trouble separating from mother. She used to walk out when I was sick. She was angry at me. For that reason I try to be on top with Margaret at all times." I pointed out that she was treating herself, not Margaret.

In the next interview she reported: "I thought of you as mother and that I couldn't discuss my boyfriend with you. I expect you to be annoyed if I tell you how much I care for him. Mother wouldn't like him. It upsets me that he doesn't get annoyed with me. The anxiety is wearing me out." I underlined that this was the very anxiety about intimacy with men that she had previously avoided by acting out. She continued, "Since mother would disapprove of this man I'm not sure I want him." I pointed out that he was forcing her to come to grips with her feelings about her mother. She replied, "I secretly wish my mother would come around." I again confronted the wish by saying, "That's really crazy."

Several interviews later Lynn was extremely distraught, crying, exhausted, hopeless, hysterical. She was overwhelmed by her anxiety about intimacy and the demands of Margaret's illness. Margaret was now throwing up every night and unable to cope.

I asked her why she allowed these traumas to build her emotions up to such a tremendous pitch and then acted hopeless, as if she couldn't cope. I suggested that she was staging a scene for me: She was hopeless and inadequate and entitled to it. She replied, "I want to do here what I couldn't do with my mother."

Thirty-sixth Month

She continued to report anxiety, anger and depression about being on her own. "I feel everything I do will turn out wrong. I know it's ridiculous. My life is OK but I am not. I threw up all night, had insomnia. I'm so upset every time I act independently."

Thirty-seventh Month

She began the next interview with a dream: "I am riding in a car with you and my mother. You ask me to drive. There is no steering wheel. I say I can't drive without a wheel. You say, 'Yes, you can.' I turn on the ignition and the car starts out of control; I am terrified. You say, 'OK, I'll drive.' I can't stop the car. I'm afraid of killing everybody. The car stops. You go into the back and return with the steering wheel."

This dream was followed by a second: "Mother telling me to go out with a man other than Irv" (a fellow teacher she was currently dating). I pointed out that she had a steering wheel but feels she doesn't and fears she would go out of control and kill herself and others. Why? She replied, "I always thought I was going to go crazy. I'm afraid I will run amok." I clarified this anxiety about autonomy by saying that she feels if she gives up following the rules and pursues self expression she will run amok.

Lynn made special arrangements for her daughter to go to camp despite her illness. She reported: "After Margaret left I was alone but I puttered around the house and enjoyed it. I'm going to stay alone. I don't know what I am going to do. No burning desire to do anything except maybe go to the movies or shopping."

I suggested that she may have to tune her ear to her inner feeling since this was such a new operation for her. She answered, "I've had headaches, knots in my stomach and anger at myself for doing nothing. I've started some new activities— swimming, going to museums. I was so guilty that I practically died; everybody will be mad at me. I know it's my mother. Yet I enjoyed it. I felt like the Thurber cartoon with my mother looking over my shoulder." I pointed out that her mother attacked her capacity to cope as well as her femininity. She replied, "I didn't realize this would be so hard."

At the next interview she reported enjoying herself trying different swimming pools, doing some knitting, working on her book. "It's very exciting for me to do things alone. I never thought or understood that people had a need to do things alone. I feel more capable. Except in my job I never felt I had the capacity to cope." After this interview she got very depressed, had fantasies of disaster but "even I don't want to stop now. I had a fantasy that mother and everybody would be mad at me. I feel guilty, not entitled. I'm a Catholic and my mother the church. I have no sense of my own physical and emotional properties."

The patient had two weeks' vacation with her boyfriend and on her return I did not want to put her under any more therapeutic pressure than absolutely necessary since the principal task was helping her manage her daughter. Lynn felt that she should cut down to once a week. I agreed, anticipating that at some point, probably after the daughter's death, she would have to come more often. Lynn reported: "I feel ready to cut down.

I have no depression, some nausea. I have to face the pain of separation some time."

Thirty-eighth Month

In the second interview at once a week she reported, "I'm angry and depressed but working well on the book. I keep dreaming about the time I couldn't get up out of bed in the morning. I guess I'm in mourning again. I'm mad but not specifically mad at anyone, even mother."

Thirty-ninth Month

Margaret had returned to school on the days she was able to function and the progress of her illness seemed temporarily arrested when she suddenly had a severe recurrence and was on the verge of death. She said to her mother, "I know I am going to die." Lynn told her, "You have to fight." Lynn was furious and terrified. Then Margaret began to respond to radiation treatment. Lynn was angry, depressed and overwhelmed. When Margaret asked her mother what was wrong, Lynn told her she had cancer and that it was curable. The patient reported, "I may die of a broken heart."

As the burden increased Lynn became more angry, tired, fed up, frustrated, and mad at everybody. She had constant headaches.

The prognosis for Margaret worsened and her hair fell out again. She couldn't sleep, woke up in cold sweats with physical shaking. She had to go to the hospital every day for treatment. She improved briefly with the radiation therapy. During this period Lynn decided not to marry Irv as he was too passive and withdrawn.

Fortieth Month

Margaret's condition took a further turn for the worse and she had to be hospitalized with a pleural effusion. Lynn reported, "She's detached. We have nothing to say to each other. It's the worst part. I feel as if I'm in shock and I don't let myself get upset."

The next few interviews were repetitions of the same theme. Margaret responded briefly to the radiation and was discharged the day before Christmas at the mother's insistence. It was now apparent that the radiation therapy was not holding the disease.

Forty-first Month

Right after Christmas Margaret was back in the hospital. Lynn reported, "I feel so lonely I'm about to die. How will I survive to support her in her ordeal?" In the meantime she had made plans to move into a long-sought-for new apartment with my encouragement. She said, "I'm finally confronted with having to do something myself alone. It frightens me." I pointed out that Margaret needs to know that Lynn doesn't feel that she will die if Margaret dies. Margaret's condition continued slowly to deteriorate.

Lynn was constantly battling for her daughter's interests against the hospital staff to make her more comfortable and to avoid unnecessary procedures. The doctors recommended heroic medication which had little chance of success. Lynn reported her dilemma: "Should I decide to go along with the doctors' suggestion and subject her to a medication that has little or no chance of helping her while at the same time it will increase her suffering, or should I tell them to stop all treatment and let her die? Am I holding on to her? Do I want them to stop to get it over with quickly for selfish reasons or is it to minimize her suffering? If it were me I would stop the treatment and die in peace."

Forty-second Month

The French refer to a person's preparing himself for death with the saying "He is packing his bag." It has often been thought that children are not able to prepare in this fashion for their own death. However Margaret, an unusual child, when faced with the reality of her own death turned to her mother and said, "What will you do with my things if I die? My rabbit, my dolls, my books and my clothes?"

Lynn replied, "If you want I will take care of them for you." Margaret continued, "What will you do with yourself?" Lynn queried, "What would you do if I died?" Margaret answered, "I guess I would be very sad and I'd go on and live my life." Lynn said, "That's what I'll do." Margaret asked, "Will you remarry?" Lynn answered, "If I find the right man I will remarry. I won't remarry just because I won't have you anymore. Does that make you feel better?" Margaret said, "Yes. What do people like about me? Who will remember me?" After this interview Margaret allowed Lynn to go home to sleep at night if Lynn would allow her to call her.

For the next month Margaret's condition continued to worsen. She attempted to get the most out of every day and was quite irritable and angry at herself when sleep caused her to miss some activity. At the same time, she became more dependent and angry, occasionally telling Lynn: "Tell me I'm not going to die. I just wanted to grow up and be a lady." At other times she was quiet and withdrawn.

Lynn reacted to Margaret's withdrawal as a kind of abandonment and requested that I see her twice a week. I agreed. She continued: "Not knowing what goes on in her mind blows my mind. She must be going through something alone and in an isolated way that I can't share." To counter Lynn's feelings that Margaret was withdrawing from her I pointed out Margaret's need to use denial and withdrawal to deal with her physical symptoms and her approaching death.

The pain and suffering that had racked Margaret's body suddenly abated, she became more comfortable and relaxed for two days, slowly slipped into a coma and died quietly with her mother at her side.

17

Mourning

Faced with the challenge of having to cope with Margaret's illness, Lynn had suppressed her feelings of anger and depression about the impending loss. She had waged a vigorous unrelenting campaign that enabled Margaret to live as fully as possible during her last two years. Furthermore, she obtained the best possible care during her declining months. The cause over, the campaign concluded, those suppressed feelings now returned in full force.

Forty-fifth Month

In the first interview after Margaret's death Lynn reported feelings of depression and uselessness with no longer having the role of Margaret's mother, and of anger that she had to go on living. But she declared that she had no regrets about how she managed Margaret's last year. She didn't want any other children because Margaret had been very special. She was glad she had moved into the new apartment, since she didn't have the old surroundings to remind her of Margaret. I reinforced her feelings about having no regrets by saying she had handled the last year in a masterful manner.

Lynn reported, "I can't recall what she looked like before three months ago. All the events that occurred in the hospital that I forced myself not to feel are returning and I'm haunted by them. All the horrible things that happened. It's worse now than when I went through it. I'm more aware now than at the time of what she suffered. She would have made out better without me than I will without her. I'm still at the hospital."

A week later Lynn reported, "I have Margaret's possessions all around me in the new apartment. It's comforting. I can't sleep. I'm ravenously hungry. I'm drinking milk and eating cookies all the time. Every time I shop it reminds me of her and I get depressed. I'm still dancing but the music has stopped and it suddenly overwhelms me. She knew she was dying. How did she do it with such control? I broke down only once when she objected to not being treated like a person. A hospital is so dehumanizing. She exercised her choices, thought about everything, preserved herself. I feel without purpose, back where I was 20 years ago. Margaret made me feel full of juice. I now feel like a dried up prune. Sometimes I feel as if she's still alive. I talk to her momentarily. I'm keeping many of her things. The hardest thing is the memories of how she looked. I could stand the burden of her illness because I had her."

I suggested that perhaps the illness had produced gratification of her wish for reunion, so that despite the reality frustration and pain she had felt a great deal of unconscious gratification.

The next week Lynn talked about some of the reactions of the hospital staff to her fight: The hospital social worker called to say that Lynn had had more courage than any mother they had ever seen and had had the closest relationship with a child that they had ever seen. She received a letter from the doctor who treated Margaret telling her how important her support had been to Margaret. Then an old boyfriend turned up and offered to take her away for a few days. Lynn said, "It helps me to see that people respect me apart from Margaret. When she died I thought I ceased to exist."

One month after Margaret's death Lynn returned to work for the first time and reported, "I feel guilty about being alive and I'm beginning to miss her. I'm afraid I will forget her completely." I pointed out the need to mourn for Margaret in order to go on and live her life. She said, "I'm guilty about enjoying myself. I miss her all the time. I have no choice now but to start to live for myself. I feel guilty about being relieved, being rid of the burden, and terrified to be on my own. I lost a job as well as a daughter: the job of being a parent. Though I'm often sad I seem to be not only surviving but managing. I'm surprised I don't feel as bad as I did when I left my husband."

Forty-sixth Month

A week later Lynn reported, "I'm crying a lot and miss her. Dreaming about the period before hospitalization. No patience. Can't concentrate or sit still. I always expected something bad would happen to her." "Yes," I pointed out, "you expected to be abandoned by her." Lynn replied, "I seem to have a need to spend time alone and don't even mind it and I seem to be beginning to get my head together. I don't feel so alone in my apartment and I'm living inside myself more than I thought I could. I'm continuously aware of missing her all the time with memories and bouts of crying. I've had my hair cut five times since she died. My life as a parent is over. I don't mind being alone in my apartment for the first time in my entire life."

Forty-seventh Month

A month later Lynn reported, "I have to keep busy. I'm feeling more pain than two months ago, dreaming about her dying, losing her hair, the clinic visits. School is ending, I have to work on my book. Will I be able to be alone in the apartment? I burst into tears when others talk about children. I feel connected only to my feelings about her, not to my daily life. When she died I thought my batteries would die with her and I would never be able to feel again for another human being. I'm surprised to feel alive and that I could feel for my old boyfriend."

This boyfriend tells the patient he would like to leave his wife and marry her. She suggests that he make up his mind and leave his wife first. By the third month after Margaret's death Lynn decided to at least give away some of Margaret's games.

A week later Lynn reported, "I'm shocked to find that living alone is OK. It's a relief to be alone and be able to get upset about Margaret. My feelings now about her are unpredictable. Still dreaming about the hospital but I'm getting organized and am getting rid of her things. I decided to take piano lessons from her teacher and am pleased about it. I'm still thinking, dreaming about the hospital and her dying. Memories of her keep me awake at night: the emergency operations, spinal taps, etc." I pointed out that she doesn't verbalize all this in her interviews, that she was synopsizing rather than verbalizing.

Two weeks later she was still dreaming about the hospital and the things the doctors did that made her mad. I suspected her anger at the doctors was splitting her anger at Margaret for leaving her. Lynn continued, "I hate other people's children; I don't like children that much; that part of me is gone. I'd like to go to bed, stay there for a month" (as she had during previous abandonment episodes). She continued, "Don't know what I want to do. The hard part is not being alone, but living without Margaret and having nothing to do and being needed by no one. I feel as if I've lost a limb, lost a mother role I like, and yet it happened to her, not me. I lost the person I loved most who loved me. I don't know who I am."

Lynn continued to work on her book. The relationship with the old boyfriend did not work out. She continued to feel depressed, had memories of Margaret prompted by seeing other people's children.

Two weeks later—four months after Margaret's death, she reported, "The book gives me something to do. I feel I have no future. I feel lovable only because she loved me. Like an old lady sitting and waiting to die. I'm not worth being responsible for. I stop existing if there isn't someone in my life who cares about me. I hear my mother saying if I got my freedom I'd hang myself but I want freedom anyway."

I pointed out that she had this tenacious stubborn drive to replace her mother with a substitute rather than grow up and that she denied reality in service of this drive. In other words, after four years of therapy, she had lost sight of the fact that she actually had made a considerable investment in a separate self.

Forty-ninth Month

Two weeks later, after a brief visit to her brother in Arizona, she reported having had a perfect time and hating to come back, feeling guilty when enjoying herself. "I'm afraid if I take life in hand I won't remember her. I'm still dreaming about her dying. I'm guilty about putting my experience with her behind me. It's hard to believe it's over. I've been feeling I left her, not vice versa. I never felt she left me. My mother lives a desolate life and I'm afraid I have traits that will make me end up the same as she is."

I point out the truth of this. Mother stubbornly and persistently saw the patient as her object and lost her. The patient changed her behavior with her daughter but continues to cling to her as a mother figure in her head in order to avoid separation and the emotional investment in a separate self. Margaret's death now forced her to invest in a separate self or have nothing.

This confrontation led to more individuation. The patient decided to do some volunteer work at the Cancer Hospital, and to make some money by writing a history book for 11-14-year-old girls. She realized she needed a vacation and time for herself and that she still only thinks about Margaret as she was in the hospital. At this point I suggested that the kinds of thoughts she was having about Margaret represented clinging, holding on to her to avoid mourning rather than mourning itself.

In the next interview Lynn reported, "It's more painful to think about her before she was sick, and having her things around makes me feel sadder. Before it made me feel better." I used this to interpret her ambivalence about mourning for Margaret. She said, "If I face my feelings about losing Margaret I will lose my mind." I pointed out her stubbornness and her unwillingness to mourn, holding on to hospital memories. I said that if she continued her only alternative would be to detach from Margaret emotionally as she had from others in the past.

This confrontation produced anger: "I haven't accepted Margaret's death. Other people may be able to do it. I've been trying to fill up the void and it doesn't work. I think seeing her in the hospital makes it easier to accept her death because she's better off. To think of her healthy makes it more difficult for me. I know I have the potential for cutting off all feelings. I did with mother and my husband. There are no emotions in my memories about mother, and it's as if I never lived with my ex-husband." I then interpreted that her daughter's illness allowed the patient to gratify fully her wish to devote herself 100 percent to her but that Margaret's death interrupted this fantasy. Lynn replied, "It was the ultimate experience with mothering; it sustained me too."

The confrontation seemed to initiate mourning, as reported in the next interview: "I'm crying all the time. It feels different. I'm accepting that she's gone. Physical pain. I feel worse, lost a limb. Bleeding inside. Want to stay in bed. It's so painful to realize she's gone. I'll never see her again. Lost a whole part of me. Feel like I had an operation and have to recuperate. Yet in the mirror I am intact. Incredible that this could have happened to me. I can't feel the void. I feel worse than the day I buried Margaret, inundated. When alone, so inundated I'm afraid I'll lose my mind or I will die. Like a constant movie in front of my eyes. Things that we did together. I feel sorry for myself. Why me? I lost my main reason for being, my main satisfaction in life."

At this point, five months after Margaret's death, Lynn left to spend a month's vacation with her brother in Tucson with my urging and support. I felt she required a neutral but supportive setting to facilitate the work of mourning.

Fifty-first Month

A month later Lynn returned from vacation, which had been a kind of "time out" from real living. The consequent return to school heightened her depression and she talked about how she could no longer distract herself or cope and had no life without Margaret. I challenged this assumption that she had no life without her daughter and pointed out that she denied much rage and anger at Margaret for leaving her. Lynn replied, "I'm angry that I no longer have a choice about expressing myself and that you were right. I have to pick up the threads of my life and there are none.

At the next interview Lynn reported the following dream: "I had driven to Kentucky and had to drive back to New York City. I was worried about driving alone after dark. I was enjoying myself and didn't want to go. I knew I had to, terrified at the long drive in the dark alone. I woke up in a sweat." Free association: "I was mad at you for the dream, for connecting my remarks with Margaret, and for being at cross purposes with me, and for Margaret's dying, which made your point about being on my own." I pointed out that life had made her give up her fantasy of permanent union with Margaret as her mother as I had predicted it would but in an entirely different way—not by Margaret's growing up but by death—and that she was mad at me and at life.

Lynn resumed teaching, resumed work on her book, and continued to mourn but also to individuate. She said, "I feel I'm right back where I was when I went to Kentucky on my first job. I should have done something with myself then. It's 16 years later. I made a mess of my life. I don't want to make the same mistake again. My mother always told me I was crazy. I couldn't go to psychotherapy at that time because I was afraid I would find out I really was crazy or as my mother predicted I might become a streetwalker."

Fifty-second Month

Lynn continued taking piano lessons from Margaret's teacher and went to a course given by an accomplished pianist, talked about being afraid that thoughts about Margaret might go out of her head, which, I pointed out, is normal. She had still done nothing about Margaret's room. I said she was still clinging to the image of Margaret and she replied, "It also means giving up the image of myself as a mother, but even if I do want to stop clinging to my image of Margaret, I feel guilty, like a monster. I'm afraid of what I will feel after I get rid of Margaret's things. I'm afraid to close the open wound, I'm afraid I'll forget her. I'm betraying her. What will I be without her?"

I pointed out, "Part of her will stay with you." I also pointed out that most of these feelings were part of her fantasy life since Margaret was gone.

Lynn's thoughts and dreams continued to be about the last two years of the illness. I questioned, "Why?" Lynn replied, "I now feel the horror and resentment that I didn't feel when she was ill. Her death confirmed that I've been singled out to be left alone. My conflict over getting rid of her things related to my anger at her. I've only been aware of the anger at everybody else." I interpreted that her need to defend against the rage at Margaret for abandoning her as a representation of her maternal object, and her clinging to her memories interfered with mourning the reality loss of her daughter. She said, "I'm mad that I'm left to cope with all of this. I reached the end of my rope the same time that she did. It's worse to recall her well, and sick she was such an affectionate child. I elected to be a mother and I was deeply satisfied. I have to find another role and am ambivalent about everything. I never was a person." I pointed out she had two tasks: 1) mourning the loss of Margaret, and 2) individuation.

A week later Lynn reported, "I'm more frightened 'to let go of her than to think about her illness. I can't do without her. I resent my whole life. Afraid I'll forget her, never remember her with pleasure." I again discussed with Lynn the difference between detachment and mourning. If she doesn't stop clinging to her memories she will have to forget her and never will remember her with pleasure. It required mourning to be able to recall the pleasant memories. She replied, "No, I will hurt Margaret if I stop feeling pain about her death. Seems monstrous to be relieved at her death." I pointed out that this is a natural process, not monstrous. She said, "I'm afraid of what comes next." I pointed out that being on her own came next and that this was Margaret's legacy to her.

Fifty-fourth Month

In the next interview Lynn reported individuating more, and more anxiety about autonomy. "Whatever I do will not turn out right because I'm flawed. When I'm playing the piano I have to battle my mother. Sometimes I win and sometimes I lose and it ruins the pleasure. My problem with shopping for clothes is better. I used to be caught between buying what mother liked or what she despised, neither of which I wanted. I lose my sense of physical boundary—what I look like, what size I am. I don't know what I look like except to mother. I believed mother when she said I couldn't make it on my own. I've been angry and depressed most of my life, guilty about doing what I want to do and scared that catastrophe will occur. I enjoy going to the opera, piano lessons and practice."

Finally, nine months after Margaret's death, Lynn reports feeling somewhat better, less of a disaster: "I grew up because Margaret was sick." I said "No! You had to do it anyway."

Over Thanksgiving memories about Margaret were exacerbated but because she made plans to be busy they were kept within manageable limits. She talked about wanting to write a children's book on food and agriculture in the middle ages: "I finally have some feeling that I'm entitled to do something by myself, but I'm still guilty about surviving."

Fifty-fifth Month

In the next interview Lynn reported, "I'm still dreaming about Margaret in the hospital." I interpreted that she wanted Margaret back and clung to her in her dreams. I added that Margaret deserved a better fate than to be enshrined in Lynn's psyche as an excuse for her not becoming herself. Lynn replied: "I put away some of her things. I got scared, depressed about living on my own and angry." I said, "Of course you're angry about having to be on your own." At the next interview the patient angrily revealed that she packed up all of Margaret's things to be gotten rid of and she recognized that stubbornness was part of her style: "If I give up Margaret it will be what mother wants. Mother was apoplectic when I got pregnant."

The confrontation with the clinging at the time that Lynn was getting rid of Margaret's possessions deepened her depression: "I can't accept the fact that all the things I want in life are gone—marriage and a family. I can't see my teaching career as a substitute. I'm ready to die, nothing is left, life is over. I've lost the only job I ever wanted: being Margaret's mother."

18

Triumph

As Lynn struggled with unabated mourning ten months after Margaret's death, fate, which had treated her so cruelly, finally intervened with kindness and a new promising theme entered— Robert. Lynn began by mentioning incidentally that she liked Robert and then talked about her fear that she would do to her memory of Margaret what she did to the memory of other relationships. I pointed out that she had three options—to detach, cling or mourn—and that mourning would preserve Margaret in memory. The patient replied, "I feel foolish and absurd to have cared so much about mother." I questioned, "Was it mother or a fantasy about mother?"

With the dawning realization that she found Robert extremely attractive and that he also liked her, she reviewed her relationships with men: "I'm afraid I'll wreck it with him. He is interesting, the kind of man who makes me anxious lest he might leave me and in a way I would be relieved if he did, because if he gets to know me better he won't think I'm attractive. With other men in my life, I didn't feel inadequate. I knew they wouldn't leave me. They didn't threaten me. Like my first husband—they made me feel bad but didn't threaten. Robert has made my entire plumbing back up. These anxieties were taken care of in other relationships for me. I feel awful but delightful. I care about him, so feelings of inadequacy surface. This anxiety would not be present with a man with whom I'm sure it wouldn't work out in advance. I always arranged it that way.

"I've accepted Margaret's death, gotten rid of her things. I'm mostly just lonesome for her. The frequency of the hospital dreams has decreased." As the clinging to the image of Margaret decreased the relationship with men surfaced as a problem. Lynn said: "Yes, she was the only person I believed loved me." She reported a dream: "I was on a subway train with my mother and got off. An aged woman wanted to borrow a book from me, *The Hobbit,* one given to Margaret. I said 'no' and got off the train."

Free association: "In my fantasy my mother is always 35 and beautiful, not aged. I left her on the train. I'd spoken to my brother on the phone and thought he was going to tell me that mother had died. I thought, 'I'd better work this out before mother dies.' Never cry about her, I'd like to kill her."

I pointed out the confusion of her feelings of revenge against the real mother with the need to separate from the psychic mother and that she wanted to deny her need for the mother. She said, "It means my mother will win." I said, "No, it means you will win." She replied, "I can't forgive her for attacking my attractiveness. It's a problem for me now. I couldn't have been as ugly as she said. Mother devoted full time to her appearance."

In the next interview she reported, "I feel like a bowl of whipped cream. Robert is the nicest thing that ever happened to me but it makes me anxious. I expect him to leave me. I don't deserve him." A few sessions later, she continued, "I'm falling in love with Robert. Like drinking champagne all the time, I can't believe it will last. He told me he loved me. He is the kind of man I always was attracted to but I never thought he would reciprocate; it's almost too good to be true. If I had met him before Margaret died I would have run away from him— too threatening. The better I feel, I have flashes of Margaret's worst times in the hospital. I feel guilty about becoming myself, being independent, enjoying Robert. I feel so at ease with Robert. I resent my mother more now because of the picture I have of myself which will do me in if I don't change it."

Fifty-sixth Month

A week later she reported, "At times I have acute memories of Margaret's death, but now I'm also beginning to remember her before she was sick and I don't dream about the hospital very much. I'm actively enjoying being alone. Amazing! It's nice to have time to do nothing and not be scheduled. I'd like to cut down my sessions with you again to once a week. I'm anxious about leaving you but I want to try it. Following my own instincts in coping with Margaret's illness taught me how to decide what's good for me, how to take care of myself. I'm afraid if I stop treatment I will do something destructive. I'd like to put my past behind me. I think I'm more of a person. I feel I could do it for myself. Maybe mother didn't like me because I was OK."

In the first interview at once a week Lynn reported that Robert proposed marriage and she was ecstatic and again reviewed her anxieties and the difference between a real relationship and clinging. "I realize I'm moving away. I feel a great sense of loss. I want to move on, move ahead. I feel as if I'm shedding my skin. Glad of it. Not as scared as I was but why did it make me so sad? I started to give up clinging to Margaret when I packed up her clothes. I was always convinced that I would die if I didn't cling to her, that I would feel like an orphan."

Between this interview and the next interview the patient went through an abandonment crisis: "I felt physically sick. I wanted to go to bed and it had to do with what's going on with Robert, with the decrease in seeing you to once a week, my guilt about having a good time, my realization that I want to put the past behind me. Only my pride kept me from calling you. But I didn't and began to feel better. I'm now at last removed from the hospital experience. It's not as painful. Robert is a product of my experience with Margaret."

I pointed out that this was true, that her mourning the loss of her relationship with Margaret and therefore separating from the maternal object and cathecting her self image rather than the object had diminished her fears of engulfment and abandonment and allowed her to take a chance on a real intimate relationship.

Lynn reported, "My relationship with Robert is so good I keep pinching myself. I keep waiting for disaster to strike." She reported the following dream: "I was led down the street by an old crone of a woman. The streets were filled with snakes. I had to jump over them. I was terrified."

Free association: "I feel I've changed, that it's all slipping away from me—Margaret, mother and you. That part of me knows what I'm doing. I'm sad about leaving a lot of things behind me like mother and Margaret. I don't mind much about my mother but I'm frightened at what my final perspective on Margaret will be. It's as if I've cast loose my moorings. I'm frightened but I'm sure of myself underneath. I'm even changing all my relationships with my girlfriends and getting rid of all the old mother symbols."

Comment: The dream expressed the patient's separation anxiety at shifting her emotional investment from the object to the self.

Fifty-seventh Month

Lynn continued to report the twin themes of feeling much better on the one hand and experiencing increasing anxiety about being abandoned on the other. "Most of the time I feel happier than I ever have in my life. My whole life is turned around. My shock absorbers are gone. I can't believe it. I am turned upside down, don't know whether I'm on my head or on my feet. I'm surprised I'm capable of feeling as happy as I do. On the other hand my stomach is constantly upset. I often feel guilty about feeling so good twelve months after Margaret died. I can no longer conjure the image of my mother. I can't understand her behavior. She disliked the fact that I was a girl. I was not enough of a doormat to her. Mother was devoted to cleanliness, perfection, beauty, flawlessness. She never touched me because I never deserved it. She married my father because he looked good to her."

In the next several interviews these themes continued: "I vacillate between drowning and missing Margaret, rage at being deprived of the role of a mother, and feeling better than I ever have in my life. I never spent a whole day in my apartment alone before unscheduled, doing just what I want. I seem to enjoy just bumming around. It's such a relief to be unplugged from my friends. I could walk out of my present life without looking back. I no longer feel that I will be leaving Margaret behind."

At the end of the month, as the first anniversary of her daughter's death approached, Lynn developed recurrent dreams about the hospital, rage about the death, and had spells of weeping, but she said, "It's painful to go on without her but not impossible. I have finally put Margaret and the hospital in perspective. I will always feel sad and I feel guilty about putting it behind me, that I have made such progress. Not only have I survived her but I am more intact than I ever was. I thought I was completely burned out. Although anything in the environment that I see around me that reminds me of Margaret makes me sad, when I'm with Robert I'm happier than I've ever been in my life. He loves me for what I am. It's like being wrapped in whipped cream."

Fifty-eighth Month

Following the last interview, Lynn reported the following dreams: "I was on a bus alone with the driver. The driver took the wrong direction and left me out in a deserted place on the edge of water and, as I stood there all alone, a snake appeared and I screamed. I woke up screaming." Free association: "I don't know what it means." I interpreted to Lynn that I felt it was an expression of her feelings that the end point of treatment, i.e., becoming herself, led to fear of being attacked. She responded with the following dream: "I went to a children's birthday party to pick up Margaret and Robert. Margaret looked as she did before she got sick. Suddenly I was in a hotel room with my mother. She kept coming closer and closer. I thought she was trying to establish contact with me. She said 'Lord & Taylor is closed.' I left relieved."

Free association: "Eight or nine years ago I saw mother but she didn't see me in Lord & Taylor. Shopping and clothes are symbols of the essence of what went on between mother and me. Symbols of mother's onslaught. The whole encounter distasteful. Just wanted to get out and knew I was going to." I reminded Lynn that she used to say that she could spend all day shopping in Lord & Taylor, i.e., with mother, and I felt the dream suggested that she was putting an end to the wish for reunion with mother at long last, i.e., Lord & Taylor is truly closed.

Fifty-ninth Month

Lynn then took a week's vacation with Robert and on her return reported that they would be married in one month. "I had a wonderful time but I had acute indigestion and vomiting half the time I was away. I can't believe it's happening. . . . No one's ever loved me like Robert, thought that I was wonderful. Life is changing in a way that it is better than I had ever dreamed. I could not have planned it better. I dream about losing Margaret and looking for her, and off and on I get hysterical about getting married.

"I now enjoy being alone; I've had the experience. I keep taking my temperature because I'm afraid I'll disappear. I bought a wedding wardrobe and spent more money on myself in one day than I have on clothes in my entire life. I have developed a 'wall of indolence'—I want to do nothing."

The patient and Robert were then married in a civil ceremony and planned to spend the summer away so the patient could no longer see me in treatment, which brought forth her anxiety about separation from me, as described in the following dream:

Dream: "I was in a terrible awful dark rain forest looking for Margaret. Nobody was there except you. You didn't realize I was looking for her. You said there were snakes all over in cages. I thought I was OK because you wouldn't let them out but you did and I woke up terrified."

Free association: "I thought I trusted you and I was wrong in the dream. Now I have the same thoughts about you and about Robert. I realize they're crazy and atrocious. I begin to get feelings he married me to be mean to me." I interpreted these feelings about Robert as an externalization of her anxiety that if she continues in the present path she will be ready to leave me. But she sees it as my leaving her, i.e., a repetition of abandonment by the mother for individuation. She continued to work through her anxiety about termination of treatment as being an abandonment until she left with her husband for the summer trip.

SUMMARY

Lynn's history illustrated how the developmental failure that occurs in the childhood of the borderline patient stunts the capacities for love (intimacy) and work and inevitably leads to an adult life which becomes a literal and horrifying repetition of the emotional deprivations of childhood.

Each effort to change the difficult and painful life situation produces only further failure and frustration. There is no way out. The borderline adult's metaphor of his or her childhood as a concentration camp becomes a prophecy for his or her entire life. Those chains formed so early and bound so firmly hobble any effort to escape.

Lynn's need to defend herself against her feelings of engulfment and abandonment associated with separation from her mother by acting out the wish for reunion through clinging became the leitmotif or guidepost of her entire life.

She managed to negotiate her adolescent and adult years through a plodding, compulsive approach to her work and by clinging first to her mother and then to an older man. When he died and she left home she experienced her second severe abandonment depression which impelled her to marry an inappropriate man with whom she lived years of frustration. The birth of her daughter brought on further clinging as she attempted to solve the deprivation at the hands of her mother through her daughter. Without the capacities for true intimacy in love and creativity in work she had to manage as best she could.

Psychotherapy entered this dismal scene and slowly, tediously, sometimes tortuously wrought change. She divorced her husband, controlled the acting out of the wish for reunion on her daughter, and finally, through the tragedy of her daughter's death, she mourned the loss of her daughter and thereby developed a capacity for object constancy.

She now had an emotional investment in her self image as well as the internal object so that she was no longer so dependent on the external object to cope and be free of anxiety. Her fears of engulfment and/or abandonment diminished. Her individuation began to flower and with it her creativity at work. Ideas began to gush forth and her writing on her textbook flowed easily.

Her newly developed capacity for object constancy enabled her to seek out and enjoy a true, loving, intimate relationship with a man without being overwhelmed by fears of engulfment or abandonment. She could now love and work.

Summary and Discussion

SUMMARY

It is now necessary to take a step back from the emotional intensity and the immediacy of the clinical situation presented in the last 12 chapters to review and summarize the principles those chapters illustrated.

An object relations theory of the developmental origin and intrapsychic structure of the borderline syndrome was described and then a therapeutic design based on that theory was presented. The theory can be summarized as follows: The borderline patient suffers from an arrest occurring at the separation-individuation phase (rapprochement subphase) of development. The arrest is due to the mother's withdrawal of her libidinal availability at the child's efforts to separate and individuate. The arrest or fixation occurs at that time because the child's individuation consti-

337

tutes a major threat to the mother's defensive need to cling to her infant and causes her to withdraw her libidinal availability. The child needs the availability of her supplies to grow; if he grows the supplies are withdrawn. This precipitates an abandonment depression in the child—who feels the withdrawal as a loss of part of himself. To defend against these feelings he denies the separation and clings to the maternal figure and thus fails to progress through the normal developmental stages of separation-individuation to autonomy. He suffers from a developmental arrest.

The twin themes of this interaction—reward for regression and clinging and withdrawal for separation-individuation—are introjected by the child as self and object representations together with the affect that linked those interactions. These form the leitmotif of the borderline's intrapsychic structure—the split object relations unit consisting of a rewarding part-unit and a withdrawing part-unit, each with its characteristic object representation, self representation and affect.

At the same time the patient develops a split ego as follows: The mother rewards those ego functions that enable her to cling—avoidance of individuation, denial of separation, projection and acting out of the wish for reunion by clinging. Thus, part of the ego fails to undergo the necessary transformation from pleasure principle to reality principle, for to do so would mean acceptance of the reality of the separation, which would bring on the abandonment depression. The mother's clinging and withdrawing and the patient's acting out of the wish for reunion promote the failure of one part of the ego to develop, resulting in an ego structure which is split—a pathologic pleasure ego which pursues relief from feelings of abandonment and a reality ego which pursues the reality principle.

An alliance develops between the RORU and the pathologic ego, the purpose of which is to promote the "good" feeling and to defend against the bad feelings of abandonment associated with the WORU. The WORU is activated by actual experiences of separation or loss, or by efforts towards separation and individuation, including those that occur as a result of therapy. The RORU-pathologic ego alliance is activated by the resurgence of the WORU to defend against the abandonment depression.

The RORU thus becomes the borderline's principal defense against the painful affective state associated with the WORU. In terms of reality, however, both part-units are pathological. It is as if the patient had but two alternatives—either to feel bad, the abandonment depression (WORU), or to feel good (RORU) at the cost of the denial of reality and the acting out of self-destructive behavior.

The transference of the borderline results from the activation and projection of the split object relations units—the RORU and the WORU—each of which the patient proceeds to alternatively project upon the therapist. When it is the WORU, the patient perceives therapy as leading to feelings of abandonment, denies the reality of therapeutic benefit and activates the RORU as a defense. When it is the RORU, the patient "feels good" but under the sway of the pathologic ego is usually acting in a self-destructive manner.

The psychotherapy compensates for the two key developmental defects of the borderline's intrapsychic structure, i.e., in object relations and ego structure, by two therapeutic techniques. The therapist must be a real person (object) who supports the patient's individuation, and he must provide a reality ego through confrontation of the denial of the destructiveness of the pathologic ego. The purpose of the confrontation is to change the patient's experience of the RORU-pathologic ego alliance from ego-syntonic to ego-alien. Insofar as confrontation promotes control of the behavior, the WORU becomes activated, which in turn reactivates the RORU with the appearance of further resistance. A circular process results sequentially including resistance, confrontation, working-through of the abandonment depression (WORU), further resistance (RORU), and further confrontation which leads to further working-through.

If this process proves successful a new alliance develops between the therapist's healthy ego and the patient's embattled reality ego as a result of the patient's having internalized the therapist as a positive object. This new alliance battles with the RORU-pathologic ego alliance for control of the patient's motivations and actions. A new object relations unit develops with the therapist as a positive object representation who approves of separation-individuation, plus a self representation as a capable, developing person, plus an affect (good feeling) which ensues from the exercise of constructive coping and mastery rather than regressive behavior. Working-through impels progressive externalization of the RORU and WORU units (together with the latter's rage and depression) and sets the stage for the coalescence of good and bad self and object representations, which is a prelude to the inception of whole object relations.

Supportive psychotherapy—which is more than supportive and more than short-term—aims to enable the patient to learn awareness and control of the defense mechanisms of his pathologic ego and thereby to strip from the reality of his life structure these defenses, along with their destructive effects. Despite the fact that it does not attempt a reconstruction of the patient's intrapsychic state, it still can bring about dramatic changes in the patient's life as he controls the pathologic ego and his motivations become more reality oriented than fantasy oriented—i.e., his life becomes dominated by efforts to master and cope with reality rather than to "feel good" at the cost of denying reality problems.

Reconstructive psychotherapy, intensive and psychoanalytically oriented, is usually an expansion and outgrowth of supportive psychotherapy. It aims at reconstruction of the patient's intrapsychic state by working through the abandonment depression associated with the original separation-individuation phase arrest. This leads to the achievement of ego autonomy, together with the transformation of the split object relations part-units into whole units and the split ego into a whole ego. As the patient's individuation flowers, new capacities for love and work emerge. Many—but not all—borderline patients can and will respond to intensive psychotherapy if given the proper therapeutic support. The enormous decrease in the vulnerability to stress (both separation and individuation stress), and the new-found capacities which enrich the person's life are persuasive arguments for attempting intensive psychotherapy where possible.

DISCUSSION

A Perspective on the Mother

It has been fashionable in some psychiatric and lay circles to blame the mother for whatever goes wrong in development. The theory described here that the mother's withdrawal produces the arrest, combined with the reports of patients' hostility to the mother in psychotherapy, may give some the impression that I share this opinion. Nothing could be farther from the truth.

There may be some borderline patients whose constitutional endowment is so defective that any withdrawal on the part of the mother would cause difficulty—i.e., it is their need, not the mother's withdrawal. Even in those patients where the mother's withdrawal seems the principal factor, the notion that it is her fault assumes that she had a choice and could have done otherwise, which is just not true. The borderline mother is caught in the same bind with her own mother that she reproduces with her child. She has no choice.

If blame must be assessed it should be placed on the human condition which requires such prolonged dependence on one individual for development to take place. This makes the child extraordinarily vulnerable to the idiosyncrasies of that person (the mother). On the other hand, the prolonged dependence on this relationship also provides the potential for the richness of the human personality.

It is a mistake, in my judgment, in psychotherapy to encourage or side with the patient's hostility to the mother. The patient has to become aware of and express it in therapy in order to grow but whatever the source of this hostility in the past—be it an actual memory or a fantasy to rationalize a feeling state—the problem is now the patient's responsibility and he must work it out.

As the patient grows in therapy, as he overcomes the splitting and establishes whole object relations, and as the wounds of the past lose some of their sting, the patient comes to see his mother as a whole object, both good and bad, as she existed in reality caught in her own existential dilemma. The ancient rage at her subsides and ebbs away, as does the patient's need to blame her. As an adult he accepts the responsibility for his past as well as his present and can see his mother as a fellow human being who was caught, as was he, in a net that was not of her own making.

Patients whose hostility to their mothers continues unabated have not attained maturity and whole object relations but, more than likely, the rage at the mother becomes a rationalization for a life of acting out to avoid the painful task of taking responsibility for and working through past traumas in order to free the present.

My Emotional Reactions as Therapist

Probably the single most difficult skill to acquire in psychotherapy with borderline patients is the ability to recognize and control one's own identification with their projections—whether it be the RORU or the WORU, to recognize that one neither "loves" (RORU) nor "hates" (WORU) the patient but rather serves as a target upon which the patient projects a repetition of his early developmental struggles, thereby revealing the signs as well as the sources of his emotional problems.

My own emotional difficulty in learning this skill is best illustrated by the work with the two patients in intensive reconstructive psychotherapy, Peter and Lynn.

Peter

In the beginning phase of therapy, before a therapeutic alliance was formed, Peter actively and cleverly engaged in a subtle campaign to flatter me by "feeding my ego" so that I would respond with the desired approval. For example, he would report having accidentally met people who knew me and my work at the hospipital, all couched in flattering terms. Peter was a true professional at this art, as evidenced by his success as a salesman. He was a master of subtlety in avoiding my initial efforts at confrontation.

I found myself under constant, intense pressure to respond in a way I knew was not therapeutic. I began to react to the manipulation involved in his maneuvers and the inner tension rose as I controlled the responses he was so doggedly trying to evoke. This led to an inhibition of the flexibility of my general emotional responsiveness in therapy that Peter felt as an emotional withdrawal. At these times he would accuse me, not entirely unjustly, of being "a cold fish." I was too caught up in trying to find a way out of my own dilemma to provide him with what was therapeutically needed.

After a while I realized that I was unconsciously identifying with his projection of the RORU on me and attempting to summon up the emotions that the projection was designed to elicit—like the resident described on pp. 106-107 I was trying to find the emotions that would support my playing the RORU role. At the same time as I was unconsciously identifying with the RORU role, I was consciously controlling its expression because my reality ego perceived that expression as not therapeutic. The tension rose, my emotional responsiveness was inhibited, which the patient felt was an emotional withdrawal, which activated a projection of the WORU on me—the patient's calling me a "cold fish."

The awareness of the identification now showed the way out of this dilemma. I began to use the occurrence of the tension in me as a *signal* that the patient was projecting the RORU on me, and rather than identifying with the projection and reacting to the patient, I used the signal to recognize the projection and to alert me to the patient's behavior, which enabled me to bring it to his attention for investigation. This drained my tension and restored my own emotional flexibility so that I was free to deal with the patient's therapeutic needs. At the same time, it brought to the center stage for investigation why he behaved as he did and thus began the therapeutic efforts to overcome the splitting and link the RORU with the WORU.

As the therapeutic alliance evolved and Peter began to work through his problems, a rich communication developed based on the joint therapeutic endeavor that was gratifying to me as well as to him. However, it carried with it the risk of my identifying too closely with his struggle and thereby becoming prone to reactions of disappointment and/or anger at the inevitable regressions that came to punctuate his slow but steady progress. On more than one occasion I would find myself angry and disappointed at his sudden loss of a previously learned insight as a temporary regression seemingly "interrupted" the therapeutic work. These emotions would impel me to overlook the meaning of his behavior (regression) and therefore I would attempt to deal with it inappropriately by repeating an interpretation to restore the lost insight. When the interpretation failed I realized something was wrong which led me back to my own over-identification and the anger and disappointment. Recognition of the over-identification freed me to diagnose the regression and deal with it appropriately through confrontation.

As Peter passed into the last phase of therapy it became necessary for me to "give up" the gratification inherent in the working-through phase. I observed myself being tempted to err on both sides in the management of this phase: to foreclose the working-through of these emotions by encouraging him to stop too soon, or to dogmatically insist that he continue for a long period to put off the process of separation. Since it seemed to me that he was defending himself against separation by the former mechanism—stopping too soon to foreclose the working-through— it became a real test of my own capacity for self and object differentiation to be able to tell who was doing what. I think I finally managed to avoid the two temptations and confront my own emotions about separation, which enabled me then to confront Peter about his defenses.

Lynn

My problems with Lynn were similar. In the initial phase of therapy Lynn employed angry demands rather than flattery to activate the desired approval. I again identified with her projections and attempted to summon the emotions they were designed to evoke, and meanwhile inhibited my responses, which again led to angry accusations on her part. The metaphor for this interaction was that she was paying her hard earned money for "help" (i.e., love, maternal supplies, etc.) from me and what she was getting was "not enough." This brief account does not convey the intensity with which Lynn insisted that her transference acting out was "real." My own efforts to deal with the transference acting out were quite impaired until I recognized that I was identifying with her projections and began to *point out* what she was doing rather than *react to* her behavior.

When her daughter became fatally ill, a far greater danger arose—that I would be influenced by my own feelings of empathy and sadness over this terrible tragedy toward efforts at reassurance and support that would go beyond the therapeutic necessity and give therapeutic reinforcement to the RORU. In addition, throughout this period I experienced a variety of withdrawal phenomenon: being late for interviews, difficulties maintaining concentration in interviews and in recalling the content from interview to interview. These reflected my own difficulty in facing the reality presented by her problem, i.e., that I could possibly lose one of my own children.

This awareness reinforced my efforts to separate the struggle with my own emotions from the technical requirements of her therapy. That does not mean that the struggle was settled but rather that as time wore on it came to have less and less influence on my therapeutic efforts with the patient.

Management of the separation phase of therapy with Lynn

seemed to present fewer than usual difficulties because of the way in which it came about. However, it is entirely possible, as I shall describe, that there were few problems because the separation was handled by a type of acting out that is very difficult to confront—a love relationship.

The objective of the therapy had been to help her to free herself from the past and her mother in order to make a freer or less contaminated object choice. The long struggle in therapy with her contaminated object choice, as seen in the transference and as portrayed in her relationship with all the men in her life, had conditioned me, as well as her, to the paradoxical fact that she badly needed a more appropriate object choice despite her difficulty in that area. The loss of her daughter further underlined this conditioning. The appearance on the scene of a new and seemingly appropriate man—against the background just described—seemed to spring right out of a fairy tale to fulfill the patient's hopes. Separation from therapy contained, therefore, a stronger than usual positive tone. It is impossible, it seems to me, to confront a woman in love in order to enable her to work through abandonment depression about separation if those feelings are possibly being managed by the love relationship in the first place. On the other hand, the relationship was not solely for that purpose and I was reassured by the thought that if it did not work out she could return.

Parents' Psychopathology

The father can seem to have any of the severe forms of character pathology as long as his behavior reinforces the mother's clinging. On the other hand, the evidence in both adolescents and adults suggests that the mother is borderline. A legitimate question can be raised as to whether or not the mother, like the father, might not also have any one of the severe forms of character pathologies as long as it results in her clinging. The final evidence is far from available on this issue and I am open to a change of opinion in the light of further evidence. In the meantime my argument is as follows: The mothers of adolescents whom we were able to observe directly and to treat were clearly borderline, and my adult patients' reports of their mothers bear striking resemblance to what we observed in the mothers of the adolescents. Their early childhood memories in the working-through phase and the repetition of their early relationships with the mother in the transference are also quite similar to the adolescents'.

Furthermore, one might speculate that the level of the developmental arrest of the child might depend upon how much individuation the mother could tolerate before withdrawing. The mother with a narcissistic disorder might require her child to exist solely as a narcissistic object and then could tolerate little individuation and would withdraw quite early, producing a developmental arrest very early in the separation-individuation phase long before the rapprochement subphase. The mother who has schizophrenia, on the other hand, as described by Lidz (131) and Bateson (7), would require the maintenance of the symbiotic relationship and would withdraw at early attempts to begin to separate. It is, I suspect, a specific and unique characteristic of the borderline that the symbiotic and early separation-individuation phases are times of rich gratification for mother and child alike (see Chapter 15). The mother's withdrawal during the rapprochement subphase then comes as a great and stark contrast to what has gone before.

The specificity of the mother's clinging and withdrawal response to the emerging individuation of her child was borne home again and again 1) by observation of mother-adolescent interaction, 2) by patients' (adolescents' and adults') reports of memories of childhood experiences once they had reached the working-through phase, and 3) by their transference relationship. The resistance of young residents to perceiving this relationship, as well as the resistance, from time to time, of audiences, to the notion suggests the possibility that this issue ranks along with infantile sexuality as one of the most repressed of human experiences. Could it be that our own ancient infantile need for this support seems to blind us to accepting the fact that for some it was faulty?

Oedipal Level of Conflict in the Borderline

For years many borderline patients whose problems revolved about separation from the mother and therefore a dyadic relationship were treated as if their problems were at the oedipal level and involved a triadic relationship. Now that this issue has been clarified and the focus has properly shifted to a dyadic relationship and separation from the mother, the question arises as to the relationship of this level to the oedipal level of development. This complex problem, focusing as it does on key developmental issues, has aroused much controversy, which can only be settled by further research.

The impression I have gathered from work with borderline patients suggests a number of possibilities. In some patients the developmental arrest is so severe that they do not reach the oedipal level; in others, such as Peter, when the patient reaches the oedipal level, hampered by his earlier fixation, his separation anxiety and castration anxiety condense and he regresses to the borderline level, i.e., there is a condensation of the pre-oedipal and the oedipal. In a woman such as Catherine the father who rescues the patient, substituting for the mother in the separation-individuation phase—probably helping the patient's growth at this time, produces a closeness which becomes very threatening in the oedipal phase so that she must regress to her relationship with her father as a care-taker to defend against her perception of him as a sexual object.

Most of the borderline patients I have treated have first resolved their separation anxiety in a transference which is dyadic. As the separation anxiety was resolved, castration anxiety and oedipal concerns came to the fore as the transference changed from dyadic to triadic.

Selection of Cases

The patients presented are more or less representative of the type of borderline patient I have seen in psychotherapy over the last ten years, with the exception of those borderline patients whose disorder was closer to the psychotic level—those with strong paranoid features or intermittent psychotic episodes. Work with these patients suggested that their intrapsychic structure differed more in degree than kind from those already described. Their developmental arrest occurred earlier in the separation-individuation phase, their pathologic ego and their WORU were stronger, their tolerance for separation stress was less, and the sensitivity to and projection on the therapist were greater. More care and consideration had to be given to the therapeutic input, particularly confrontations, which had to be carefully phrased and well-timed in order to avoid providing fodder for the patient's paranoid projections.

It is my hunch that the limits of the borderline spectrum are much wider than presently conceived and probably include, as Kernberg (99) suggests, many patients with symptom pictures of anorexia nervosa, phobias, alcoholism, drug addiction, impulse disorders and possibly perversions. These have not been presented here. Again, however, my own work with adolescents with anorexia nervosa and school phobia and with adults with alcoholism, drug addiction or impulse disorders suggests that the same theoretical and therapeutic considerations apply.

The Boundaries of Theory and Clinical Research

One of the sources from which theory springs is the therapist's need to find some conceptual framework upon which to base the decisions he makes in his daily task of trying to help patients. Theory represents an organic living body of knowledge, a residue of hypothesis formulation, clinical testing, and then hypothesis revision. It is open-ended and subject to constant revision based on further clinical tests. For example, Freud first theorized that his hysterical patients had been seduced and then, on the basis of later evidence, changed the theory to a fantasy of seduction. Both steps in this process were vital to theory construction—his entertaining the first theory and later changing it in the light of further evidence. The more the tests confirm the theory the greater its validity. One must be careful, however, to avoid the trap of assuming that the theory is fact and requires no further validation. Theory is vital to our therapeutic task, but it is equally vital that we keep in mind its limitations.

Clinical research is probably the best instrument for studying the human personality, because it can evaluate all the variables acting at one time in the patient. However, the phenomena it studies are so complex and the observer who is involved in psychotherapy with the patient is so subject to distortions, both unconscious and conscious, that the process defies the application of a rigorous scientific methodology, which therefore limits the generalization of the findings. Does this mean that because it is not so-called scientifically controlled for the bias of the observer and the variable under study that the findings have no meaning?

The answer to this question revolves about the differences between the two basic types of research—hypothesis gathering and hypothesis testing. The former is the first stage of any research where general observations are made about the phenomena under study in order to formulate a hypothesis. This phase of research can be of an indeterminate length and does not require rigorous controls. The second stage of hypothesis testing requires those controls in order to make sure that the research design provides a true test of the theory. The research presented here, like most clinical research, falls under the heading of hypothesis gathering and the scientific validity of the findings applies only at that level. It will require many similar studies at verifying the same phenomena before the stage is even set for hypothesis testing research (82, 85).

This, however, does not mean that no efforts were made to control for the bias of the researcher. All patients in psychotherapy have a tendency to tell the therapist what they think he wants to hear, and borderline patients are probably more tempted to do this than most patients. The need for therapeutic confrontation and communicative matching make this an even more sensitive issue. What efforts were made to avoid this dilemma— to avoid fitting the patient to the theory rather than vice versa? What efforts were made to avoid manipulation or programing of the patient?

In his relationship with his mother in his early development the borderline patient was accustomed to defending against his own feelings by avoidance, denial and splitting. As a consequence he often is completely unaware of his *own* feelings. It is vital to his therapy that the patient *experience* the therapy as emanating from his own feelings or coming from his own head, with the therapist facilitating the process, rather than the other way round. The patient must feel that the direction and continuity of the process come mostly from within, not from without. Winnicott's (235) statement that his own pleasure at a particularly apt interpretation was replaced in time by his pleasure in seeing the patient acquire an insight serves as a useful guide. Similarly, Bruch's (25) comments about psychotherapy with patients with anorexia nervosa are also useful: The therapist must restrain his therapeutic impatience and create an environment in which the patient can learn to identify and distinguish between his feelings.

Confrontation and communicative matching must be in response to the patient's feeling state and not the need of the therapist and should result from the therapist's being "tuned in" and empathetic to that feeling state. Otherwise they can become manipulations. However, even if these therapeutic activities are performed in an ideal manner, it is still necessary at some point in the therapy that their effect on the patient become a subject of investigation. The degree to which the patient has consciously or unconsciously succumbed to the temptation to utilize these activities as a program or set of rules with which to comply in order to please his therapist and incidentally also to avoid individuation must be analyzed. This analysis serves to make the patient aware of his own motivations and helps to limit their harmful effects.

There is no question that suggestions are involved in confrontation—i.e., suggestions antithetic to the nature of the patient's pathogenic interest. The confrontation suggests that it is in the patient's therapeutic interest to control his destructive impulse in order to analyze it rather than to act it out. Although the suggestive element is limited to destructive behavior it raises the question of whether the patient's improvement has been due to the fact that he has incorporated the suggestion into his defensive system, which has brought about a symptomatic improvement at the cost of greater resistance to deeper analysis and working-through. It is a moot question for patients in supportive psychotherapy since they never get to the point of deeper analysis. The evidence from those patients in reconstructive therapy would imply that this is a minimal influence. Once acting out behavior is controlled the working-through process takes a course of its own, powered by the patient's feelings and associations, as the confrontations of the therapist are relegated to a minor role. He then limits himself to cautious interpretation of resistance. The emotional effect of the suggestions themselves becomes a subject for analysis. It is my impression that, if the therapist has handled his confrontations properly in the initial stage of therapy, the patient increasingly takes over the direction of his treatment and makes his own interpretation of his feeling state. At that point the therapist actively deals mainly with resistances.

Therapist's Conviction

Could the therapeutic effect be solely a result of the therapist's conviction? This is a difficult question for any therapy or therapist to answer. This theory and technique have now been taught to over 100 psychiatrists whose results are similar if not the same. They would also claim the theoretical understanding as the reason, but it cannot be denied that they might also be getting the results from conviction rather than theory.

CONCLUSION

To return to the clinical level, I would like to emphasize that the kind of clinical improvement demonstrated in these patients is dramatic and at this moment appears to be enduring. Whatever the scientific reason for this change, at the clinical level it represents such a vast improvement in therapeutic possibilities for the borderline patient that it warrants further serious study and widespread application.

The fruits of successful psychotherapeutic labor with the borderline adult are rich and varied for patient and therapist alike —freeing the patient from the chains of childhood conflicts to enable him to grow and discover for himself the magic and mystery of life—to love and to work.

APPENDIX: Opening Remarks of Paper Presented at Margaret Mahler Symposium

This occasion* has a double meaning for me. It weaves together two prominent threads in my own life—the city of Philadelphia and the work of Margaret Mahler. I would like to take a moment to share this meaning with you.

I found no small degree of irony in the fact that I was asked to present this work on developmental failure in this city of all cities where I was born, where my own emotional conflicts began and where my ties are so deep. Except for college and the war years I lived here until I moved to New York City at the age of 26, going to high school nearby. The city became a great symbol of emotional conflict for me—an externalization, you will say. And you are right.

I had more than a little trouble leaving at 26. For example, when I left to go to New York I developed a fetish, a transitional object.

---

* This paper was presented at the Margaret Mahler Symposium, Philadelphia Psychoanalytic Institute, April, 1973.

I ordered and received the *Philadelphia Evening Bulletin* every night and on Sunday for the first six months in New York City. I suppose in retrospect I was just checking to be sure the city was still there.

In New York City I spent more years of my young adult life than I care to remember metaphorically attempting to get out of Philadelphia or to get Philadelphia out of me. The achievement of this seemingly gargantuan task catapulted me into the kind of activities which led me to the work of Margaret Mahler, which led me to write a book, which I suppose led me to be invited back to Philadelphia —throwing countless years of analysis into jeopardy. The more things change the more they stay the same. It would seem that I can't win.

I am happy to report, however, that this visit to Philadelphia reveals a profound difference. It's much like visiting a personal disaster area 30 years later with the tools that could have prevented the disaster had you only known how to use them in the first place. It provides a unique feeling of fulfillment akin to that of completing a cycle, closing a circle or mastering a trauma.

Since symbiosis and separation-individuation are on the agenda for today I'd like to report one other personal experience. My father was a lawyer and I have two younger brothers who are lawyers. The story is told that when I was born my mother said, "This one's going to be a doctor." I can't recall her mentioning it during childhood or adolescence, but such is the power of symbiotic cuing and matching that here I am nevertheless.

However, there is more to the story. I feel certain my mother had in mind that I would be a laying-on hands type of doctor, perhaps OB-GYN or maybe an internist. I'm sure that the next to last thing in her mind was that I would be a psychiatrist who pried into mother's heads to determine how they mother. The fact that I am such a psychiatrist testifies to the power of separation-individuation.

Now, as to my encounter with Dr. Mahler's work. I am not by nature a flatterer, as my staff will readily attest and will even show the bruises to prove it. However, once in a very great while the reality of life events does correspond to the magic of a dream. Once in a very great while a man has an encounter that changes his life so completely, so dramatically, inexorably and irreversibly that he is never the same again. Such was the effect on me of my encounter with the work of Dr. Mahler.

Let me briefly explain. I had been struggling for years to understand and to treat what at the time were called personality disorders in adolescence. The results were neither very helpful for the patient nor flattering to my therapeutic skill. I had read everything I could get my hands on but could find nothing that would shed enough light to change this state of affairs. Then I happened upon the work of Dr. Mahler. I can still remember the electricity I felt on reading the first paper, "Autism and Symbiosis—Two Extreme Disturbances of Identity." After that I followed her papers like a hungry kid waiting outside the bakery to wolf down the next batch of pastry. I devoured every article and immediately applied it. Gradually the door opened and the mysteries of the borderline syndrome were revealed.

When I conveyed this understanding to my patients they began to improve at a rapid rate. So today I stand here as a spokesman not just for myself, but also for the many patients whom I've treated and who are now able to lead much improved, constructive lives and for the residents I've taught who are now able to give these patients the help they need. In the name of all these I say to Dr. Mahler that we owe you a profound debt of gratitude for your work which can never be repaid directly. Hopefully, we can make some inroads on this debt by participating in meetings of this sort.

Bibliography

1. ABELIN, E. "The Role of the Father in the Separation-Individuation Process," in Settlage, C. F. and McDevitt, J. B. (Eds.), *Separation-Individuation—Essays in Honor of Margaret S. Mahler*. New York: Int. Univ. Press, 1971. 229-252.
2. ADLER, G. "Hospital Treatment of Borderline Patients," *Amer. J. Psych.*, 130: 32-36, 1973.
3. ADLER, G. and MYERSON, P. *Confrontation in Psychotherapy*. New York: Science House, 1973.
4. ATKIN, S. "Ego Synthesis and Cognition in a Borderline Case," *Psa. Quart.*, 44:29-61, 1975.
5. ATKINS, N. B. "Comments on Severe and Psychotic Regressions in Analysis," *J. Amer. Psa. Ass.*, 15:584-605, 1967.
6. BAK, R. C. "Being in Love and Object Loss," *Int. J. Psa.*, 54:1-8, 1973.
7. BATESON, C. F., MISHLER, E. G. and WAXLER, N. E. *Family Processes and Schizophrenia*. New York: Science House, 1968.
8. BENEDEK, T. "Adaptation of Reality in Early Infancy," *Psa. Quart.*, 7:200-215, 1938.
9. BENEDEK, T. "The Psychosomatic Implications of the Primary Unit: Mother-Child," *Amer. J. Orthopsychiat.*, 19:642-654, 1949.
10. BENEDEK, T. "Psychobiological Aspects of Mothering," *Amer. J. Orthopsychiat.*, 26:272-278, 1956.

11. BENEDEK, T. "Parenthood As a Developmental Phase," *J. Amer. Psa. Ass.,* 7:389-417, 1959.
12. BLANCK, G. "Some Technical Implications of Ego Psychology," *Int. J. Psa.,* 47:6-13, 1966.
13. BLANCK, G. *Ego Psychology.* New York: Columbia Univ. Press, 1974.
14. BLOS, P. *On Adolescence.* New York: The Free Press of Glencoe, 1962.
15. BONNARD, A. "Primary Process Phenomena in the Case of a Borderline Psychotic Child," *Int. J. Psa.,* 48:221-236, 1967.
16. BOWLBY, J. "Separation Anxiety," *Int. J. Psa.,* 41:89-113, 1960.
17. BOWLBY, J. "Grief and Mourning in Infancy and Early Childhood," *Psa. Study Child,* 15:9-52, 19660.
18. BOWLBY, J. *Attachment and Loss, Vol. I, Attachment.* New York: Basic Books, 1969.
19. BOWLBY, J. "The Nature of the Child's Tie to His Mother," *Int. J. Psa.,* 39:350-371, 1958.
20. BOWLBY, J. "Process of Mourning," *Int. J. Psa.,* 42:317-340, 1961.
21. BOWLBY, J. *Attachment and Loss, Vol. II, Separation.* New York: Basic Books, 1973.
22. BAOYER, L. B. and GIOVACCHINI, P. L. *Psychoanalytic Treatment of Characterological and Schizophrenic Disorders.* New York: Science Books, 1967.
23. BRADY, N. "Vulture as a Mother Symbol," *Amer. Imago,* 22:47-57, 1965.
24. BRODEY, W. M. "On the Dynamics of Narcissism: I. Externalization and Early Ego Deviation," *Psa. Study Child,* 20:165-193, 1965.
25. BRUCH, H. "Psychotherapy in Primary Anorexia Nervosa," *J. Nervous and Mental Disease,* 150:51-67, 1970.
26. BYCHOWSKI, G. "The Problem of Latent Psychosis," *J. Amer. Psa. Assn.,* 1: 484-503, 1953.
27. BYCHOWSKI, G. "Obsessive Compulsive Façade in Schizophrenia," *Int. J. Psa.,* 47:189-202, 1966.
28. CAIN, A. C. "On the Meaning of 'Playing Crazy' in Borderline Children," *Psychiatry,* 27:278-289, 1964.
29. CHASE, L. S., and HIRE, A. W. "The Borderline Character Disorder." Unpublished manuscript, 1969.
30. CHASE, L. S. and HIRE, A. W. "Countertransference in the Analysis of Borderlines," *Bull. Phila. Assn. for Psa.,* 17:48-51, 1967.
31. CHASE, L. S. "Countertransference in the Psychoanalysis of Borderline Personality Disorders." Paper read at the Boston Psychoanalytic Society and Institute, March 23, 1966.
32. CHATTERJI, N. N. "Delusional Ideas in a Case of Borderland Psychosis," *Samiksa,* 14:1-4, 9-23, 1960.
33. CHESSICK, R. D. "Defective Ego Feeling and the Quest for Being in the Borderline Patient," *Int. J. Psa. Psychother.,* 3:73-89, 1974.
34. CHESSICK, R. D. "The Psychotherapy of Borderline Patients," *Amer. J. Psychother.,* 20:600-614, 1966.
35. CLARK, L. P. "Some Practical Remarks Upon the Use of Modified Psychoanalysis in the Treatment of Borderland Neuroses and Psychoses," *Psa. Rev.,* 6:306-308, 1919.
36. DEUTSCH, H. "Some Forms of Emotional Disturbances and Their Relationship to Schizophrenia," *Psa. Quart.,* 11:301-321, 1942. Also (Rev.) in: Deutsch, H. (Ed.), *Neuroses and Character Types.* New York: Int. Univ. Press, 262-281, 1965.

37. DEUTSCH, H. *The Psychology of Woman*, Vol. 1. New York: Grune & Stratton, 3-23, 1944.
38. DICKES, R. "Severe Regressive Disruptions of the Therapeutic Alliance," *J. Amer. Psa. Assn.*, 15:508-533, 1967.
39. EDER, M. D. "Borderland Cases (London)," *University Med. Records*, 5:1-10, 1914.
40. EISENSTEIN, V. W. "Differential Psychotherapy of Borderline States," in: Bychowski, G. and Despert, J. L. (Eds.), *Specialized Techniques in Psychotherapy*. New York: Basic Books, 1952. Also *Psych. Quart.*, 25:379-401, 1951.
41. EISSLER, K. "The Effects of the Structure of the Ego on Psychoanalytic Technique," *J. Amer. Psa. Assn.*, 1:104, 1953.
42. EKSTEIN, R. *Children of Time and Space*. New York: Appleton-Century-Crofts, 1966.
43. EKSTEIN, R. and RANGELL, L. "Reconstruction and Theory Formation," *J. Amer. Psa. Assn.*, 9:684-697, 1961.
44. EKSTEIN, R. and WALLERSTEIN, J. "Vicissitudes of the Internal Image in the Recovery of a Borderline Schizophrenic Adolescent," *Bull. Menn. Clin.*, 9:86-92, 1955.
45. EKSTEIN, R. and WALLERSTEIN, J. "Observations on the Psychology of Borderline and Psychotic Children," *Psa. Study Child*, 9:344-369, 1954.
46. EKSTEIN, R. and WALLERSTEIN, J. "Special Training Problems in Psychotherapeutic Work with Psychotic and Borderline Children," *Amer. J. Orth.*, 32:569-583, 1962.
47. EKSTEIN, R. and WALLERSTEIN, J. "Choice of Interpretation in the Treatment of Borderline and Psychotic Children," *Bull. Menn. Clin.*, 21:199-208, 1957.
48. ERIKSON, E. H. *Dimensions of a New Identity*. New York: Norton, 1974.
49. ERSNITZ, A. J. "Narcissistic Object Choice and Self-Representation," *Int. J. Psa.*, 50:15-25, 1969. Discussed in *Int. J. Psychoanal.*, 51:151-157, 1970.
50. FAIRBAIRN, W. R. D. "A Revised Psychopathology of the Psychoses and Psychoneuroses," in: *Psychoanalytic Studies of the Personality* (An Object-Relations Theory of the Personality). London: Tavistock, 1952; New York: Basic Books, 1954.
51. FEDERN, P. *Ego Psychology and the Psychoses*. New York: Basic Books, 1952.
52. FRAIBERG, S. "Libidinal Object Constancy and Mental Representation," *Psa. Study Child*, 24:9-47, 1969.
53. FREEMAN, T. "Some Aspects of Pathological Narcissism," *J. Amer. Psa. Assn.*, 12:540-561, 1964.
54. FREUD, A. and DANN, S. "An Experiment in Group Upbringing," *Psa. Study Child*, 6:127-168, 1951.
55. FREUD, S. "Fetishism" (1927), in: Strachey, J. (Ed.), *Collected Papers*, Vol. V. London: Hogarth Press, 198-204, 1950.
56. FREUD, S. "Splitting of the Ego in the Defensive Process" (1938), in: Strachey, J. (Ed.), *Collected Papers*, Vol. V. London: Hogarth Press, 372-375, 1950.
57. FREUD, S. "On Narcissism: An Introduction" (1914), in: Riviere, J. (Ed.), *Collected Papers*, Vol. IV. London: Hogarth Press, 30-59, 1948.
58. FREUD, S. "Formulations on the Two Principles of Mental Functioning," in: *Standard Edition*, 12:218-226, 1911.
59. FREUD, S. "Three Essays on the Theory of Sexuality," in: *Standard Edition*, 7:125-244, 1953.
60. FRIEDMAN, H. J. "Some Problems of Inpatient Management with Borderline Patients," *Amer. J. Psych.*, 126:47-52, 1969.

61. FRIEDMAN, H. J. "Current Psychoanalytic Object Relations Theory and Its Clinical Implications," *Int. J. Psa.*, 56:137-146, 1975.

62. FROSCH, J. "Severe Regressive States During Analysis," *J. Amer. Psa. Assn.*, 15:491-507, 1967.

63. FROSCH, J. "The Psychotic Character: Clinical Psychiatric Consideration," *J. Psych. Quart.*, 38:81-96, 1964.

64. FROSCH, J. "Psychoanalytic Considerations of the Psychotic Character," *J. Amer. Psa. Assn.*, 15:606-625, 1967.

65. FROSCH, J. "Severe Regressive States During Analysis Summary," *J. Amer. Psa. Assn.*, 15:606-625, 1967.

66. FRYLING-SCHREUDER, E. C. M. "Borderline States in Children," *Psa. Study Child*, 11:336-351, 1956.

67. GABRIEL, E. "Analytic Group Psychotherapy with Borderline Psychotic Women," *Int. J. Group Psychother.*, 1:243-253, 1951.

68. GEDO, J. and GOLDBERG, A. *Models of the Mind.* Chicago: Univ. Chicago Press, 1973.

69. GELEERD, E. R. "Borderline States in Childhood and Adolescence," *Psa. Study Child.*, 11:336-351, 1956.

70. GIOVACCHINI, P. L. "The Submerged Ego," *J. Amer. Child Psych.*, 3:430-442, 1964.

71. GIOVACCHINI, P. L. "Maternal Introjection and Ego Defect," *J. Amer. Acad. Child Psych.*, 4:279-292, 1965.

72. GIOVACCHINI, P. L., "Transference Incorporation and Synthesis," *Int. J. Psa.*, 46:287-296, 1965.

73. GIOVACCHINI, P. L. "Frustration and Externalization," *Psa. Quart.*, 36:571-583, 1967.

74. GIOVACCHINI, P. L. "The Frozen Introject," *Int. J. Psa.*, 48:61-67., 1967.

75. GIOVACCHINI, P. L. et al. "On Regression: A Workshop," in: Lindon, J. A. (Ed.), *The Psychoanalytic Forum*, Winter, 1967, 2 (4).

76. GIOVACCHINI, P. L. "Effects of Adaptive and Disruptive Aspects of Early Object Relationships and Later Parental Functioning," in: Anthony, E. and Benedek, T. (Eds.), *Parenthood.* Boston: Little, Brown, Inc. 1970.

77. GLOVER, E. "A Psycho-Analytical Approach to the Classification of Mental Disorders," *J. Mental Sci.*, 78:819-842, 1932.

78. GLOVER, E. *The Technique of Psychoanalysis.* New York: Int. Univ. Press, 353-367, 1955.

79. GOLDFARB, W. "Psychological Privation in Infancy and Subsequent Adjustment," *Amer. J. Orthopsychiat.*, 15:247-255, 1945.

80. GREENACRE, P.: "Regression and Fixation," *J. Amer. Psa.*, 8:703-723, 1960.

81. GREENACRE, P. "The Predisposition to Anxiety," in: *Trauma, Growth and Personality.* New York: Int. Univ. Press, 27-82, 1952.

82. GUNDERSON, J. G. and SINGER, M. T. "Defining Borderline Patients: An Overview," *Amer. J. Psych.*, 132:1-9, 1975.

83. GUNTRIP, H. *Personality Structure and Human Interaction.* London: Hogarth Press; New York: Int. Univ. Press, 1964.

84. GUNTRIP, H. *Schizoid Phenomena, Object Relations and the Self.* New York: Int. Univ. Press, 1968.

85. GUZE, S. "Differential Diagnosis of the Borderline Syndrome," in: Mack, J. (Ed.), *Borderline States.* New York: Grune & Stratton, 69-74, 1975.

86. HAMMERMAN, S. "Conception of Superego Development," *J. Amer. Psa. Assn.*, 13:320-355, 1965.

87. HAVENS, L. L. "Some Difficulties in Giving Schizophrenic and Borderline Patients Medication," *Psych.*, 31:44-50, 1968.
88. HAYMAN, A. "Verbalization and Identity," *Int. J. Psa.*, 46:455-466, 1966.
89. HAYMAN, M. "Traumatic Elements in the Analysis of a Borderline Case," *Int. J. Psa.*, 39:9-21, 1958.
90. HOCH, P. H. and CATTELL, J. P. "The Diagnosis of Pseudoneurotic Schizophrenia," *Psych. Quart.*, 33:17-43, 1959.
91. HOCH, P. H., CATTELL, J. P., STRAHL, M. O. et al. "The Course and Outcome of Pseudoneurotic Schizophrenia," *Amer. J. Psych.*, 11:106-115, 1962.
92. HUNTER, R. C. A. "The Analysis of Episodes of Depersonalization in Borderline Patients," *Int. J. Psa.*, 47:32-41, 1966.
93. JACOBSON, E. "Denial and Repression," *J. Amer. Psa. Assn.*, 5:61-92, 1957.
94. JACOBSON, E. *The Self and the Object World.* New York: Int. Univ. Press, 1964.
95. KALINA, E. "Aspects of a Clinical Case Transferential Relations in Face of Separations," presented April 19, 1966 to the Argentina Psychoanalytical Association.
96. KALINA, E. "The Analytical Process of an Adolescent with an 'As If' State. Diagnostic Problems and Psychotherapy," presented November 11, 1969 to the Argentina Psychoanalytic Association.
97. KAUFMAN, I. "Some Considerations of the 'Borderline' Personality Structure and the Psychodynamics of the Therapeutic Process," *Smith College Studies in Social Work*, 26:7-17, 1956.
98. KAYWIN, L. "The Evocation of a Genie: The Study of an As If Character Type," *Psa. Quart.*, 37:22-41, 1968.
99. KERNBERG, O. "Borderline Personality Organization." *J. Amer. Psa. Assn.*, 15:641-685, 1967.
100. KERNBERG, O. "A Psychoanalytic Classification of Character Pathology, *J. Amer. Psa. Assn.*, 18:800-822, 1970.
101. KERNBERG, O. "The Treatment of Patients with Borderline Personality Organization," *Int. J. Psa.*, 49:600-619, 1968.
102. KERNBERG, O. "Notes on Countertransference," *J. Amer. Psa. Assn.*, 13:38-56, 1965.
103. KERNBERG, O. "Prognostic Considerations Regarding Borderline Personality Organization," presented at the 57th Annual Meeting of the American Psychoanalytic Assn., San Francisco, Calif., 1970.
104. KERNBERG, O. "Factors in the Psychoanalytic Treatment of Narcissistic Personalities," *J. Amer. Psa. Assn.*, 18:51-85, 1970.
105. KERNBERG, O. "New Developments in Psychoanalytic Object Relations Theory," presented at the 58th Annual Meeting of the American Psychoanalytic Assn., Washington, D.C., 1971.
106. KERNBERG,, O. "Early Ego Integration and Object Relations," *Ann. N.Y. Acad. Sci.*, 193:233-247, 1972.
107. KERNBERG, O. "Structural Derivatives of Object Relationships," *Int. J. Psa.*, 47:236-253, 1966.
108. KERNBERG, O. "Further Considerations to the Treatment of Narcissistic Personalities," *Int. J. Psa.*, 55:215-240, 1974.
109. KERNBERG, O. *Borderline Conditions and Pathological Narcissism.* New York: Science House, 163-177, 1975.
110. KHAN, M. M. R. "On Symbiotic Omnipotence," in: *The Privacy of the Self.* New York: Int. Univ. Press, 82-92, 1974.

111. KHAN, M. M. R. "The Finding and Becoming of Self," in: *The Privacy of the Self*. New York: Int. Univ. Press, 294-305, 1974.
112. KHAN, M. M. R. "Dread of Surrender to Resourceless Dependence in the Analytic Situation," in: *The Privacy of the Self*. New York: Int. Univ. Press, 270-279, 1974.
113. KLEIN, M. *The Psychoanalysis of Children*. London: Hogarth Press, 1932.
114. KLEIN, M. "Contribution to the Psychogenesis of Manic Depressive States," in: *Contributions to Psychoanalysis 1921-1945*. London: Hogarth Press, 1948.
115. KLEIN, M. "Mourning and Its Relation to Manic Depressive States," in: *Contribution to Psychoanalysis 1921-1945*. London: Hogarth Press, 1948.
116. KLEIN, M. "Notes on Some Schizoid Mechanisms," in: Riviere, J. (Ed.), *Developments in Psychoanalysis*. London: Hogarth Press, 1946.
117. KNIGHT, R. P. "Borderline States," in: *Psychoanalytic Psychiatry and Psychology*. New York: Int. Univ. Press, 1954.
118. KNIGHT, R. P. "Management and Psychotherapy of the Borderline Schizophrenic Patient," *Bull. Menn. Clin.*, 17:139-150, 1953.
119. KOHUT, H. "Autonomy and Integration," *J. Amer. Psa. Assn.*, 13:851-856, 1965.
120. KOHUT, H. "Forms and Transformations of Narcissism," *J. Amer. Psa. Assn.*, 14:243-272, 1966.
121. KOHUT, H. "Psychoanalytic Treatment of Narcissistic Personality Disorder: Outline of a Systematic Approach," *Psa. Study Child*, 23:86-113, 1968.
122. KOHUT, H. "Panel on Narcissistic Resistance," (N. P. Segal, Reporter), *J. Amer. Psa. Assn.*, 17:941-954, 1969.
123. KOHUT, H. *The Analysis of the Self: A Systematic Approach to the Psychoanalytic Treatment of Narcissistic Personality Disorders*. New York: Int. Univ. Press, 1971.
124. KRIS, E. "The Development of Ego Psychology," *Samiksa*, 5:153-168, 1952.
125. KUT (ROSENFELD), S. "Some Thoughts on the Technical Handling of Borderline Children," *Psa. Study Child*, 20:494-517, 1965.
126. KUT (ROSENFELD), S. and SPRINCE, M. P. "An Attempt to Formulate the Meaning of the Concept 'Borderline,'" *Psa. Study Child*, 20:495-500, 1963.
127. LAZAR, N. "Nature and Significance of Changes in Patients in a Psychoanalytic Clinic," *Psa. Quart.*, 42:579-600, 1973.
128. LEWIS, A. B. "Perception of Self in Borderline States," *Amer. J. Psych.*, 124:-1491-1498, 1968.
129. LIBOWITZ, N. A. and NEWMAN, K. M. "Borderline Personality and the Theatre of the Absurd," *Arch. Gen. Psychiat.*, 16:268-280, 1967.
130. LICHTENSTEIN, H. "Identity and Sexuality: A Study of Their Interrelationship in Man," *J. Amer. Psa. Assn.*, 9:179-260, 1961.
131. LIDZ, T., *The Origin and Treatment of Schizophrenic Disorders*. New York: Basic Books, 1973.
132. LITTLE, M. "Transference in Borderline States," *Int. J. Psa.*, 47:476-485, 1966.
133. LITTLE, M. "On Basic Unity," *Int. J. Psa.*, 41:377-384, 1960.
134. LITTLE, M. "On Delusional Transference," *Int. J. Psa.*, 39:134-138, 1958.
135. LITTLE, M. "Countertransference and the Patient's Response to It," *Int. J. Psa.*, 32:32-40, 1951.
136. MACK, J. (Ed.). *Borderline States*. New York: Grune & Stratton, 1975.
137. MAENCHEN, A. "Object Cathexis in a Borderline Twin," *Psa. Study Child*, 23:438-456, 1968.

138. MAHLER, M. S. *On Human Symbiosis and the Vicissitudes of Individuation.* New York: Int. Univ. Press, 1968.

139. MAHLER, M. S. "Thoughts About Development and Individuation," *Psa. Study Child,* 18:307-324, 1963.

140. MAHLER, M. S. "Autism and Symbiosis—Two Extreme Disturbances of Identity," *Int. J. Psa.,* 39:77-83, 1958.

141. MAHLER, M. S. "On the Significance of the Normal Separation-Individuation Phase," in: Schur, M. (Ed.), *Drives, Affects and Behavior,* Vol. 2. New York: Int. Univ. Press, 161-169, 1965.

142. MAHLER, M. S. and FURER, M. "Certain Aspects of the Separation-Individuation Phase," *Psa. Quart.,* 32:1-14, 1963.

143. MAHLER, M. S. and LAPERRIERE, R. "Mother-Child Interactions During Separation-Individuation," *Psa. Quart.,* 34:483-489, 1965.

144. MAHLER, M. S. and McDEVITT, J. "Observations on Adaptation and Defense in Statu Nascendi," *Psa. Quart.,* 37:1-21, 1968.

145. MAHLER, M. S., PINE, F. and BERGMAN, A. "The Mother's Reaction to Her Toddler's Drive for Individuation," in: Anthony, E. and Benedek, T. (Eds.), *Parenthood.* Boston: Little, Brown, 1970.

146. MAHLER, M. S. *The Psychological Birth of the Human Infant.* New York: Basic Books, 1975.

147. MAHLER, M. S. "A Study of the Separation-Individuation Process and Its Possible Application to Borderline Phenomena in the Psychoanalytic Situation," *Psa. Study Child,* 26:403-424, 1971.

148. MARCUS, J. "Borderline States in Childhood," *J. Child Psychol. Psych.,* 4:3-4, 207-218, 1963.

149. MASTERSON, J. F. *Treatment of the Borderline Adolescent: A Developmental Approach.* New York: John Wiley & Sons, Inc. 1972.

150. MASTERSON, J. F. *Psychiatric Dilemma of Adolescence.* Boston: Little, Brown, 1967.

151. MASTERSON, J. F. "The Psychiatric Significance of Adolescent Turmoil," *Amer. J. Psych.,* 124:1549-1554, 1968.

152. MASTERSON, J. F. "Intensive Psychotherapy of the Adolescent with a Borderline Syndrome," in: Kaplan, G. (Ed.), *American Handbook of Psychiatry* (Special Edition on Adolescence), New York: Basic Books, 250-263, 1975.

153. MASTERSON, J. F. "Intensive Psychotherapy of the Borderline Adolescent," *Annals of Adolescent Psychiatry,* Vol. 2, 240-268, 1975.

154. MASTERSON, J. F. "Treatment of the Adolescent with Borderline Syndrome (A Problem in Separation-Individuation)," *Bull. Menn. Clin.,* 35:5-18, 1971.

155. MASTERSON, J. F. "Diagnosis and Treatment of the Borderline Syndrome in Adolescents." Paris: *Confrontations Psychiatriques,* 7.

156. MASTERSON, J. F. "Intensive Psychotherapy of the Adolescent with a Borderline Syndrome." Buenos Aires: *Cuadernos de la A.S.S.A.P.P.I.A.,* 3.

157. MASTERSON, J. F. "The Splitting Defense Mechanism of the Borderline Adolescent: Developmental and Clinical Aspects," in: Mack, J. (Ed.), *Borderline States.* New York: Grune & Stratton, 1975.

158. MASTERSON, J. F. and RINSLEY, D. B. "The Borderline Syndrome: The Role of the Mother in the Genesis and Psychic Structure of the Borderline Personality," *Int. J. Psa.,* 56:163-178, 1975.

159. McDEVITT, J. B. "Separation-Individuation and Object Constancy," *J. Amer. Psa. Assn.,* 23:713-742, 1975.

160. MODELL, A. H. "Primitive Object Relationships and the Predisposition to Schizophrenia," *Int. J. Psa.*, 44:282-292, 1963.
161. MODELL, A. H. "Denial and the Sense of Separateness," *J. Amer. Psa. Assn.*, 9:533-547, 1961.
162. MODELL, A. H. "A Narcissistic Defense Against Affect and the Illusion of Self-Sufficiency." Talk presented at the Boston Psychoanalytic Society and Institute, October 12, 1974.
163. MOORE, T. V. "The Parataxes: A Study and Analysis of a Certain Borderline Mental State," *Psa. Rev.*, 8:252-283, 1921.
164. MURPHY, W. F. "The Borderline Patient: A Case of Impulsive Acting Out," in: *The Tactics of Psychotherapy.* New York: Int. Univ. Press, Chapt. 14, 1965.
165. MURPHY, W. F. *The Tactics of Psychotherapy: The Application of Psychoanalytic Theory to Psychotherapy.* New York: Int. Univ. Press, 1965.
166. NELSON, M. C. "Effect of Paradigmatic Techniques on the Psychic Economy of Borderline Patients." *Psych.*, 25:119-134, 1962.
167. NOVEY, S. "The Principle of 'Working Through' in Psychoanalysis," *J. Amer. Psa. Assn.*, 10:658-676, 1962.
168. OBERNDORF, C. P. "The Psychoanalysis of Borderline Cases," *N.Y. State Med. J.*, 30:648-651, 1930.
169. OLINICK, S. "Negative Therapeutic Reaction," *J. Amer. Psa. Assn.*, 18:655-672, 1970.
170. PANEL: "The Borderline Case," *J. Amer. Psa. Assn.*, 3:528-533, 1955.
171. PANEL: "The Traditional Psychoanalytic Technique and Its Variations," *J. Amer. Psa. Assn.*, 1:526-37, 1953.
172. PANEL: "Depression and Object Loss"; a panel report on a presentation at the Annual Meeting of the Amer. Psa. Assn. N.Y., April 1965. Also *J. Amer. Psa.*, 14:142-153, 1966.
173. PARENS, H. and SAUL, L. J. *Dependency in Man: A Psychoanalytic Study.* New York: Int. Univ. Press, 1971.
174. PARENS, H. "A Contribution of Separation-Individuation to the Development of Psychic Structure," in: McDevitt, J. and Settlage, C. (Eds.), *Separation-Individuation.* New York: Int. Univ. Press, 100-112, 1971.
175. PETO, A. "Dedifferentiations of the Therapeutic Alliance," *J. Amer. Psa. Assn.*, 15:534-550, 1967.
176. PETO, A. "Variations of Archaic Thinking in Neurotics, Borderlines, and in Schizophrenics." Paper presented at N.Y. Psa. Society meetings, January 28, 1964. *Abst. Psa. Quart.*, 33:461-463, 1964.
177. PIAGET, J. *The Construction of Reality in the Child.* New York: Basic Books, 1954.
178. PIAGET, J. *Play, Dream and Imitation in Childhood.* New York: Norton, 1951.
179. PIAGET, J. *The Psychology of Intelligence.* London: Routledge and Kegan, P. 1950.
180. PINE, F. and FURER, M. "Studies of the Separation-Individuation Phase: A Methodological Overview," *Psa. Study Child.*, 18:325-342, 1963.
181. POLLACK, G. H. "On Symbiosis and Symbiotic Neurosis," *Int. J. Psa.*, 45:1-30, 1964.
182. PROVENCE, S. "Some Aspects of Early Ego Development: Data from a Longitudinal Study," in: Loewenstein, R. M., Newman, L. M., Schur, M. and Solnit, A. J. (Eds.), *Psychoanalysis—A General Psychology.* New York: Int. Univ. Press, 107-122, 1966.

183. RANGELL, L. "The Role of Early Psychic Functioning in Psychoanalysis," *J. Amer. Psa. Assn.*, 9:595-609, 1962.

184. RANGELL, L. "The Borderline Case," *J. Amer. Psa. Assn.*, 3:285-298, 1955.

185. REICH, A. "Further Remarks on Counter-Transference," *Int. J. Psa.*, 41:389-395, 1965.

186. REICH, A. "On Counter-Transference," *Int. J. Psa.*, 32:25-40, 1951.

187. RICKMAN, J. *The Development of the Psycho-Analytic Theory of the Psychoses 1893-1926.* London: Bailliere, Tindall & Cox, for the Institute of Psychoanalysis, 1928.

188. RINSLEY, D. B. "Economic Aspects of the Object Relations," *Int. J. Psa.* 49:38-48, 1968.

189. RINSLEY, D. B. "The Adolescent Inpatient: Patterns of Depersonification," *Psych. Quart.*, 45:1-20, 1971.

190. RINSLEY, D. B. "An Object Relations View of Borderline Personality," presented at International Meeting on Borderline Disorders. The Menninger Foundation and the National Institute of Mental Health, Topeka, Kansas, March 19-21, 1976.

191. RINSLEY, D. B. "Intensive Psychiatric Hospital Treatment of Adolescents: An Object Relations View," *Psych. Quart.*, 39:405-429, 1965.

191a. RINSLEY, D. B. "Residential Treatment of Adolescents," in: Arieti, S. (Ed.), *American Handbook of Psychiatry, Second Revised Edition*, Vol. II. New York: Basic Books, 353-366, 1974.

192. ROBBINS, L. L. "The Borderline Case," *J. Amer. Psa. Assn.*, 4:550-562, 1956.

193. ROSENFELD, S. K. and SPRINCE, M. P. "Some Thoughts on the Technical Handling of Borderline Children," *Psa. Study Child*, 20:495-517, 1965.

194. ROSHCO, M. "Perception Denial and Depersonalization," *J. Amer. Psa. Assn.*, 15:243-260, 1967.

195. ROSS, N. "An Examination of Nosology, According to Psychoanalytic Concept," *J. Amer. Psa. Assn.*, 8:535-551, 1960.

196. SANDLER, J. and JOFFE, W. G. "Notes on Childhood Depression," *Int. J. Psa.*, 46:88-95, 1965.

197. SAVITT, R. A. "Transference Somatization and Symbiotic Need," *J. Amer. Psa. Assn.*, 17:1030-1054, 1969.

198. SAVITT, R. A. "Turning Point in the Analysis of a Borderline Problem," *J. Hillside Hosp.* 10:3/4, 256-260, July-Oct. 1961.

199. SCHER, J. M. II. "Primary Gain: The Game of Illness and the Communicative Compact in the Borderline Patient," *Psych. Quart.* 35:532-543, 1961.

200. SCHMIDEBERG, M. "The Borderline Patient," in: Arieti, S. (Ed.), *American Handbook of Psychiatry*, Vol. I. New York: Basic Books, 398-416, 1959.

201. SCHMIDEBERG, M. "The Treatment of Psychopathic and Borderline Patients," *Amer. J. Psychother.*, 1:45-71, 1947.

202. SEGAL, N. P. (Reporter). "Narcissistic Resistance," *J. Amer. Psa. Assn.*, 18:941-954, 1969.

203. SHAPIRO, E. and SHAPIRO, R. "Protective Identification as a Model of Perception and Behavior in Families of Adolescents," *Int. J. Psa.*, 53:523-529, 1972.

204. SHAPIRO, R. and ZINNER, J. "Family Organization and Adolescents' Development," in: Miller, E. (Ed.), *Task and Organization*. New York: John Wiley & Sons, Inc. 1975.

205. SIEGMAN, A. J. "Denial and Screening of Object Images," *J. Amer. Psa. Assn.*, 15:261-280, 1967.

206. SINGER, M. B. "Fantasies of a Borderline Patient," *Psa. Study Child*, 15:310-356, 1960.

207. SPIEGEL, L. "Acting Out and Defensive Instinctual Gratification," *J. Amer. Psa. Assn.*, 2:107-119, 1954.
208. SPITZ, R. A. "Anaclitic Depression," *Psa. Study Child*, 2:313-341, 1946.
209. SPITZ, R. A. *The First Year of Life (A Psychoanalytic Study of Normal and Deviant Development of Object Relations)*. New York: Int. Univ. Press, 1965.
210. SPITZ, R. A. *The Smiling Response: A Contribution to the Ontogenesis of Social Relations, Genet. Psychol. Monog.* Vol. 34. Provincetown, Mass.: Journal Press, 1957.
211. SPITZ, R. A. *No and Yes*. New York: Int. Univ. Press, 1957.
212. SPITZ, R. A. "The Evolution of Dialogue," in: Schur, M. (Ed.), *Drives, Affects, Behavior*, Second Edition. New York: Int. Univ. Press, 170-190, 1965.
213. SPITZ, R. A. "Relevancy of Direct Infant Observations," *Psa. Study Child*, 5:66-75, 1950.
214. SPITZ, R. A. "Hospitalism: An Inquiry Into the Genesis of Psychiatric Conditions of Early Childhood," *Psa. Study Child*, 1:53-74, 1945.
215. SPITZ, R. A. "Hospitalism: A Follow-Up Report," *Psa. Study Child*, 2:313-342, 1946.
216. STERN, A. "Psychoanalytic Investigation of and Therapy in the Borderline Group of Neuroses," *Psa. Quart.* 7:467-489, 1938.
217. STERN, A. "Psychoanalytic Therapy in the Borderline Neurosis," *Psa. Quart.*, 14:190-198, 1945.
218. STERN, A. "Transference in Borderline Neuroses," *Psa. Quart.*, 17:527-528, 1948. *Yearbook Psa.*, 5:84-85, 1949.
219. STERN, A. "The Transference in the Borderline Group of Neuroses," *J. Amer. Psa. Assn.*, 5:348-350, 1957.
220. STEWART, W. A. "The Split Ego and the Mechanism of Disavowal," *Psa. Quart.*, 36:1-16, 1970.
221. STEWART, W. A. "An Inquiry into the Concept of Working Through," *J. Amer. Psa. Assn.*, 11:474-499, 1963.
222. STONE, L. "The Widening Scope of Indications for Psychoanalysis," *J. Amer. Psa. Assn.*, 2:567-594, 1954.
223. VAILLANT, G. "Five Ego Mechanisms Underlying Character Disorders or Wisdom is Never Having to Call a Patient Borderline." Talk presented at Cambridge Hospital (Mass.), September 23, 1974.
224. WALLERSTEIN, R. S. "Reconstruction and Mastery in the Transference Psychosis," *J. Amer. Psa. Assn.*, 15:551-583, 1967.
225. WEIL, J. "The Basic Core," *Psa. Study Child*, 25:442-460, 1970.
226. WEINBERGER, J. "Basic Concepts in Diagnosis and Treatment of Borderline States," *Smith College Studies in Social Work*, 26:18-23, 1956.
227. WEISS, J. "Clinical and Theoretical Aspects of 'As If' Characters," A Panel Report, *J. Amer. Psa. Assn.*, 14:569-590, 1966.
228. WINNICOTT, D. W. "The Capacity to be Alone," in: *The Maturational Processes and the Facilitating Environment*. New York: Int. Univ. Press, 29-36, 1965.
229. WINNICOTT, D. W. "The Theory of the Parent-Infant Relationship," in: *The Maturational Processes and the Facilitating Environment*. New York: Int. Univ. Press, 37-55, 1965.
230. WINNICOTT, D. W. "Ego Integration in Child Development," in: *The Maturational Processes and the Facilitating Environment*. New York: Int. Univ. Press, 56-63, 1965.
231. WINNICOTT, D. W. "The Development of the Capacity for Concern," in: *The Maturational Processes and the Facilitating Environment*. New York: Int. Univ. Press, 73-82, 1965.

232. WINNICOTT, D. W. "From Dependence Towards Independence in the Development of the Individual," in: *The Maturational Processes and the Facilitating Environment*. New York: Int. Univ. Press, 83-92, 1965.
233. WINNICOTT, D. W. "Psychotherapy of Character Disorder," in: *The Maturational Processes and the Facilitating Environment*. New York: Int. Univ. Press, 203-216, 1965.
234. WINNICOTT, D. W. "Hospital Care Supplementing Intensive Psychotherapy in Adolescence," in: *The Maturational Processes and the Facilitating Environment*. New York: Int. Univ. Press, 242-248, 1965.
235. WINNICOTT, D. W. "The Use of an Object," *Int. J. Psa.*, 50:711-716, 1969.
236. WINNICOTT, D. W. "Ego Distortions in Terms of True and False Self," in: *The Maturational Processes and the Facilitating Environment*. New York: Int. Univ. Press, 140-152, 1965.
237. WINNICOTT, D. W. "Transitional Objects and Transitional Phenomena." *Int. J. Psa.*, 34:89-99, 1953.
238. WINNICOTT, D. W. "Hate in the Countertransference," *Int. J. Psa.*, 30:69-74, 1949.
239. WOLBERG, A. R. "The Borderline Patient," *Amer. J. Psychother.*, 6:694-710, 1952.
240. WOLBERG, A. R. "The Psychoanalytic Treatment of the Borderline Patient in the Individual and Group Setting," *Tropical Probl. Psychother.*, 2:174-197, 1960.
241. WOLBERG, A. R. *The Borderline Patient*. New York: Intercontinental Medical Book, 1973.
242. YATMATSU, T., et al. "An Analytic Study of the Process of Psychotherapy with a Borderline Schizophrenic Child," *Japanese J. Clin. Psychol.*, 2:74-83, 1963. *Psychol. Abst.* 39:1, 230, No. 2096, Feb. 1965.
243. ZENTNER, E. B. and APONTE, H. J. "The Amorphous Family Nexus," *Psych. Quart.*, 44:91-113, 1970.
244. ZETZEL, E. R. "A Developmental Approach to the Borderline Patient," *Amer. J. Psych.*, 127:867-871, 1971.
245. ZETZEL, E. R. "A Developmental Model and the Theory of Therapy (1965)," in: *The Capacity for Emotional Growth*. New York: Int. Univ. Press, 246-270, 1970.
246. ZETZEL, E. R. "Therapeutic Alliance in the Analysis of Hysteria (1958)," in: *The Capacity for Emotional Growth*. New York: Int. Univ. Press, 182-196, 1970.
247. ZETZEL, E. R. "The Concept of Transference (1956)," in: *The Capacity for Emotional Growth*. New York: Int. Univ. Press, 168-181, 1970.
248. ZETZEL, E. R. "On the Incapacity to Bear Depression (1965)," in: *The Capacity for Emotional Growth*. New York: Int. Univ. Press, 82-114, 1970.
249. ZETZEL, E. R. "The Depressive Position (1953)," in: *The Capacity for Emotional Growth*. New York: Int. Univ. Press, 63-81, 1970.
250. ZETZEL, E. R. "Depressive Illness (1960)," in: *The Capacity for Emotional Growth*. New York: Int. Univ. Press, 53-62, 1970.
251. ZETZEL, E. R. "Anxiety and the Capacity to Bear It (1949)," in: *The Capacity for Emotional Growth*. New York: Int. Univ. Press, 33-52, 1970.
252. ZILBOORG, G. "Ambulatory Schizophrenias." *Psychiatry*, 4:149-155, 1941.
253. ZINNER, J. and SHAPIRO, R. "The Family Group as a Single Psychic Entity: Implications for Acting Out in Adolescence," *Int. Rev. Psa.*, 1:179-186.

Index

371